P. E. T.
PARENT
EFFECTIVENESS
TRAINING

P. E. T.
PARENT
EFFECTIVENESS
TRAINING

The Tested New Way
To Raise Responsible Children

by Dr. Thomas Gordon

DAVID MCKAY, INC.
NEW YORK

P.E.T.: PARENT EFFECTIVENESS TRAINING

Copyright © 1970 by THOMAS GORDON

Quotation on page 287 from "On Children" in THE PROPHET, by Kahlil
Gibran, with permission of the publisher, Alfred A. Knopf, Inc. Copyright
1923 by Kahlil Gibran; renewal copyright 1951 by Administrators C.T.A.
of Kahlil Gibran Estate and Mary G. Gibran.

.

ISBN: 0-679-26039-0

30

Library of Congress Catalog Card Number: 74-130756

MANUFACTURED IN THE UNITED STATES OF AMERICA

To my Judy, and to the hundreds of children I have counseled, who provided me the opportunity to learn about parenthood.

To Elaine, my companion, counselor, and colleague in parenthood, whose penetrating insights so frequently enriched my own thinking and contributed immeasurably to the development and growth of Parent Effectiveness Training.

To the group of dedicated P.E.T. instructors, whose faith and inspired efforts as pioneers of our program in their own communities helped shape my dream into a reality.

Contents

P. E. T.
PARENT
EFFECTIVENESS
TRAINING

1

Parents Are Blamed but Not Trained

Everybody blames parents for the troubles of youth and for the troubles that young people appear to be causing society. It's all the fault of parents, mental health experts lament, after examining the frightening statistics on the rapidly increasing number of children and youth who develop serious or crippling emotional problems, who become victims of drug addiction, or commit suicide. Political leaders and law-enforcement officials blame parents for raising a generation of ingrates, rebels, protestors, hippies, peace demonstrators, and draft-card burners. And when kids fail in school or become hopeless drop-outs, teachers and school administrators claim that the parents are at fault.

Yet who is helping parents? How much effort is being made to assist parents to become more effective in raising children? Where can parents learn what they are doing wrong and what they might do differently?

Parents are blamed, but not trained. Millions of new mothers and fathers take on a job each year that ranks among the most difficult anyone can have, taking an infant, a little person who is almost totally helpless, assuming full responsibility for his physical and psychological health and raising him so he will become a productive, cooperative, and contributing citizen. What more difficult and demanding job is there?

Yet how many parents are effectively trained for it? What "job training program" is available for parents; where can they acquire the knowledge and the skills to be effective at this job?

In 1962, in Pasadena, California, I took a very small step toward filling this void in my own community. Initially I designed a course with the idea of training parents who already were encountering problems with their children, and invited a few parents to enroll. Eight years later, this "school for parents" has spread to more than two hundred communities in eighteen states, taught by over three hundred dedicated instructors who have been given special training to teach in this program. Called Parent Effectiveness Training, the course has been taken by more than fifteen thousand mothers and fathers, and it will soon bring training to many more parents as it continues its expansion into other states and countries. No longer a training program solely for parents whose children already have developed problems, Parent Effectiveness Training (P.E.T.) attracts many parents of very young children and even couples who have not yet started having their children. For these young parents, P.E.T. serves a preventive function—*training before trouble*.

We have demonstrated in this exciting program that with a certain kind of special training many parents can greatly increase their effectiveness in parenthood. They can acquire very specific skills that will keep the channels of communication open between parents and children—both ways. And they can learn a new method of resolving parent-child conflicts that brings about a strengthening rather than a deterioration of the relationship.

This program has convinced those of us who are involved that parents and their children can develop a warm, intimate relationship based on mutual love and respect. It has also demonstrated that the "generation gap" need not exist in families.

A decade ago I was as convinced as most parents and professionals that the period of the "terrible teens" is all but inevitable—the consequence of children's natural need to establish their independence. I was sure that adolescence, as most studies have shown, was invariably a time of storm and stress in families. Our experience with P.E.T. has proven me wrong. Time and time again, parents trained in P.E.T. have reported the surprising absence of rebellion and turmoil in their families.

I am now convinced that *adolescents do not rebel against parents.* They only rebel against certain destructive methods of discipline almost universally employed by parents. Turmoil and dissension in families can be the exception, not the rule, when parents learn to substitute a new method of resolving conflicts.

The P.E.T. program has also thrown new light on punishment in child-rearing. Many of our P.E.T. parents have proven to us that punishment can be discarded forever in disciplining children—and I mean *all kinds of punishment,* not just the physical kind. Parents can raise children who are responsible, self-disciplined, and cooperative without relying on the weapon of fear; they can learn how to influence children to behave out of genuine consideration for the needs of parents rather than out of fear of punishment or withdrawal of privileges.

Does this sound too good to be true? Probably it does. It did to me before I had the experience of personally training parents in P.E.T. Like most professionals, I had underestimated parents. P.E.T. parents have taught me how much they are capable of changing, given the opportunity for training. I have a new trust in the ability of mothers and fathers to comprehend new knowledge and acquire new skills. Our P.E.T. parents, with few exceptions, have been eager to learn a new approach to child-rearing, but first they have to be convinced that the new methods will work. Most parents already know their old methods have been ineffective. So today's parents are ready for change, and our P.E.T. program has demonstrated they can change.

We have been rewarded by one other outcome of the P.E.T. program. One of our earliest objectives was to teach parents some of the very skills used by professional counselors and therapists with formal training in helping children overcome emotional problems and maladaptive behavior. It may seem strange or even presumptuous that we had such aspirations. Preposterous though it may sound to some parents (and to quite a few professionals), we know now that even parents who have never taken a basic college course in psychology can be taught these proven skills and can learn how and when to employ them effectively to help their own children.

During the growth of P.E.T. we have come to accept a reality that sometimes makes us discouraged, yet more often makes us feel all the more challenged: parents today rely almost universally on the same methods of raising children and dealing with problems in their families that were used by their own parents, by their parents' parents, by their grandparents' parents. Unlike almost all other institutions of civilization, the parent-child relationship seems to have remained unchanged. Parents depend on methods used two thousand years ago!

Not that the human race has acquired no new knowledge about human relationships. Quite the contrary. Psychology, child development, and other behavioral sciences have amassed impressive new knowledge about children, parents, interpersonal relationships, how to help another person grow, how to create a psychologically healthy climate for people. A lot is known about effective person-to-person communications, the effects of power in human relationships, constructive conflict resolution, and so on.

Unfortunately, those who have uncovered new facts and developed new methods have not done a very good job of telling parents about them. We communicate to our colleagues in books and professional journals, but do not communicate as well with parents, the rightful consumers of these new methods.

A few professionals* certainly have tried to pass on new ideas and methods to parents, particularly Haim Ginott, who pointed out in his book, *Between Parent and Child*, how parents can talk more therapeutically to a child and avoid damage to his self-esteem. However, even those relatively few parents who have read this and other books show little evidence in our classes of having modified their behavior very significantly, *particularly their approach to discipline and handling parent-child conflicts*.

This book might prove to have some of the same limitations as previous ones, but it is my hope that it will not, because it presents a more comprehensive philosophy of what it takes to establish and maintain an effective *total relationship* with a child, in any and all circumstances.

In this book parents can learn not only methods and skills but also when and why they are to be used and for what purpose. As in our P.E.T. classes, parents will be given a *complete system*—principles as well as techniques. It is my conviction that parents must be told the whole story—all that we know about creating effective parent-child relationships, beginning with some fundamentals about what goes on in all relationships between two people. Then they will understand why they are using the P.E.T. methods, when it is appropriate to use them, and what the outcomes will be. Parents will be given a chance to become *experts themselves* in dealing with the inevitable problems that come up in all parent-child relationships.

* See references to these books in the list of suggested readings for parents in the appendix.

In this book, as in our P.E.T. program, parents will be given *everything we know*, not just bits and pieces. A complete model of effective parent-child relationships will be described in detail and will frequently be illustrated with case material from our experience. Most parents consider P.E.T. quite revolutionary because it differs dramatically from tradition. Yet it fits parents with very young children as well as those with teen-agers, parents with handicapped children or those with "normal" children.

As in our classroom program, P.E.T. will be described in terms familiar to everyone, not in technical jargon. Some parents may find themselves initially disagreeing with some of the newer concepts, but very few will find themselves not understanding them.

Since readers will not be able to express their concerns face-to-face with an instructor, here are some questions and answers that may be helpful at the start.

QUESTION:　Is this another permissive approach to raising children?

ANSWER:　Definitely not. Permissive parents get into as much trouble as overly strict parents, for their kids often turn out to be selfish, unmanageable, uncooperative, and inconsiderate of the needs of their parents.

QUESTION:　Can one parent use this new approach effectively if the other sticks to the old approach?

ANSWER:　Yes and no. If only one parent starts to use this new approach, there will be a definite improvement in the relationship between that parent and the children. But the relationship between the other parent and the children may get worse. Far better then, for both parents to learn the new methods. Furthermore, when both parents try to learn this new approach together, they can help each other a great deal.

QUESTION:　Will parents lose their influence over the children with this new approach? Will they abdicate the responsibility to give guidance and direction to their childrens' lives?

ANSWER:　As parents read the first chapters, they may get this impression. A book can only present a system step by step. The early chapters deal with ways to help children find *their own* solutions to problems *they encounter*. In these situations, the role of an effective parent will seem different—much more passive or "nondirective" than parents are accustomed to. Later chapters, however, deal with how to modify unacceptable behavior of children and how to influence them to be considerate of your needs as parents. In these situations, you will be shown specific ways of being an even more responsible parent—acquiring even more influence than you have now. It might be helpful to check the Table of Contents for the subjects covered in later chapters.

This book—as does the P.E.T. course—teaches parents a rather easy-to-learn method of encouraging kids to accept responsibility for finding their own solutions to their own problems, and illustrates how parents can put that method to work right away in the home. Parents who learn this method (called "active listening") may experience what P.E.T.-trained parents have described:

> "It's such a relief not to think I have to have all the answers to my children's problems."
> "P.E.T. has made me have a much greater appreciation of the capacities of my children for solving their own problems."
> "I was amazed at how the active listening method worked. My kids come up with solutions to their problems that are often far better than any I could have given them."
> "I guess I've always been very uncomfortable about playing the role of God—feeling that I should be knowing what my kids should do when they have problems."

Today, thousands of adolescents have fired their parents, and for good reason as far as the kids are concerned.

"My parents don't understand kids my age."

"I just hate to go home and get lectured to every night."

"I never tell my parents anything; if I did they wouldn't understand."

"I wish my parents would get off my back."

"As soon as I can, I'm going to leave home—I can't stand their constantly hassling me about everything."

The parents of these kids are usually well aware of having lost their jobs, as evidenced by these statements made in our P.E.T. classes:

"I have absolutely no more influence over my sixteen-year-old boy."

"We've given up with Sally."

"Tim won't ever eat with us, and he hardly ever says a word to us. Now he wants a room out in the garage."

"Mark is never home. And he'll never tell us where he goes or what he's doing. If I ever ask him, he tells me it's none of my business."

To me it is a tragedy that one of the potentially most intimate and satisfying relationships in life, so often creates bad blood. Why do so many adolescents come to see their parents as "the enemy"? Why is the generation gap so prevalent in homes today? Why are parents and youth in our society literally at war with each other?

Chapter 14 will deal with these questions and show why it is unnecessary for kids to rebel and revolt against their parents. P.E.T. is *revolutionary, yes, but not a method that invites revolution*. Rather, it is a method that can help parents avoid being fired, can prevent war in the home, and bring parents and children closer rather than grouped against each other as hostile antagonists.

Parents who at first may be inclined to reject our methods as too revolutionary may find the motivation to study them with an open mind by reading the following excerpt from a history submitted by a mother and father after they had taken P.E.T.

"Bill, at sixteen, was our greatest problem. He was estranged. He was running wild and was completely irresponsible. He was getting his first *D*'s and *F*'s in school. He never came home from dates at the agreed times, offering as excuses flat tires, unwound watches, and empty gas tanks. We spied on him, he lied to us. We grounded him. We took away his license. We docked his allowance. Our conversations were full of recriminations. All to no avail. After one violent argument, he lay on the kitchen floor and kicked and screamed and shouted that he was going crazy. At that point we enrolled in Dr. Gordon's class for parents. Change did not come overnight . . . We never had felt like a unit, a warm and loving, deeply caring, family. This only came about after great changes in our attitudes and values. . . . This new idea of being a person—a strong separate person, expressing his own values but not forcing them on another, but being a good model—this was the turning point. We had much greater influence. . . . From rebellion and fits of rage, from failure in school, Bill changed to an open, friendly, loving person who calls his parents 'two of my favorite people.' . . . He is finally back in the family. . . . I have a relationship with him I never believed possible, full of love and trust and independence. He is strongly internally motivated and,

when each one of us is also, we really live and grow
as a family."

Parents who learn to use our new ways of communicating
their feelings are not likely to produce a child like the six-
teen-year old boy who sat in my office and announced with a
straight face:

"I don't have to do anything around the house.
Why should I? It's my parents' duty to take care of
me. They are legally required to. I didn't ask to be
born, did I? As long as I am a minor, they have to
feed me and clothe me. And I don't have to do a
darn thing. I'm not required to please them at all."

When I heard what this young man said and obviously
believed, I could not help but think, "What kind of persons
are we producing if children are permitted to grow up with
the attitude that the world owes them so much even though
they give back so little? What kind of citizen are parents
sending out into the world? What kind of society will these
selfish human beings make?"

Almost without exception parents can be categorized
roughly into three groups—the "winners," the "losers," and
the "oscillators." Parents in the first group strongly defend
and persuasively justify their right to exercise authority or
power over the child. They believe in restricting, setting
limits, demanding certain behaviors, giving commands, and
expecting obedience. They use threats of punishment to influence the child to obey, and mete out punishments when he
does not. When conflict arises between the needs of the parents and those of the child, these parents consistently resolve
the conflict in such a way that *the parent wins and the child
loses.* Generally, these parents rationalize their "winning" by

such stereotyped thinking as "Father knows best," "It's for the good of the child," "Children actually want parental authority," or simply the vague notion that "It is the responsibility of parents to use their authority for the good of the child, because parents know best what is right and wrong."

The second group of parents, somewhat fewer in number than the "winners," allow their children a great deal of freedom most of the time. They consciously avoid setting limits and proudly admit that they do not condone authoritarian methods. When conflict occurs between the needs of the parent and those of the child, rather consistently it is *the child who wins and the parent who loses,* because such parents believe it is harmful to frustrate the child's needs.

Probably the largest group of parents is made up of those who find it impossible to follow consistently either one of the first two approaches. Consequently, in trying to arrive at a "judicious mixture" of each they oscillate back and forth between being strict and lenient, tough and easy, restrictive and permissive, winning and losing. As one mother told us:

> "I try to be permissive with my children until they get so bad I can't stand them. Then I feel I have to change and start using my authority until I get so strict I can't stand myself."

The parents who shared these feelings in one of the P.E.T. classes unknowingly spoke for the large number in the "oscillating group." These are the parents who are probably most confused and uncertain, and, as we shall show later, whose children are often the most disturbed.

The major dilemma of today's parents is that they perceive only two approaches to handling conflicts in the home—conflicts that inevitably arise between parent and child. They see but two alternatives in child-rearing. Some choose the "I win—you lose" approach, some the· "You win—I lose" approach, while others seemingly cannot decide between the two.

Parents in P.E.T. are surprised to learn that there is an alternative to the two "win-lose" methods. We call it the "no-lose" method of resolving conflicts, and helping parents learn how to use it effectively is one of the principal aims of the P.E.T. program. While this method has been used for years for resolving other conflicts, few parents have ever thought of it as a method for resolving parent-child conflicts.

Many husbands and wives resolve their conflicts by mutual problem-solving. So do business partners. Labor unions and management negotiate contracts binding to both. Property settlements in divorces are often arrived at by joint decision-making. Even children frequently work out their conflicts by mutual agreement or informal contracts acceptable to both ("If you do this, then I'll agree to that"). With increasing frequency, industrial organizations are training executives to use participative decision-making in resolving conflicts.

No gimmick or quick road to effective parenthood, the "no-lose" method requires a rather basic change in the attitudes of most parents toward their children. It takes time to use it in the home, and it requires that parents first learn the skills of nonevaluative listening and honest communication of their own feelings. Consequently, the no-lose method is described and illustrated in later chapters of this book.

Its position in the book, however, does not reflect the true importance of the no-lose method in our total approach to child rearing. In fact, this new method of bringing discipline into the home through effective management of conflict is the heart and soul of our philosophy. It is the master key to parent effectiveness. Parents who take the time to understand it and then conscientiously employ it at home as the alternative to the two win-lose methods are richly rewarded, usually far beyond their hopes and expectations.

2

Parents Are Persons, Not Gods

When people become parents, something strange and unfortunate happens. They begin to assume a role or act a part and forget that they are persons. Now that they have entered the sacred realm of parenthood, they feel they must take up the mantle of "parents." Now they earnestly try to behave in certain ways because they think that is how parents should behave. Frank and Helen Bates, two human beings, suddenly become transformed into Mr. and Mrs. Bates, Parents.

In a very serious way, this transformation is unfortunate, because it so often results in parents forgetting they are still humans with human faults, persons with personal limitations, real people with real feelings. Forgetting the reality of their own human-ness, when people become parents they frequently cease to be human. They no longer feel free to be themselves, whatever they may happen to be feeling at different moments. As parents now, they have a responsibility to be something better than mere persons.

This terrible burden of responsibility brings a challenge to these persons-turned-parents. They feel they must always be consistent in their feelings, must always be loving of their children, must be unconditionally accepting and tolerant, must put aside their own selfish needs and sacrifice for the children, must be fair at all times, and above all must not make the mistakes their own parents made with them.

While these good intentions are understandable and admirable, they usually make parents less rather than more effective. Forgetting one's human-ness is the first serious mistake one can make on entering parenthood. An effective parent lets himself be a person—a real person. Children deeply appreciate this quality of realness and human-ness in their parents. They often say so: "My father is a *real* guy," or "My mother is a nice *person*." As they move into adolescence, kids sometimes say, "My parents are more like *friends* than parents. They're groovy people. They've got faults like everyone else, but I like them the way they are."

What are these kids saying? It is fairly obvious they like their parents to be persons, not gods. They respond favorably to their parents as people, not as actors playing some part, pretending to be something they are not.

How can parents *be* persons to their children? How can they maintain the quality of realness in their parenthood? In this chapter, we want to show parents that to be an effective parent it is not necessary to throw away their human-ness. You can accept yourself as a person who has positive as well as negative feelings toward children. *You don't even have to be consistent to be an effective parent.* You don't have to pretend to feel accepting or loving toward a child when you genuinely do not feel that way. You also don't have to feel the same degree of lovingness and acceptance toward all your children. Finally, you and your spouse don't have to put up a common front in your dealings with the children. But it is essential that you learn to know what it is you *are* feeling. In our P.E.T. classes we found that a few diagrams help parents to recognize what they are feeling and what causes them to feel in various ways in various situations.

"Acceptance Diagrams" for Parents

All parents are persons who will from time to time have two different kinds of feelings toward their children—acceptance and nonacceptance. "Real-person" parents sometimes feel accepting of what a child is doing and sometimes feel unaccepting.

All of your child's possible behaviors—everything he might possibly do or say—can be represented by a rectangular area.

```
┌─────────────────┐
│       All        │
│    Possible      │
│    Behaviors     │
│     of Your      │
│      Child       │
└─────────────────┘
```

Obviously, some of his behaviors you can readily accept; some you cannot. We can represent this difference by dividing the rectangle into an *area of acceptance* and an *area of nonacceptance*.

```
┌─────────────────┐
│     Area of      │
│   Acceptance     │
├─────────────────┤
│     Area of      │
│  Nonacceptance   │
└─────────────────┘
```

Your child's watching TV on Saturday morning, leaving you free to do housework, would fall into the Area of Acceptance. If he has the volume on the TV up so loud that it is driving you up the wall, that behavior would fall into the Area of Nonacceptance.

Where the line of demarcation is drawn in the rectangle obviously will be different for different parents. One mother may find very few behaviors of her child unacceptable to her and thus quite frequently feels warm and accepting toward her child.

A relatively
"accepting"
parent

| Area of Acceptance |
| Area of Nonacceptance |

Another mother may find many behaviors of her child unacceptable to her and will quite *infrequently* be able to feel warm and accepting toward her child.

A relatively
"unaccepting"
parent

| Area of Acceptance |
| Area of Nonacceptance |

How accepting a parent is toward a child is *partly* a function of the kind of person that parent is. Some parents, simply because of their own make-up, have the capacity to be very accepting toward children. Such parents, interestingly enough, are usually very accepting toward people in general. Being accepting is a characteristic of their own personality— their inner security, their high tolerance level, the fact that they like themselves, the fact that their feelings about themselves are quite independent of what happens around them, and a host of other personality variables. Everybody has known such people; although you may not have known what made them that way, you regard them as "accepting people." One feels good around such people—you can talk openly to them, let your hair down. One can be oneself.

Other parents, as persons, are just plain unaccepting toward others. They somehow find much of other people's behavior unacceptable to them. When you observe them with their children you may be puzzled as to why so much behavior that seems acceptable to you is unacceptable to them. Inwardly you may say to yourself, "Oh come on, let the children alone—they aren't bothering anyone!"

Often these are people with very strong and rigid notions about how others "should" behave, what behavior is "right" and "wrong"—not just about children but about everyone. You may feel vaguely uncomfortable around such people because you probably have doubts about whether they accept you.

Recently, I observed a mother with her two young sons in a supermarket. To me, the boys seemed rather well-behaved. They were not boisterous, nor were they causing any trouble. Yet that mother was incessantly telling the boys what they should or shouldn't be doing: "Keep up with me, now." "Hands off the cart." "Stand aside, you're in the way." "Hurry up!" "Don't touch the food." "Leave those sacks alone." It was as if this mother could not accept *anything* those children were doing.

While the line that divides the areas of acceptance and unacceptance is partly influenced by factors solely *within the parent*, the degree of acceptance is also determined by *the child*. It is harder to feel accepting toward some children. They may be highly aggressive and active, or physically unattractive, or they may exhibit certain traits that one does not particularly admire. A child who begins life with illnesses, or doesn't go to sleep easily or cries frequently or has colic would, understandably, be more difficult for most parents to accept.

The idea, advocated in many books and articles written for parents, that a parent should feel equally accepting of each child, is not only fallacious, but has caused many parents to feel guilty when they do experience different degrees of acceptance toward their children. Most people would readily agree that they feel different degrees of acceptance toward the adults they meet. Why should it be any different in the way they feel toward children?

The fact that parental acceptance of a particular child is influenced by the characteristics of that child can be shown as follows:

Area of Acceptance
Area of Nonacceptance

Parent with child
A

Area of Acceptance
Area of Nonacceptance

Parent with child
B

Some parents find it easier to accept girls than boys—others the opposite. Highly mobile children are harder for some parents to accept. Children who are actively curious and like to explore many things independently are harder to accept by some parents than children who are more passive and dependent. I have known some children who inexplicably had such charm and appeal for me that it seemed I could accept almost anything they would do. I have also had the misfortune to encounter some whose very presence was unpleasant to me and much of the behavior of these children seemed unacceptable to me.

Another fact of great significance is that the dividing line between acceptance and nonacceptance does not remain stationary but moves up and down. It is affected by many factors, including the current state of mind of the parent and the situation in which the parent and child find themselves.

A parent who at a particular moment is feeling energetic, healthy, and happy with himself most likely can feel accepting of much of his child's behavior. Fewer things that the child does will bother the parent when he is feeling good about himself.

<table>
<tr><td>Parent feeling good
about himself.</td><td>Area of
Acceptance

Area of
Nonacceptance</td></tr>
</table>

When the parent feels dead tired through loss of sleep, or has a headache, or is feeling irritable toward himself, a great many things that the child does might bother this father or mother.

This inconsistency can be illustrated as follows:

<table>
<tr><td>Parent feeling
bad about himself.</td><td>Area of
Acceptance

Area of
Nonacceptance</td></tr>
</table>

A parent's feeling of acceptance will also change from one situation to the next. All parents recognize in themselves that they are usually much less accepting of their children's behavior when the family is visiting friends than when they are all at home. And how parents' level of tolerance for their children's behavior changes suddenly when the grandparents come to visit!

It must often seem puzzling to children that their parents get angry at their table manners when company is visiting, even though these same manners are acceptable when the family is not entertaining.

This inconsistency may be illustrated as follows:

| Area of Acceptance |
| Area of Nonacceptance |

Situation A

| Area of Acceptance |
| Area of Nonacceptance |

Situation B

The existence of two parents adds to the complexity of the acceptance picture in families. To begin with, one parent often is basically more accepting than the other.

> Jack, a strong, active five-year-old boy, picks up a football and starts throwing it to his brother in the living room. Mother gets upset and finds this quite unacceptable because of her fears that Jack will damage something in the room. Dad, however, not only accepts the behavior but proudly says, "Look at Jack—he's going to be a real ballplayer. Look at that forward pass, will you!"

Furthermore, the line of demarcation of each parent moves up and down at different times depending upon the situation and also the state of mind of each parent. So a mother and father cannot *always* feel the same way about the same behavior of their child at a particular moment.

Parents Can and Will Be Inconsistent

Inevitably, then, parents will be *inconsistent*. How could they be anything else, when their feelings are changing from day to day, from child to child, from situation to situation? If parents tried to be consistent, they could not be real. The traditional admonition to parents that they must be consistent with their children at all costs ignores the fact that situations are different, children are different, and Mom and Dad are humans who are different. Furthermore, such advice has had the harmful effect of influencing parents to pretend, to act the part of a person whose feelings are always the same.

Parents Don't Have to Put up a "United Front"

Even more important, the advice to be consistent has led many a mother and father to think that they should always be together in their feelings, presenting a united parental front to their children. This is nonsense. Yet, it is one of the most entrenched beliefs in child-rearing. Parents, according to this traditional notion, should always back each other up so that the child is led to believe that both parents feel the same way about a particular behavior.

Apart from the utter unfairness of this strategy—ganging up on the child in a two-against-one alignment—it often promotes "unrealness" on the part of one of the parents.

> A 16-year-old girl's room is generally not kept clean enough to meet her mother's standards. This daughter's cleaning habits are unacceptable to mother (in her area of nonacceptance). Her father, however, finds the room acceptably clean and neat. The same behavior is within his area of acceptance. Mother puts pressure on Father to feel the same

way about the room as she does, so that they can have a united front (and thus have more influence on the daughter). If Father goes along, he is being untrue to his real feelings.

A six-year-old boy is playing with his truck and making more racket than his father can accept. Mother, however, is not bothered at all. She is delighted that the child is playing independently instead of hanging around her as he did all day. Father approaches Mother. "Why don't you do something to stop him making all that noise?" If Mother goes along, she is being untrue to her real feelings.

False Acceptance

No parent ever feels accepting toward all the behavior of a child. Some behaviors of a child will always be in the "area of nonacceptance" of the parent. I have known parents whose "acceptance line" is very low on our rectangle, but I have never met an "unconditionally accepting" parent. Some parents pretend to be accepting of much of their children's behavior, but these parents too are playing a role at being a good parent. Therefore, a certain amount of their acceptance is false. Outwardly they may act in an accepting way, but inwardly they are really feeling unaccepting.

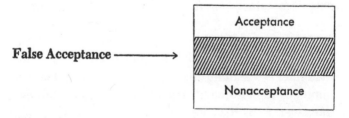

Suppose a parent is feeling irritated because the five-year-old is staying up late. The parent has needs of her own—say, to read a new book. She would much prefer doing this to devoting time to the child. Also, she is worried about the child's not getting enough sleep and then being irritable the next day or perhaps catching a cold. Yet this mother, trying to follow the "permissive" approach, is reluctant to make demands on the child for fear this might be inconsistent with her principles. This parent cannot help but show "false acceptance." She may act as if she is accepting of the child's staying up, but inside she is not accepting of it at all; she is feeling quite irritated, perhaps angry, and undoubtedly frustrated because her own needs are not being met.

What are the effects on a child when a parent is being falsely accepting? Children, as everybody knows, are amazingly sensitive to the attitudes of their parents. They are rather uncanny in sensing the parents' true feelings because parents send "nonverbal messages" to their children—cues that are perceived by the children, sometimes consciously, sometimes unconsciously. A parent whose inner attitude is one of irritation or anger cannot help but give off subtle cues, perhaps a frown, a lifted eyebrow, a particular tone of voice, a certain posture, a tenseness of the facial muscles. Even very young children pick up such cues, learning from their experience that these cues usually mean that Mother is not really accepting what they are doing. Consequently, the child is apt to feel disapproval—at that particular moment he feels that his parent does not like him.

What happens when Mother genuinely feels unaccepting but her *behavior* appears to the child to be accepting? The child gets this behavioral message, too. Now he is really confused. He is receiving "mixed messages" or contradictory cues—*behavior* that tells him it is all right to stay up but also *nonverbal* cues that tell him mother does not actually like him for staying up. This child is "in a bind." He wants to stay up, but he also wants to be loved (accepted). His staying up seems to be acceptable to mother, yet there is that frown on mother's face. Now what should he do?

Putting a child in such a bind can seriously affect his psychological health. Everyone knows how frustrating and uncomfortable it is when you don't know which behavior to choose because you get mixed messages from another person. Suppose you ask a hostess if it is all right to smoke your pipe in her house. She replies, "I don't mind." Yet, when you light up, her eyes and face give off nonverbal cues that tell you she does indeed mind. What do you do? You may ask, "Are you sure you don't mind?" Or you put your pipe back in your pocket and feel resentful. Or you go ahead and smoke, all the time feeling that your hostess does not like this behavior.

Children experience the same sort of dilemma, confronted with acceptance that appears to them to be dishonest. Frequent exposure to such situations can cause children to feel unloved. It can bring on frequent "testing" on the part of the child, can cause children to carry around a heavy load of anxiety, foster in children feelings of insecurity, and so on.

I have come to believe that the most difficult parent for children to cope with may be the honey-mouthed, "permissive," undemanding parent who acts as if she is accepting but subtly communicates unacceptance.

There is a serious by-product of being falsely accepting, and in the long run this may be even more harmful to the relationship between parent and child. When a child receives "mixed messages," he may begin to have grave doubts about the honesty or genuineness of his parent. He learns from many experiences that mother often says one thing when she feels another. Eventually the child grows to distrust such a parent. Here are some feelings teen-agers have shared with me:

> "My mother is a phony. She acts so sweet but she really isn't."
> "I can never trust my parents, because even though they don't say so, I know that they don't

approve of a lot of the things I do."

"I go along thinking my parents don't care what time I get in. Then if I get in too late I get the silent treatment the next day."

"My parents are not strict at all. They let me do pretty much what I want to do. But I can tell what they disapprove of."

"Everytime I come to the table barefooted, my mother gets a disgusted look on her face. But she doesn't ever say anything."

"My mother is so darned sweet and so understanding all the time, but I know she doesn't like the kind of person I am. She likes my brother because he is more like her."

When children have such feelings, it is evident that their parents have not really concealed their true feelings or attitudes, even though they may have thought they were doing it. *In a relationship as close and enduring as the parent-child relationship, the parent's true feelings seldom can be hidden from the child.*

So when parents have been influenced by the advocates of "permissiveness" to try to act in an accepting way far beyond their own true attitudes, they have seriously harmed the relationship with their children, as well as produced psychological damage to the children themselves. Parents need to understand that they had better not try to extend their area of acceptance beyond what their true attitudes are. Far better for parents to realize when they are not feeling accepting and not pretend that they are.

Can You Accept the Child but Not His Behavior?

I don't know where this idea originated, but it has had wide acceptance and great appeal, particularly for parents who have been influenced by the advocates of permissive-

ness, yet who are honest enough with themselves to realize
they do not always accept their children's behavior. I have
come to believe that this is another fallacious and harmful
idea—one that prevents parents from being real. While it may
have relieved some of the guilt that parents have been made
to feel when they are unaccepting of their children, this idea
has been damaging to many parent-child relationships.

It has given professional sanction for parents to use their
authority or power to restrict ("set limits" on) certain behaviors that they cannot accept. Parents have interpreted this to
mean that it is all right to control, restrict, prohibit, demand,
or deny, as long as they do it in some clever way so that the
child perceives it as not rejecting of *him* but of his *behavior*.
Herein lies the fallacy.

How can you be accepting of your *child*, independent of
and contrary to your unaccepting feelings toward *whatever
the child is doing or saying?* What is "the child" if it is not the
behaving child, acting in a particular way at a particular
moment in time? It is a *behaving child* toward whom a
parent has feelings, whether accepting or nonaccepting, not
some abstraction called "child."

I am certain that from the child's own viewpoint it appears
the same to him. If he senses that you are not feeling accepting of his putting his dirty shoes on your new couch, I doubt
very much that he then makes the high-level inference that
even though you do not like his feet-on-the-couch behavior,
you nevertheless feel very accepting of him "as a person."
Quite the contrary—he undoubtedly feels that because of
what he as a total person *is doing* as of this moment, you are
not at all accepting of *him*.

To try to get a child to understand that his parent accepts
him but does not accept what *he does*, even if it were possible
for the parent to separate the two, must be as difficult as
getting a child to believe that a spanking he is being administered is "hurting his parent more than it is him."

Whether a child feels that *he as a person* is unaccepted will be determined by how many of his behaviors are unacceptable. Parents who find unacceptable a great many things that their children do or say will inevitably foster in these children a deep feeling that they are unacceptable as persons. Conversely, parents who are accepting of a great many things their children do or say will produce children who are more likely to feel acceptable as persons.

It is best for you to admit to yourself (and to the child) that you don't accept him as a person when he is doing or saying something in a particular way at a particular moment. That way the child will learn to perceive you as open and honest, because you are being real.

Also, when you tell a child, "I accept you, but stop what you are doing", you are not likely to alter his reaction to this use of your power one bit. Children hate to be denied, restricted, or prohibited by their parents, no matter what sort of explanation accompanies the use of such authority and power. "Setting limits" has a high probability of backfiring on parents in the form of resistance, rebellion, lying, and resentment. Furthermore, there are far more effective methods for influencing children to modify behavior unacceptable to their parents than using parental power to "set limits" or restrict.

Our Definition of Parents Who Are Real Persons

Our "Acceptance Diagrams" help parents understand their own inevitable feelings and the conditions that influence these feelings to change continuously. Real parents will inevitably feel both accepting and unaccepting toward their children; their attitude toward the same behavior cannot be consistent; it must vary from time to time. They should not (and cannot) hide their true feelings; they should accept the fact that one parent may feel accepting and the other unaccepting of the same behavior; and they should realize that each will inevitably feel different degrees of acceptance toward each of their children.

In short, parents *are* people, not gods. They do not have to act unconditionally accepting, or even consistently accepting. Neither should they pretend to be accepting when they are not. While children undoubtedly *prefer* to be accepted, they can constructively handle their parent's unaccepting feelings when parents send clear and honest messages that match their true feelings. Not only will this make it easier for children to cope, but it will help each child to see his parent as a real person—transparent, human, someone with whom he would like to have a relationship.

3

How to Listen So Kids Will Talk to You: The Language of Acceptance

A fifteen-year-old girl, at the conclusion of one of her weekly counseling sessions with me, gets up from her chair, pauses before heading for the door and says:

> "It feels good to be able to talk to someone about how I really feel. I've never talked about these things with anyone else before. I could never talk with my parents like this."

A mother and father of a sixteen-year-old boy who is failing in school ask me:

> "How can we get Frankie to confide in us? We never know what he's thinking. We know he's unhappy, but we have no idea what's going on inside that boy."

A bright, attractive thirteen-year-old girl, brought to me just after she ran away from home with two of her girl friends, made this telling comment about her relationship with her mother:

> "It got to the point where we just couldn't confide
> at all about even the littlest things ... like school
> work. I'd be afraid I flunked a test, and I'd tell her I
> didn't do well. And she'd say, 'Well, why not?' and
> then get mad at me. So I just started lying. I didn't
> like to lie but I did it, and it got so it didn't really
> bother me ... Finally it was just like two different
> people talking to each other—neither of us would
> show our real feelings ... what we *really* thought."

These are not unusual examples of how children pull down
the shades on their parents, refusing to share with them what
really goes on inside. Kids learn that talking to their parents
is not helpful and often not safe. Consequently, many parents
miss thousands of chances to help their children with problems they encounter in life.

Why do so many parents get "written off" by their children
as a source of help? Why do children stop talking to their
parents about the things that really bother them? Why are so
few parents successful in maintaining a helping relationship
with their children?

And why do children find it so much easier to talk to competent professional counselors than to talk to their parents?
What does the professional counselor do differently that
enables him to foster a helping relationship with the children?

In recent years, psychologists have been finding some
answers to these questions. Through research and clinical
experience, we are beginning to understand the necessary
ingredients for an effective helping relationship. Perhaps the
most essential of these is the *"language of acceptance."*

THE POWER OF THE LANGUAGE OF ACCEPTANCE

When a person is able to feel and communicate genuine
acceptance of another, he possesses a capacity for being a
powerful helping agent for the other. His acceptance of the

other, as he is, is an important factor in fostering a relationship in which the other person can grow, develop, make constructive changes, learn to solve problems, move in the direction of psychological health, become more productive and
creative, and actualize his fullest potential. It is one of those
simple but beautiful paradoxes of life: When a person feels
that he is truly accepted by another, as he is, then he is freed
to move from there and to begin to think about how he wants
to change, how he wants to grow, how he can become
different, how he might become more of what he is capable of
being.

Acceptance is like the fertile soil that permits a tiny seed to
develop into the lovely flower it is capable of becoming. The
soil only *enables* the seed to become the flower. It *releases*
the capacity of the seed to grow, but the capacity is entirely
within the seed. As with the seed, a child contains entirely
within his organism the capacity to develop. Acceptance is
like the soil—it merely enables the child to actualize his
potential.

Why is parental acceptance such a significant positive
influence on the child? This is not generally understood by
parents. Most people have been brought up to believe that if
you accept a child he will remain just the way he is; that the
best way to help a child become something better in the
future is to tell him what you *don't* accept about him now.

Therefore, most parents rely heavily on the language of
unacceptance in rearing children, believing this is the best
way to help them. The soil that most parents provide for their
children's growth is heavy with evaluation, judgment, criticism, preaching, moralizing, admonishing, and commanding—messages that convey *unacceptance* of the child as he is.

I recall the words of a thirteen-year-old girl who was just
starting to rebel against her parents' values and standards:

> "They tell me so often how bad I am and how
> stupid my ideas are and how I can't be trusted that

> I just do more things they don't like. If they already
> think I'm bad and stupid, I might as well go ahead
> and do all these things anyway."

This bright girl was wise enough to understand the old
adage, "Tell a child often enough how bad he is and he will
most certainly become bad." Children often become what
their parents tell them they are.

Apart from this effect, the language of unacceptance turns
kids off. They stop talking to their parents. They learn that it
is far more comfortable to keep their feelings and problems to
themselves.

The language of acceptance opens kids up. It frees them to
share their feelings and problems. Professional therapists and
counselors have shown just how powerful such acceptance
can be. Those therapists and counselors who are most effective are the ones who can convey to the people who come to
them for help that they are truly accepted. This is why one
often hears people say that in counseling or therapy they felt
totally free of the counselor's judgment. They report that
they experienced a freedom to tell him the worst about themselves—they felt their counselor would *accept them* no matter
what they said or felt. Such acceptance is one of the most
important elements contributing to the growth and change
that takes place in people through counseling and therapy.

Conversely, we also have learned from these "professional
change agents" that unacceptance too often closes people up,
makes them feel defensive, produces discomfort, makes them
afraid to talk or to take a look at themselves. Thus, part of the
"secret of success" of the professional therapist's ability to
foster change and growth in troubled people is the absence of
unacceptance in his relationship with them and his ability to
talk the language of acceptance so it is genuinely felt by the
other.

In working with parents in our Parent Effectiveness Training course, we have demonstrated that parents can be taught these same skills used by professional counselors. Most of these parents drastically reduce the frequency of messages that convey unacceptance and acquire a surprisingly high level of skill in employing the language of acceptance.

When parents learn how to demonstrate through their words an inner feeling of acceptance toward a child, they are in possession of a tool that can produce some startling effects. They can be influential in his learning to accept and like himself and to acquire a sense of his own worth. They can greatly facilitate his developing and actualizing the potential with which he was genetically endowed. They can accelerate his movement away from dependence and toward independence and self-direction. They can help him learn to solve for himself the problems that life inevitably brings, and they can give him the strength to deal constructively with the usual disappointments and pain of childhood and adolescence.

Of all the effects of acceptance none is as important as the inner feeling of the child that he is loved. For to accept another "as he is" is truly an act of love; to feel accepted is to feel loved. And in psychology, we have only begun to realize the tremendous power of feeling loved: It can promote the growth of mind and body, and is probably the most effective therapeutic force we know for repairing both psychological and physical damage.

Acceptance Must Be Demonstrated

It is one thing for a parent to feel acceptance toward a child; it is another thing to make that acceptance felt. Unless a parent's acceptance comes through to the child, it can have no influence on him. A parent must learn how to demonstrate his acceptance so that the child feels it.

Specific skills are required to be able to do this. Most parents, however, tend to think of acceptance as a passive thing—a state of mind, an attitude, a feeling. True, acceptance does originate from within, but to be an effective force in influencing another, it must be actively communicated or demonstrated. I can never be certain that I am accepted by another until he demonstrates it in some active way.

The professional psychological counselor or psychotherapist, whose effectiveness as a helping agent is so greatly dependent on his being able to demonstrate his acceptance of the client, spends years learning ways to implement this attitude through his own habits of communication. Through formal training and long experience, professional counselors acquire specific skills in communicating acceptance. They learn that what they say makes the difference between their being helpful or not.

Talk can cure, and talk can foster constructive change. But it must be the right kind of talk.

The same is true for parents. How they talk to their children will determine whether they will be helpful or destructive. The effective parent, like the effective counselor, must learn how to communicate his acceptance and acquire the same communication skills.

Parents in our classes skeptically ask, "Is it possible for a nonprofessional like myself to learn the skills of a professional counselor?" Ten years ago we would have said, "No." However, in our classes we have demonstrated that it is possible for most parents to learn how to become effective helping agents for their children. We know now that it is not knowledge of psychology or an intellectual understanding *about* people that makes a good counselor. It is primarily a matter of learning how to talk to people in a "constructive" way.

Psychologists call this "therapeutic communication," meaning that certain kinds of messages have a "therapeutic" or healthy effect on people. They make them feel better, encourage them to talk, help them express their feelings, foster a feeling of worth or self-esteem, reduce threat or fear, facilitate growth and constructive change.

Other kinds of talk are "nontherapeutic" or destructive. These messages tend to make people feel judged or guilty; they restrict expression of honest feelings, threaten the person, foster feelings of unworthiness or low self-esteem, block growth and constructive change by making the person defend more strongly the way he is.

While a very small number of parents possess this therapeutic skill intuitively and hence are "naturals", most parents have to go through a process of first unlearning their destructive ways of communicating and then learning more constructive ways. This means that parents first have to expose their typical habits of communication to see for themselves how their talk is destructive or nontherapeutic. Then they need to be taught some new ways of responding to children.

COMMUNICATING ACCEPTANCE NON-VERBALLY

We send messages via the spoken word (what we say) or what social scientists call *nonverbal messages* (what we do not say). Nonverbal messages are communicated via gestures, postures, facial expressions, or other behaviors. Wave your right hand away from you with the palm toward the child and it is highly probable that the child will interpret this gesture as "Go away" or "Get away from me" or "I don't want to be bothered right now." Turn the palm away from the child and wave your hand toward you and the child will probably perceive this gesture as a message to "Come on over," "Come closer," or "I would like you here with me." The first gesture communicated nonacceptance; the second, acceptance.

Nonintervention to Show Acceptance

Parents can show acceptance of a child by not intervening in his activities. Take a child who is attempting to build a castle of sand at the beach. The parent who keeps away from the child and occupies himself with an activity of his own, permitting the child to make "mistakes" or create his own unique design for a castle (which will probably not be like the parent's design or, for that matter, may not even look like a castle)—that parent is sending a nonverbal message of acceptance.

The child will feel, "What I am doing is okay," "My castle-building behavior is acceptable," "Mother accepts me doing what I am doing as of now."

Keeping hands off when a child is engaged in some activity is a strong nonverbal way of communicating acceptance. Many parents fail to realize how frequently they communicate nonacceptance to their children simply by interfering, intruding, moving in, checking up, joining in. Too often adults do not let children just be. They invade the privacy of their rooms, or move into their own personal and private thoughts, refusing to permit them a separateness. Often this is the result of parental fears and anxieties, their own feelings of insecurity.

Parents want children to learn ("Here's what a castle should really look like"). They are uncomfortable when children make a mistake ("Build the castle farther from the water so a wave won't topple the castle wall"). They want to be proud of their children's accomplishments ("Look at the fine castle our Jimmy made"). They impose on kids rigid adult concepts of right and wrong ("Shouldn't your castle have a moat?"). They have secret ambitions for their children ("You're never going to learn anything, building that thing all afternoon"). They are overly concerned about what others think of their children ("That's not as good a castle as you're capable of making"). They want to feel that their child needs them ("Let Daddy help"), and so on.

Thus, *doing nothing* in a situation when the child is engaged in an activity can communicate clearly that the parents accept him. It is my experience that parents do not permit this kind of "separateness" frequently enough. Understandably, a "hands off" attitude comes hard.

At the first boy-girl party that our daughter gave during her first year in high school, I remember feeling very rejected after being told by her that my highly imaginative and constructive suggestions for the entertainment of her guests were quite unwelcome. Only after recovering from my mild depression after being asked to stay out could I comprehend how I was communicating nonverbal messages of nonacceptance—"You can't give a good party by yourself," "You need my help," "I don't trust your judgment," "You are not being a perfect hostess," "You might make a mistake," "I don't want this party to be a failure," and so on.

Passive Listening to Show Acceptance

Saying nothing can also clearly communicate acceptance. Silence—"passive listening"—is a potent nonverbal message and can be used effectively to make a person feel genuinely accepted. Professional helping agents know this well and make extensive use of silence in their interviews. A person who describes his first interview with a psychologist or a psychiatrist frequently reports, "He didn't say anything; I did all the talking." Or, "I told him all the horrible things about me, but he didn't even criticize." Or, "I didn't think I could tell him anything, but I talked the whole hour."

What these people are describing is their experience—more than likely their *first* experience—talking with someone who merely *listened* to them. It can be a wonderful experience when a person's silence makes you feel accepted. Not communicating, then, actually does communicate something, as in this encounter between a parent and her daughter just home from junior high school:

CHILD: I got sent down to the vice-principal's office today.
PARENT: Oh?
CHILD: Yeah. Mr. Franks said I was talking too much in class.
PARENT: I see.
CHILD: I can't stand that old fossil. He sits up there and talks about his troubles or his grandchildren and expects us to be interested. It's so boring you'd never believe it.
PARENT: Mm—hmm.
CHILD: You just can't sit in that class doing nothing! You'd go crazy. Jeannie and I sit there and make jokes when he's talking. Oh, he's just the worst teacher you can imagine. It makes me mad when I get a lousy teacher.
PARENT: (Silence).
CHILD: I do good with a good teacher, but if I get someone like Mr. Franks I just don't feel like learning anything. Why do they let a guy like that teach?
PARENT: (Shrugs).
CHILD: I suppose I'd better get used to it, 'cause I'm not always going to get good teachers. There are more lousy ones than good ones and if I let the lousy ones get me down, I'm not going to get the grades I need to get into a good college. I'm really hurting myself, I guess.

In this brief episode, the value of silence is clearly demonstrated. The parent's passive listening enabled the child to move beyond the initial factual report of being sent to the vice-principal. It permitted her to admit why she was punished, to release her angry and hateful feelings toward her teacher, to contemplate the consequences of continuing to react to bad teachers, and finally to come to her own independent conclusion that she was actually hurting herself by this kind of behavior. During the short period when this child was *accepted*, she *grew*. She was allowed to express her feelings; she was helped to move *alone* into a kind of self-initiated problem-solving. From this emerged her own constructive solution, tentative though it may have been.

The parent's silence facilitated this "moment of development," this small "increment of growth," this instance of an organism in the process of self-directed change. What a tragedy for the parent to have missed this opportunity to contribute to the growth of that child, if she had interfered with the child's communication by interjecting such typical nonaccepting responses as:

> "You what? You were sent to the vice-principal! Oh dear!"
> "Well, that should teach you a lesson!"
> "Now, Mr. Franks is not that bad, is he?"
> "Darling, you just have to learn some self-control."
> "You better learn to adjust to all kinds of teachers."

All these messages, and the many more that parents typically send in situations like this, not only would have communicated nonacceptance of the child; they would have stopped further communication and prevented any problem-solving on her part.

So, saying nothing, as well as doing nothing, can communicate acceptance. And acceptance fosters constructive growth and change.

COMMUNICATING ACCEPTANCE VERBALLY

Most parents realize that one cannot remain silent very long in a human interaction. People want some kind of verbal interaction. Obviously, parents must talk to their children, and their children need talk from them, if they are to have an intimate, vital relationship.

Talk is essential, but *how* parents talk to children is crucial. I can tell a great deal about a parent-child relationship simply by observing the kinds of verbal communication that occur between that parent and child, particularly the way the parent responds to the child's communications. Parents need to examine how they respond verbally to children, because the key to any parent's effectiveness is found here.

In our P.E.T. classes we use an exercise to help parents recognize what kinds of verbal responses they use when their kids come to them with feelings or problems. If you would like to try this exercise now, all you need is a sheet of blank paper and a pencil or pen. Suppose your fifteen-year-old announces one night at the dinner table:

> "This school is for the birds. All you learn is a lot of unimportant facts that don't do you any good. I've decided not to go to college at all. You don't need a college education to be someone important. There are a lot of other ways to get ahead in the world."

Now, write down on the paper exactly how you would respond verbally to that message. Write down your verbal communication—the exact words you would use in responding to that message from your child.

Now, when you have done that, try another situation. Your ten-year-old daughter says to you:

> "I don't know what's wrong with me. Ginny used to like me, but now she doesn't. She never comes down here to play anymore. And if I go up there she's always playing with Joyce and the two of them play together and have fun, and I just stand there all by myself. I hate them both."

Again, write down exactly what you would say to your daughter in response to that message.

Now, another situation in which your eleven-year-old says to you:

"How come I have to take care of the yard and take the garbage out? Johnny's mother doesn't make him do all that stuff! You're not fair! Kids shouldn't have to do that much work. Nobody is made to do as much as I have to do."

Write down your response.

One last situation. Your five-year-old boy becomes more and more frustrated when he can't get the attention of his mother and father and your two guests after dinner. The four of you are talking intently, renewing your friendship after a long separation. Suddenly you are shocked when your little boy loudly shouts:

"You're all a bunch of dirty old smelly stinkbugs. I hate you."

Again, write down exactly what you would say in response to this vibrant message.

The various ways you have just responded to these messages can be classified into categories. There are only about a dozen different categories into which parents' verbal responses fall. These are listed below. Take the responses you wrote down on your sheet of paper and try to classify each into whichever category fits your responses best.

1. ORDERING, DIRECTING, COMMANDING

Telling the child to do something, giving him an order or a command:

"I don't care what other parents do, you have to do the yard work!"
"Don't talk to your mother like that!"
"Now you go back up there and play with Ginny and Joyce!"
"Stop complaining!"

2. WARNING, ADMONISHING, THREATENING

Telling the child what consequences will occur if he does something:

> "If you do that, you'll be sorry!"
> "One more statement like that and you'll leave the room!"
> "You'd better not do that if you know what's good for you!"

3. EXHORTING, MORALIZING, PREACHING

Telling the child what he *should* or *ought* to do:

> "You shouldn't act like that."
> "You ought to do this. . . ."
> "You must always respect your elders."

4. ADVISING, GIVING SOLUTIONS OR SUGGESTIONS

Telling the child how to solve a problem, giving him advice or suggestions; providing answers or solutions for him:

> "Why don't you ask both Ginny and Joyce to play down here?"
> "Just wait a couple of years before deciding on college."
> "I suggest you talk to your teachers about that."
> "Go make friends with some other girls."

5. LECTURING, TEACHING, GIVING LOGICAL ARGUMENTS

Trying to influence the child with facts, counterarguments, logic, information, or your own opinions:

> "College can be the most wonderful experience you'll ever have."
> "Children must learn how to get along with each other."
> "Let's look at the facts about college graduates."
> "If kids learn to take responsibility around the house, they'll grow up to be responsible adults."
> "Look at it this way—your mother needs help around the house."
> "When I was your age, I had twice as much to do as you."

6. JUDGING, CRITICIZING, DISAGREEING, BLAMING

Making a negative judgment or evaluation of the child:

> "You're not thinking clearly."

"That's an immature point of view."
"You're very wrong about that."
"I couldn't disagree with you more."

7. PRAISING, AGREEING

Offering a positive evaluation or judgment, agreeing:

"Well, I think you're pretty."
"You have the ability to do well."
"I think you're right."
"I agree with you."

8. NAME-CALLING, RIDICULING, SHAMING

Making the child feel foolish, putting the child into a category, shaming him:

"You're a spoiled brat."
"Look here, Mr. Smarty."
"You're acting like a wild animal."
"Okay, little baby."

9. INTERPRETING, ANALYZING, DIAGNOSING

Telling the child what his motives are or analyzing why he is doing or saying something; communicating that you have him figured out or have him diagnosed:

"You're just jealous of Ginny."
"You're saying that to bug me."
"You really don't believe that at all."
"You feel that way because you're not doing well in school."

10. REASSURING, SYMPATHIZING, CONSOLING, SUPPORTING

Trying to make the child feel better, talking him out of his feelings, trying to make his feelings go away, denying the strength of his feelings:

"You'll feel different tomorrow."
"All kids go through this sometime."
Don't worry, things'll work out."
"You could be an excellent student, with your potential."
"I used to think that too."

"I know, school can be pretty boring sometimes."
"You usually get along with other kids very well."

11. PROBING, QUESTIONING, INTERROGATING

Trying to find reasons, motives, causes; searching for more information to help you solve the problem:

"When did you start feeling this way?"
"Why do you suppose you hate school?"
"Do the kids ever tell you why they don't want to play with you?"
"How many other kids have you talked to about the work they have to do?"
"Who put that idea into your head?"
"What will you do if you don't go to college?"

12. WITHDRAWING, DISTRACTING, HUMORING, DIVERTING

Trying to get the child away from the problem; withdrawing from the problem yourself; distracting the child, kidding him out of it, pushing the problem aside:

"Just forget about it."
"Let's not talk about it at the table."
"Come on—let's talk about something more pleasant."
"How's it going with your basketball?"
"Why don't you try burning the school building down?"
"We've been through all this before."

If you were able to fit each of your responses into one of these categories, you are a fairly typical parent. If one of your responses did not fit into any of the twelve categories, hold on to it until later when we introduce some other categories of responses to children's messages. Perhaps they will fit into one of those.

When parents do this exercise in our classes, over ninety per cent of most parents' responses fall into these twelve categories. Most of these mothers and fathers are surprised at the unanimity. Also, most of them have never had anyone point out just how they talk to their children—what modes of communication they use when responding to their children's feelings and problems.

Invariably, one of the parents asks, "Well now that we know how we talk, what about it? What are we supposed to learn from finding we all use the "Typical Twelve" categories?"

What About the "Typical Twelve"?

To understand what effects the "Typical Twelve" have on children or what they do to the parent-child relationship, parents must first be shown that their verbal responses usually carry more than one meaning or one message. For example, to say to a child who has just complained that her friend doesn't like her or doesn't play with her anymore, "I would suggest you try to treat Ginny better and then maybe she will want to play with you" conveys much more to a child than simply the "content" of your suggestion. The child may "hear" any or all of these hidden messages:

> "You don't accept my feeling the way I do, so you want me to change."
> "You don't trust me to work out this problem myself."
> "You think it's my fault, then."
> "You think I'm not as smart as you."
> "You think I'm doing something bad or wrong."

Or, when a child says, "I just can't stand school or anything about school" and you respond by saying, "Oh, we all felt that way about school at some time or another—you'll get over it," the child may pick up these additional messages:

> "You don't think my feelings are very important, then."
> "You can't accept me, feeling as I do."

"You feel it's not the school, it's me."
"You don't take me very seriously, then."
"You don't feel my judgment of school is legitimate."
"You don't seem to care how I'm feeling."

When parents say something *to* a child they often say something *about* him. This is why communication to a child has such an impact on him as a person and ultimately upon the relationship between you and him. Every time you talk to a child you are adding another brick to define the relationship that is being built between the two of you. And each message says something to the child about what you think of him. He gradually builds up a picture of how you are perceiving him as a person. Talk can be *constructive* to the child and to the relationship, or it can be *destructive*.

One way we help parents understand how the "typical twelve" can be destructive is to ask them to remember their own reactions when they shared their feelings with a friend. Invariably, the parents in our classes report that most of the time the "Typical Twelve" have a destructive effect on them or on their relationship with the person they are telling their troubles to. Here are some of the effects our parents report:

They make me stop talking, shut me off.
They make me defensive and resistive.
They make me argue, counterattack.
They make me feel inadequate, inferior.
They make me feel resentful or angry.
They make me feel guilty or bad.
They make me feel I'm being pressured to change—not accepted as I am.
They make me feel the other person doesn't trust me to solve my problem.
They make me feel I'm being treated paternalistically, as if I were a child.

They make me feel I'm not being understood.
They make me feel my feelings aren't justified.
They make me feel I've been interrupted.
They make me feel frustrated.
They make me feel I'm on the witness stand being cross-examined.
They make me feel the listener is just not interested.

The parents in our classes immediately recognize that if the "Typical Twelve" have these effects on *them* in their relationships with others, they would probably have the same effects on their *children*.

And they are right. These twelve kinds of verbal responses are the very ones professional therapists and counselors have learned to avoid when they work with children. These ways of responding are potentially "nontherapeutic" or "destructive." Professionals learn to rely on other ways of responding to children's messages that seem to carry far less risk of causing the child to stop talking, making him feel guilty or inadequate, reducing his self-esteem, producing defensiveness, triggering resentment, making him feel unaccepted, and so on.

In the Appendix of this book we have catalogued these "Typical Twelve," going into more detail about the destructive effects that each may have.

When parents realize how much they rely on the "Typical Twelve," they invariably ask with some impatience, "How else can we respond? What ways are left?" Most parents cannot think of alternative responses. But there are some.

SIMPLE DOOR-OPENERS

One of the most effective and constructive ways of responding to children's feeling-messages or problem-messages is the "door-opener" or "invitation to say more." These are responses that do not communicate any of the listener's own ideas or judgments or feelings, yet they invite the child to share his own ideas, judgments, or feelings. They open the door for him, they invite him to talk. The simplest of these are such noncommittal responses as:

"I see   "Really."
"Oh."   "You don't say."
"Mm hmmm."   "No fooling."
"How about that."   "You did, huh."
"Interesting."   "Is that so!"

Others are somewhat more explicit in conveying an invitation to talk or to say more, such as:

"Tell me about it."
"I'd like to hear about it."
"Tell me more."
"I'd be interested in your point of view."
"Would you like to talk about it?"
"Let's discuss it."
"Let's hear what you have to say."
"Tell me the whole story."
"Shoot, I'm listening."
"Sounds like you've got something to say about this."
"This seems like something important to *you*."

These door-openers or invitations to talk can be potent facilitators of another person's communication. They encourage people to start or to continue talking. They also "keep the ball with him." They don't have the effect of your grabbing the ball away from him, as do messages of your own, such as asking questions, giving advice, teaching, moralizing, and so on. These door-openers keep your own feelings and thoughts out of the communication process. The responses of children and adolescents to these simple door-openers will surprise parents. The youngsters feel encouraged to move in closer, open up, and literally pour out their feelings and ideas. Like adults, young people love to talk and usually do when anyone extends an invitation.

These door-openers also convey acceptance of the child and respect for him as a person by telling him, in effect:

> "You have a right to express how you feel."
> "I respect you as a person with ideas and feel-
> ings."
> "I might learn something from you."
> "I really want to hear your point of view."
> "Your ideas are worthy of being listened to."
> "I am interested in you."
> "I want to relate to you, get to know you better."

Who doesn't react favorably to such attitudes? What adult doesn't feel good when he is made to feel worthy, respected, significant, accepted, interesting? Children are no different. Offer them a verbal invitation and then you'd better jump back to get out of the way of their expressiveness and expansiveness. You also might learn something about them or about yourself in the process.

ACTIVE LISTENING

There is another way of responding to young people's messages that is infinitely more effective than the door-openers that are merely invitations to talk. They merely *open* the door for the child to talk. But parents need to learn how to *keep the door open.*

Far more effective than *passive listening* (silence), *active listening* is a remarkable way to involve the "sender" with the "receiver." The *receiver is active* in the process as well as the sender. But to learn how to listen actively, parents usually need to understand more about the communication process between two persons. A few diagrams will help.

Whenever a child decides to communicate with his parent, he does so because he has a *need*. Always it is because something is going on inside him. He wants something, he feels discomfort, he has a feeling about something, or he is upset about something—we say that the child's organism is in some kind of *disequilibrium*. In order to bring the organism back to a state of equilibrium, the child decides to talk. Say the child feels hunger.

CHILD

In order to get rid of the hunger (state of disequilibrium), the child becomes a "sender," communicating something that he thinks might bring him food. He cannot communicate what is actually going on inside him (his hunger) for hunger is a complex set of physiological processes going on *inside the organism* where it must always remain. Therefore, to *communicate to someone else* about his hunger, he must select some signal that he thinks might represent "I am hungry" to another. This selection process is called "encoding"—the child picks a *code*.

CHILD

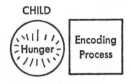

Let's say this particular child selects the code "When's dinner ready, Mom?" This code or combination of verbal symbols is then transmitted into the atmosphere where the receiver (Mother) might pick it up.

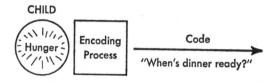

When Mother receives the coded message, she must then go through a process of *decoding* it so that she can understand its meaning in terms of what is going on inside the child.

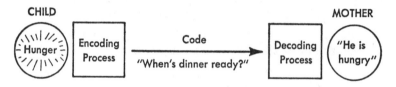

If the mother decodes accurately, she will understand that the child is hungry. But if Mother happens to decode the message to mean that the child is anxious to eat so he can go out and play before bedtime, she would be misunderstanding; the communication process has broken down. But here is the rub—the child does not know this, nor does Mother, because the child cannot see the thoughts inside Mother any more than Mother can see inside the child.

This is what so often goes wrong in the communication process between two people: There is a misunderstanding of the sender's message on the part of the receiver and neither is aware that the misunderstanding exists.

Suppose, however, that Mother decides to check on the accuracy of her decoding just to make sure she has not misunderstood. She can do this by actually telling the child her thoughts—the result of her decoding process, "You want a chance to play outside before bedtime." Now, having heard his mother's "feedback," the child is able to tell his mother that she decoded incorrectly:

CHILD: No, I didn't mean that, Mother. I meant I'm real hungry and want dinner to be ready soon.

MOTHER: Oh, I see. You're very hungry. How about some crackers and peanut butter to hold you over? We can't eat until your father gets home—about an hour from now.

CHILD: That's a good idea. I think I'll have some.

When the mother first "fed back" her understanding of the child's initial message she engaged in active listening.

In this particular case, she first misunderstood the child's message, but her feedback told him just that, so he sent another code that finally brought real understanding of his message. If she had accurately decoded the first time, the process might be diagrammed as follows:

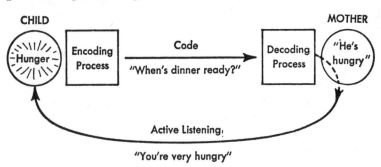

Here are some other examples of active listening:

1.

CHILD: (crying): Jimmy took my truck away from me.

PARENT: You sure feel bad about that—you don't like it when he does that.

CHILD: That's right.

2.

CHILD: I don't have anyone to play with since Billy went on vacation with his family. I just don't know what to do around here for fun.

PARENT: You miss having Billy to play with and you're wondering what you might do to have some fun.

CHILD: Yeah. Wish I could think of something.

3.

CHILD: Boy, do I have a lousy teacher this year. I don't like her. She's an old grouch.

PARENT: Sounds like you are really disappointed with your teacher.

CHILD: I sure am.

4.

CHILD: Guess what, Dad? I made the basketball team.

PARENT: You're really feeling great about that.

CHILD: Am I!

5.

CHILD: Daddy, when you were a boy what did you like in a girl? What made you really like a girl?

PARENT: Sounds like you're wondering what you need to get boys to like you, is that right?

CHILD: Yeah. For some reason they don't seem to like me and I don't know why.

In each of these illustrations, the parent has accurately decoded the child's feelings—what was "inside" the child. The child in each case then verified the accuracy of the parent's decoding by some expression indicating "You heard me-correctly."

In active listening, then, the receiver tries to understand what it is the sender is feeling or what his message means. Then he puts his understanding into his own words (code) and feeds it back for the sender's verification. The receiver *does not* send a message of his own—such as an evaluation, opinion, advice, logic, analysis, or question. He feeds back *only what he feels the sender's message meant*—nothing more, nothing less.

Here is a longer exchange where the parent is consistently using active listening. Note how the child each time verifies the feedback of the parent. Also notice how active listening makes it easier for the child to say more, to go deeper, to develop her thoughts further. Can you feel the movement? Watch the child begin to redefine her problem on her own; then tentively develop some insights about herself, and make a good start toward solving her problem.

SALLY: I wish I could get a cold once in a while like Barbie. She's lucky.

FATHER: You feel you're sort of getting gypped.

SALLY: Yes. She gets to stay out of school and I never do.

FATHER: You really would like to stay out of school more.

SALLY: Yes. I don't like to go to school every day—day after day after day. I get sick of it.

FATHER: You really get tired of school.

SALLY: Sometimes I just hate it.

FATHER: It's more than not liking it, sometimes you really hate school.

SALLY: That's right. I hate the homework, I hate the classes, and I hate the teachers.

FATHER: You just hate everything about school.

SALLY: I don't really hate all the teachers—just two of them. One of them I can't stand. She's the worst.

FATHER: You hate one in particular, huh?

SALLY: Do I ever! It's that Mrs. Barnes. I hate the sight of her. I got her for the whole year, too.

FATHER: You're stuck with her for a long time.

SALLY: Yes. I don't know how I'll ever stand it. You know what she does! Every day we get a long lecture—she stands up there smiling like this [demonstrates] and tells us how a responsible student is supposed to behave, and she reads off all these things you have to do to get an *A* in her class. It's sickening.

FATHER: You sure hate to hear all that stuff.

SALLY: Yeah. She makes it seem impossible to get an *A*—unless you're some kind of genius or a teacher's pet.

FATHER: You feel defeated before you even start, because you don't think you can possibly get an *A*.

SALLY: Yeah. I'm not going to be one of those teacher's pets

—the other kids hate them. I'm already not very popular with the kids. I just don't feel too many of the girls like me [tears].

FATHER: You don't feel popular and that upsets you.

SALLY: Yeah, it sure does. There's this group of girls that are the top ones in school. They are the most popular girls. I wish I could get in their group. But I don't know how.

FATHER: You really would like to belong to this group, but you're stumped about how to do it.

SALLY: That's right. I don't honestly know how girls get into this group. They're not the prettiest—not all of them. They're not always the ones with the best grades. Some in the group get high grades, but most of them get lower grades than I get. I just don't know.

FATHER: You're sort of puzzled about what it takes to get into this group.

SALLY: Well, one thing is that they're all pretty friendly— they talk a lot and, you know, make friends. They say hello to you first and talk real easy. I can't do that. I'm just not good at that stuff.

FATHER: You think maybe that's what they have that you don't have.

SALLY: I know I'm not good at talking. I can talk easily with one girl but not when there's a whole bunch of girls. I just keep quiet. It's hard for me to think of something to say.

FATHER: You feel okay with one girl but with a lot of girls you feel different.

SALLY: I'm always afraid I'll say something that will be silly or wrong or something. So I just stand there and feel kind of left out. It's terrible.

FATHER: You sure hate that feeling.

SALLY: I hate to be on the outside, but I'm afraid to try to get into the conversation.

In this brief encounter between Dad and Sally, Dad is putting aside his own thoughts and feelings ("I"-messages) in order to listen, decode, and understand Sally's thoughts and feelings. Note how the father's feedbacks generally begin with "you." Note also that Sally's father refrained from using any of the "typical twelve." By consistently relying on active listening, he showed understanding and empathy for Sally's feelings but allowed her to retain the responsibility for her problem.

Why Should Parents Learn Active Listening?

Some parents who are introduced to this new technique in our P.E.T. course say:

> "It seems so unnatural to me."
> "That isn't the way people talk."
> "What's the purpose of active listening?"
> "I'd feel like a dope responding to my kid that way."
> "My daughter would think I flipped my lid if I started to use active listening with her."

These are understandable reactions because parents are so accustomed to telling, preaching, questioning, judging, threatening, admonishing, or reassuring. It is certainly natural for them to ask if it will be worth the trouble to change and learn active listening?

One of the more skeptical fathers in a P.E.T. class became convinced after an experience with his daughter, aged fifteen, during the week following the class session in which he was introduced to this new way of listening.

> "I want to report to the class an amazing experience I had this week. My daughter, Jean, and I haven't said a civil word to each other for about two years, except maybe, 'Pass the bread,' or 'Can I have the salt and pepper?' The other night she and her boy friend were sitting at the table in the kitchen when I came home. I overheard my daughter telling her boy friend how much she hated school and how she was disgusted with most of her girl friends. I

decided right then and there I would sit down and do nothing but active listen, even if it killed me. Now, I'm not going to say I did a perfect job, but I surprised myself. I wasn't too bad. Well, will you believe it, they both started talking to me and never stopped for two hours. I learned more about my daughter and what she is like in those two hours than I had in the past five years. On top of that, the rest of the week she was downright friendly to me. What a change!"

This amazed father is not unique. Many parents have immediate success when they try out the new technique. Even before they acquire a reasonable level of competence at active listening, they often report some startling results.

Many people think that they can get rid of their feelings by suppressing them, forgetting them, or thinking about something else. Actually, people free themselves of troublesome feelings when they are encouraged to express them openly. *Active listening fosters this kind of catharsis.* It helps children to find out exactly what they are feeling. After they express their feelings, the feelings often seem to disappear almost like magic.

Active listening helps children become less afraid of negative feelings. "Feelings are friendly" is an expression we use in our classes to help parents come to realize feelings are not "bad." When a parent shows by active listening that he accepts a child's feelings, the child is also helped to accept them. He learns from the parent's response that feelings *are* friendly.

Active listening promotes a relationship of warmth between parent and child. The experience of being heard and understood by another person is so satisfying that it invariably makes the sender feel warm toward the listener. Children, particularly, respond with loving ideas and feelings. Sim-

ilar feelings are evoked within the listener—he begins to feel
warmer and closer to the sender. When one listens empathically and accurately to another, he gets to understand that
person, to appreciate his way of looking at the world—in a
sense, he *becomes that person* during the period of putting
himself in his shoes. Invariably, by allowing oneself to "get
inside" the other person, one produces feelings of closeness,
caring and love. To empathize with another is to see him as a
separate person, yet be willing to join with him or be with
him. It means "becoming a companion" to him for a brief
period in his journey through life. Such an act involves deep
caring and love. Parents who learn empathic active listening
discover a new kind of appreciation and respect, a deeper
feeling of caring; in turn, the child responds to the parent
with similar feelings.

Active listening facilitates problem-solving by the child.
We know that people do a better job of thinking a problem
through and toward a solution when they can "talk it out" as
opposed to merely thinking about it. Because active listening
is so effective in facilitating talking, it helps a person in his
search for solutions to his problems. Everybody had heard
such expressions as "Let me use you as a sounding board" or
"I'd like to kick this problem around with you" or "Maybe it
would help me to talk it out with you."

*Active listening influences the child to be more willing to
listen to the parents' thoughts and ideas.* It is a universal
experience that when someone will listen to one's own point
of view, it is then easier to listen to *his.* Children are more
likely to open themselves up to receive their parents' messages if their parents first hear them out. When parents complain that their kids don't listen to them, it's a good bet that
the parents are not doing an effective job of listening to the
kids.

Active listening "keeps the ball with the child." When parents respond to their kids' problems by active listening, they

will observe how often kids start thinking for themselves. A child will start to analyze his problem on his own, eventually arriving at some constructive solutions. Active listening encourages the child to think for himself, to find his own diagnosis of his problem, to discover his own solutions. Active listening conveys trust, while messages of advice, logic, instruction, and the like convey distrust by taking over the problem-solving responsibility from the child. Active listening is therefore one of the most effective ways of helping a child become more self-directing, self-responsible and independent.

Attitudes Required to Use Active Listening

Active listening is not a simple technique that parents pull out of their "tool kit" whenever their children have problems. It is a method for putting to work a set of basic attitudes. Without these attitudes, the method seldom will be effective; it will sound false, empty, mechanical, insincere. Here are some basic attitudes that must be present when a parent is using active listening. Whenever these attitudes are not present, a parent cannot be an effective active listener.

1. You must *want* to hear what the child has to say. This means you are willing to take the time to listen. If you don't have time, you need only say so.
2. You must genuinely *want* to be helpful to him with his particular problem at that time. If you don't want to, wait until you do.
3. You must genuinely be able to *accept his feelings,* whatever they may be or however different they may be from your own feelings or from the feelings you think a child "should" feel. This attitude takes time to develop.
4. You must have a deep feeling of *trust* in the child's capacity to handle his feelings, to work through them, and to find solutions to his problems. You'll acquire this trust by watching your child solve his own problems.

5. You must appreciate that feelings are *transitory,* not permanent. Feelings change—hate can turn into love, discouragement may quickly be replaced by hope. Consequently, you need not be afraid of feelings getting expressed; they will not become forever fixed inside the child. Active listening will demonstrate this to you.

6. You must be able to see your child as *someone separate* from you—a unique person no longer joined to you, a separate individual having been given by you his *own* life and his *own* identity. This "separateness" will enable you to "permit" the child to have his *own* feelings, his *own* way of perceiving things. Only by feeling "separateness" will you be able to be a helping agent for the child. You must be "with" him as he experiences his problems, but not joined to him.

The Risk of Active Listening

Active listening obviously requires the receiver to suspend his own thoughts and feelings in order to attend exclusively to the message of the child. It *forces* accurate receiving; if the parent is to understand the message in terms of the child's meaning, he must put himself into the child's shoes (into his frame of reference, into his world of reality), and he can then hear the meaning *intended* by the sender. The "feedback" part of active listening is nothing more than the parent's ultimate check on the accuracy of his listening, although it also assures the sender (child) that he has been understood when he hears his own "message" fed back to him accurately.

Something happens to a person when he practices active listening. To understand accurately how *another person* thinks or feels from his point of view, to put yourself momentarily into his shoes, to see the world as *he* is seeing it—you as a listener run the risk of having your own opinions and attitudes changed. In other words, people actually become changed by what they *really understand.* To be "open to the experience" of another invites the possibility of having to reinterpret your own experiences. This can be scary. A "defensive" person cannot afford to expose himself to ideas and views that are different from his own. A flexible person, however, is not as afraid of being changed. And kids who have flexible parents respond positively when they see their mothers and fathers willing to change, willing to be human.

4

Putting Your Active Listening Skill to Work

Parents are usually amazed when they discover what active listening can accomplish, but it takes effort to put it to work. And, difficult as it may seem at first, active listening must be used frequently. "Will I know when to use it?" parents ask. "Can I get good enough at it to become an effective counselor for my own children?"

Mrs. T., an intelligent, well-educated mother of three, confessed to the other parents in her P.E.T. class, "I now realize how strong my habit is to give my children advice or tell them my solutions to their problems. It's a habit I have with other people, too—my friends, my husband. Can I change from being Mrs. Know-it-all?"

Our answer is a somewhat qualified "Yes." Yes, most parents can change and learn when to use active listening appropriately, provided they take the plunge and start putting it to work. Practice makes perfect—or, at least, practice will bring to most parents a reasonably effective level of competence. To hesitant parents who at first feel inadequate about trying this new method of talking to kids, we say, "Give it the old college try—the rewards will be worth the effort."

In this chapter, we will show how parents have learned to use active listening. As in learning any new activity, people inevitably encounter difficulties and even failures. But we now know that parents who seriously work at developing their skills and sensitivity will see progress in their children's growth toward independence and maturity, and will enjoy new warmth and intimacy with them.

WHEN DOES THE CHILD "OWN" THE PROBLEM?

Active listening is most appropriately used when the child *reveals he has a problem.* Usually, the parent will spot these situations because they will hear the child express feelings.

All children encounter situations in their lives that are disappointing, frustrating, painful, or shattering: problems with their friends, their brothers or sisters, their parents, their teachers, their environment, and problems with themselves. Children who find help in solving such problems maintain their psychological health and continue to acquire more strength and self-confidence. Children who do not, develop emotional problems.

To recognize when it is appropriate to put active listening to work, parents need to get tuned in to hearing these I've-got-a-problem kind of feelings. But, first, we need to make them aware of a very important principle—the principle of *problem ownership.*

In every human relationship there are times when one person (A) "owns the problem"—that is, some need of his is not being met or he is not satisfied with his behavior. At some particular moment in the relationship he may be bothered, frustrated, deprived, needful, or disturbed. Because of this, the relationship at the moment is unsatisfying to A. *A owns the problem.*

At other times, A's needs are being met by his behavior, but that behavior is interfering with B's satisfying some need of his own. It is now *B* who is bothered, frustrated, deprived, needful, or disturbed because of *A*'s behavior. Consequently, at that moment in time, *B owns the problem.*

In the parent-child relationship three situations occur that we will shortly illustrate with case histories:

1. The child has a problem because he is thwarted in satisfying a need. It is not a problem for the parent because the child's behavior in no tangible way interferes with the parent's satisfying his own needs. Therefore, THE CHILD OWNS THE PROBLEM.

2. The child is satisfying his own needs (he is not thwarted) and his behavior is not interfering with the parent's own needs. Therefore, THERE IS NO PROBLEM IN THE RELATIONSHIP.

3. The child is satisfying his own needs (he is not thwarted). But his behavior is a problem to the parent because it is interfering in some tangible way with the parent's satisfying a need of his own. NOW THE PARENT OWNS THE PROBLEM.

It is critical that parents always classify each situation that occurs in the relationship. Which of these three categories does the situation fall into? It helps to remember this diagram:

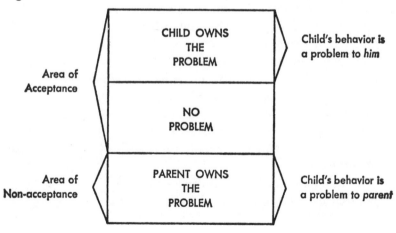

Active listening by the parent is most appropriate and helpful when the child owns the problem, but often very inappropriate when the parent owns the problem; it helps the *child* find solutions to *his own* problems, but seldom helps the parent find solutions when the child's behavior is causing the parent a problem. (In the next chapter we will introduce methods for parents to solve problems they own.)

Such problems as these would be *owned by the child*:

> Jimmy is feeling rejected by one of his friends.
>
> Billy is sad because he didn't make the tennis team.
>
> Linda is frustrated because boys are not dating her.
>
> Bonnie is unable to decide what her vocation is to be.
>
> Ralph is uncertain about whether to go to college.
>
> Bruce is suspended for two days for ditching school.
>
> Fran is unhappy with taking piano lessons.
>
> Bobby is getting angry when he loses a game to his brother.
>
> Ricky is doing poor work in school because he hates his teacher.
>
> Barbara is feeling shy because of her height.
>
> Betsy is feeling troubled because she may flunk two courses.
>
> John is finding it hard to do his homework.

Problems such as these are the ones children inevitably encounter as they attempt to cope with life—their *own* life. Children's frustrations, puzzlements, deprivations, concerns and, yes, even their failures belong to them, not their parents.

This concept is one that parents at first find hard to accept. Most mothers and fathers are inclined to make too many of their children's problems their own. By doing so, as we shall demonstrate later, they cause themselves unnecessary grief, contribute to the deterioration of their relationship with their children, and miss countless opportunities to be effective counselors to their children.

When a parent accepts the fact that problems are owned by the child, this in no way means he, the parent, cannot be *concerned*, *care*, or offer *help*. A professional counselor has real concern for, and genuinely cares about, each child he is trying to help. But, unlike most parents, he leaves the responsibility for solving the child's problem *with the child*. He allows the child to *own the problem*. He accepts the child's having the problems. He accepts the child as a person *separate from himself*. And he relies heavily upon and basically *trusts* the child's own inner resources for solving his own problem. Only because he lets the child own his problem is the professional counselor able to employ active listening.

Active listening is a powerful method for helping another person solve a problem that he owns, provided the listener can accept the other's ownership and consistently allow the person to find his own solutions. Active listening can greatly increase the effectiveness of parents as helping agents for their children, but it is a different kind of help from that which parents usually try to give.

Paradoxically, this method will *increase* the parent's influence on the child, but it is an influence that differs from the kind that most parents try to exert over their children. *Active listening is a method of influencing children to find their own solutions to their own problems.* Most parents, however, are tempted to take over ownership of their children's problems, as in the following case:

JOHNNY: Tommy won't play with me today. He won't ever do what I want to do.

MOTHER: Well, why don't you offer to do what he wants to do? You've got to learn to get along with your little friends. [ADVISING, MORALIZING.]

JOHNNY: I don't like to do things he wants to do and besides I don't want to get along with that dope.

MOTHER: Well, go find someone else to play with then if you're going to be a spoilsport. [OFFERING A SOLUTION; NAME-CALLING.]

JOHNNY: He's the spoilsport, not me. And there isn't anyone else to play with.

MOTHER: You're just upset because you're tired. You'll feel better about this tomorrow. [INTERPRETING, REASSURING.]

JOHNNY: I'm not tired, and I won't feel different tomorrow. You just don't understand how much I hate the little squirt.

MOTHER: Now stop talking like that! If I ever hear you talk about one of your friends like that again, you'll be sorry . . . [ORDERING, THREATENING.]

JOHNNY (walking away and sulking): I hate this neighborhood. I wish we would move.

Here is how the parent can help the same boy with active listening:

JOHNNY: Tommy won't play with me today. He won't ever do what I want to do.

MOTHER: You're kinda angry with Tommy. [ACTIVE LISTENING.]

JOHNNY: I sure am. I never want to play with him again. I don't want him for a friend.

MOTHER: You're so angry you feel like never seeing him again. [ACTIVE LISTENING.]

JOHNNY: That's right. But if I don't have him for a friend, I won't have anyone to play with then.

MOTHER: You would hate to be left with no one. [ACTIVE LISTENING.]

JOHNNY: Yeah. I guess I just have to get along with him someway. But it's so hard for me to stop getting mad at him.

MOTHER: You want to get along better but it's hard for you to keep from getting mad with Tommy. [ACTIVE LISTENING.]

JOHNNY: I never used to—but that's when he was always willing to do what I wanted to do. He won't let me boss him anymore.

MOTHER: Tommy's not so easy to influence now. [ACTIVE LISTENING.]

JOHNNY: He sure isn't. He's not such a baby now. He's more fun though.

MOTHER: You really like him better this way. [ACTIVE LISTENING.]

JOHNNY: Yeah. But it's hard to stop bossing him—I'm so used to it. Maybe we wouldn't fight so much if I let him have his way once in a while. Think that would work?

MOTHER: You're thinking that if you might give in occasionally, it might help. [ACTIVE LISTENING.]

JOHNNY: Yeah, maybe it would. I'll try it.

In the first version, the mother used eight of the "Typical Twelve" categories of responding. In the second, the mother consistently used active listening. In the first, the mother "took over the problem;" in the second, her active listening kept ownership of the problem with Johnny. In the first, Johnny resisted his mother's suggestions, his anger and frustration were never dissipated, the problem remained unresolved, and there was no growth on Johnny's part. In the second, his anger left, he initiated problem-solving, and took a deeper look at himself. He arrived at his own solution and obviously grew a notch toward becoming a responsible, self-directing problem-solver.

Here is another situation to illustrate how parents typically try to help children.

KATHY: I don't want any dinner tonight.

DAD: Come on. Kids your age need to have three meals a day. [INSTRUCTING, PERSUADING WITH LOGIC.]

KATHY: Well, I had a big lunch.

DAD: Well, just come to the table anyway and see what we're having. [SUGGESTING.]

KATHY: I'm sure I won't eat anything.

DAD: What's the matter with you tonight? [PROBING.]

KATHY: Nothing.

DAD: Well, then get to the table. [ORDERING.]

KATHY: I'm not hungry and I don't want to go to the table.

Now here is how the same girl can be helped with active listening:

KATHY: I don't want any dinner tonight.

DAD: You don't feel like eating tonight. [ACTIVE LISTENING.]

KATHY: I sure don't. My stomach is in knots today.

DAD: You're feeling sorta tense today, is that right? [ACTIVE LISTENING.)

KATHY: Tense is no word for it—I'm really scared.

DAD: You're really frightened about something. [ACTIVE LISTENING.]

KATHY: I sure am. Bob called me today and said he wanted to talk to me tonight. He sounded real serious, not like him.

DAD: Makes you feel something's up, huh. [ACTIVE LISTENING.]

KATHY: I'm afraid he wants to break up.

DAD: You'd hate to have that happen. [ACTIVE LISTENING.]

KATHY: It would kill me! Especially because I think he'd like to go with Sue. That would be the worst!

DAD: That's really what scares you—that Sue might get him. [ACTIVE LISTENING.]

KATHY: Yeah. She gets all the good guys. She's sickening—always talking to boys and making them laugh. They all fall for it. She's always got three or four boys hanging around her in the halls. I don't know how she does it—I can't ever think of anything to talk about around boys.

DAD: You wish you could talk as easily as Sue around boys. [ACTIVE LISTENING.]

KATHY: Yeah. I'm a plain old flop. Guess I'm so anxious to have them like me I'm afraid I'll say something wrong.

DAD: You want so badly to be popular that you're afraid you'll make a mistake. [ACTIVE LISTENING.]

KATHY: Yeah. But I couldn't do any worse than I'm doing now
—standing around like a dope.

DAD: You feel maybe you are worse off now than if you did
go ahead and talk. [ACTIVE LISTENING.]

KATHY: I am, for sure. I'm sick of saying nothing.

In the first version Kathy's father failed to decode her message right at the start, and so the conversation got hung up
on the eating problem. In the second go-around, Dad's sensitive active listening helped uncover the basic problem,
encouraged problem-solving on Kathy's part, and eventually
helped her to consider making a change.

HOW PARENTS MAKE ACTIVE LISTENING WORK

Here is a chance to watch some parents putting active
listening to work at home when they are confronted with
nitty-gritty problems that mothers and fathers encounter. It
is wise not to get so involved in these authentic situations
that you forget to take note of the active listening these parents are using.

Danny: The Child Afraid to Go to Sleep

In handling this situation, this mother, a P.E.T. graduate,
used a few of the "Typical Twelve" responses, but she also
relied heavily on active listening. The child, age eight, had
been having increasing trouble getting to sleep since he was
five years old. About eight months before the following dia-
logue took place, he moved out of a room he had been sharing with two younger brothers. Although eager for a room of
his own, Danny found his sleeping problem intensified.

MOTHER: It's late. Turn out the light and go to sleep.

DANNY: I'm not going to sleep.

MOTHER: You have to, it's late. You'll be tired tomorrow.

DANNY: I'm not going to sleep.

MOTHER   (harshly): Turn that light off immediately!

DANNY   (flatly): I'm *never* going to sleep.

MOTHER   (I feel like strangling him. I'm so tired, I can't stand this tonight . . . I go into the kitchen, smoke a cigarette, decide that I'm going in there and try active listening even if it kills me! Entering Danny's room): "C'mon, it's late but I'll sit on your bed for a while and rest my feet before I do the dishes. [She takes the book from him, turns off the light, closes the door, and sits on the bed beside him, leaning back against the wall.]

DANNY: Gimme that book! Don't turn off the light. Get out of here. I don't want you in here. I'm not going to sleep. I hate you!

MOTHER: You're feeling angry.

DANNY: Yeah, I hate school, and I'll never go back, never!

MOTHER   (He loves school.): You're fed up with school.

DANNY: It's horrible. I'm not good in school. Don't know anything. I ought to be in second grade. [He's in third.] Math, I don't know it. [He is very good at it.] The teacher must think we're in a high school or something.

MOTHER: Math's pretty hard for you.

DANNY: No! It's easy. Just don't feel like doing it.

MOTHER: Oh.

DANNY   (sudden shift): I sure like baseball. Much rather play baseball than go to school.

MOTHER: You really like baseball.

DANNY: Do you *have* to go to college? [Oldest brother will soon enter college and there is much family talk about it.]

MOTHER: No.

DANNY: How long do you have to go to school?

MOTHER: You have to finish high school.

DANNY: Well, I'm not going to college. Don't have to, right?

MOTHER: Right.

DANNY: Good, I'll play baseball.

MOTHER: Baseball's really fun.

DANNY: Sure is. [Completely calmed down, talking comfortably, no anger.] Well, good night.

MOTHER: Good night.

DANNY: Will you sit up with me some more?

MOTHER: Uh huh.

DANNY   (pulls up covers which had been kicked off; carefully covers up Mother's knees and pats them): Comfortable?

MOTHER: Yes, thank you.

DANNY: You're welcome. [Period of quiet, then Danny starts snorting and sniffing with much exaggerated clearing of throat and nose.] Snort, snort, snort. [Danny does have slight allergy with stuffy nose, but the symptoms are never acute. Mother has never heard Danny snort like this before.]

MOTHER: Nose bugging you?

DANNY: Yeah, sure is. Think I need the stuffy nose medicine?

MOTHER: Do you think it would help?

DANNY: No. (Snort, snort.)

MOTHER: Nose really bugs you.

DANNY: Yeah [snort]. [Sigh of anguish.] Oh, I wish you didn't have to breathe through your nose when you sleep.

MOTHER   (very surprised at this, tempted to ask where that idea came from): You think you have to breathe through your nose when you sleep?

DANNY: I *know* I have to.

MOTHER: You feel sure about it.

DANNY: I know it. Tommy told me, a long time ago. [Much admired friend, two years older.] He said you have to. You can't breathe through your mouth when you sleep.

MOTHER: You mean you aren't supposed to?

DANNY: You just *can't* [snort]. Mommy, that's so, isn't it? I mean, you *gotta* breathe through your nose when you sleep, don't you? [Long explanation—many questions from Danny about admired friend. "He wouldn't lie to me."]

MOTHER   (explains that friend is probably trying to help but kids get false information sometimes. Much emphasis from Mother that everyone breathes through the mouth when sleeping.)

DANNY   (very relieved): Well, good night.

MOTHER: Good night. [Danny breathing easily through mouth.]

DANNY   (suddenly): Snort.

MOTHER: Still scary.

DANNY: Uh huh. Mommy, what if I go to sleep breathing through my mouth—and my nose is stuffy—and what if in the middle of the night when I'm sound asleep—what if I closed my mouth?

MOTHER   (realizes that he has been afraid to go to sleep for years because he is afraid he would choke to death; thinks, "Oh, my poor baby"): You're afraid you might choke maybe?

DANNY: Uh huh. You *gotta* breathe. [He couldn't say, "I might die."]

MOTHER   (more explaining): It simply couldn't happen. Your mouth would open—just like your heart pumps blood or your eyes blink.

DANNY: Are you *sure?*

MOTHER: Yes, I'm sure.

DANNY: Well, good night.

MOTHER: Good night, dear. [Kiss. Danny is asleep in minutes.]

The case of Danny is not a unique example of a parent whose active listening brought about the dramatic resolution of an emotional problem. Reports like these from parents in our classes confirm our belief that most parents can learn the skill employed by professional counselors well enough to put it to work to help their own children solve rather deep-seated problems that used to be considered the exclusive province of professionals.

Sometimes this kind of therapeutic listening brings only a cathartic release of a child's feelings; all the child seems to need is an empathic ear or a sounding board, as with Betty, a very bright ten-year-old. Betty's mother suggested that the session be tape recorded so she could bring the tape to her P.E.T. class. We encourage parents to do this in our course, so we can use the tape for coaching the mother and teaching others. As you read the verbatim transcript, try to imagine how most untrained parents would have used the "Typical Twelve" in responding to Betty's feelings about her teacher.

MOTHER: Betty, you don't feel like going school tomorrow, huh?

BETTY: There's nothing to look forward to there.

MOTHER: You mean it's sort of boring. . . .

BETTY: Yeah—there's nothing to do except watch Mrs. Stupid—she's so fat and saggy and so stupid looking!

MOTHER: So she really annoys you with the things she does . . .

BETTY: Yeah—and then she goes around, "Okay, I'll give this to you tomorrow. So it's tomorrow and she says, "Oh, I forgot it. I'll give it to you some other time."

MOTHER: So she makes promises that she's going to do things . . .

BETTY: And she never does them. . . .

MOTHER: And she doesn't follow through, and this makes you very upset. . . .

BETTY: Yeah, she still hasn't given me that paper fastener she promised me in September.

MOTHER: She says she's going to do things and you count on her and she doesn't do them.

BETTY: And all sorts of trips we're supposed to go on and she says we're going to go to the library one of these days . . . then after she says something like that she never gives us anything else about it—she says it and that's all—and then she goes on to make other promises. . . .

MOTHER: So she gets your hopes up and you really think things are going to be better and something fun is going to happen and it doesn't happen.

BETTY: Right—it's dumb all over.

MOTHER: Then you're really disappointed about what does go on in the course of the day.

BETTY: Yeah, the only period I like is Art because at least she's not nagging you about your writing or something. She's always on top of me—"Oh, your writing is *so* terrible! Why can't you make your writing better? Why are you so careless?"

MOTHER: Like she's on your back all the time. . . .

BETTY: Yeah, and in Art she tells me what colors to use and I don't use them. . . . I make it look pretty and she just shows me how to put shadows in. . . .

MOTHER: The rest of the time she leaves you pretty much alone in Art.

BETTY: Uh huh, except for on the tile roofs. . . .

MOTHER: She makes you do those a certain way. . . .

BETTY: Uh huh. I don't do them that way, though. . . .

MOTHER: It really bothers you that she tells you her ideas that you have to follow. . . .

BETTY: I'm not going to—I'm going to ignore them—then I get in trouble. . . .

MOTHER: When you ignore her ideas you're afraid you're going to get in trouble.

BETTY: Uh huh—I don't most of the time. I always have to do what she wants—the way she makes me number in Math: one *A*, one *B*, and ughh. . . .

MOTHER: You really would like to ignore her ideas, but you go ahead anyway and do them and then you're mad. . . .

BETTY: She makes everything take so long—she has to explain everything and do one or two with the kids and tell them how to do it and make me feel like we're babies—"this is a brand new step"—she treats us like little kindergarteners.

It is sometimes hard for parents to let a session like this end on an inconclusive or incomplete note. When parents understand that this frequently happens in counseling sessions conducted by professional counselors, they are much more able to allow the child to stop, trusting her to find her own solution later. Professionals learn from experience that you can have faith in the capacity of children to deal constructively with their own life problems. Parents underestimate this capacity.

Following is an example, drawn from an interview I had with an adolescent. It illustrates the point that active listening does not always bring about an on-the-spot change. Frequently, active listening merely starts a chain of events, and the conclusion may never be known to the parent or may not become apparent for some time. This happens because children often work out a solution afterward on their own. Professional counselors see this happening all the time. A child may end a counseling hour still in the middle of discussing a prob-

lem, only to return a week later to report that he has solved
it.

   This occurred with Ed, a sixteen-year-old who was brought
to me for counseling because his parents were worried about
his utter disregard for school, his rebellion against adults, his
use of drugs, and his lack of cooperation at home:

> For several weeks, Ed spent the counseling hour
> defending his smoking marijuana and criticizing
> adults for their own use of alcohol and tobacco. He
> saw nothing wrong with using pot. He thought
> everyone should try it because it was such a marvel-
> ous experience for him. He also strongly questioned
> the value of school. He regarded it only as prepara-
> tion for getting a job so that you could earn money
> and be in the same trap that everyone else in society
> was in. He had been getting *D*'s and *F*'s in school.
> For Ed, doing anything constructive seemed futile.
> One day he came in for his counseling hour and sud-
> denly announced that he had decided to stop smok-
> ing pot—he was through "ruining his life." While he
> still did not know what he wanted to do in life, he
> said he was sure he did not want to throw his life
> away by going the "hippie route." He also
> announced that he was working hard on the two
> courses he was taking in summer school, after
> flunking all but one of his courses during the year.
> Eventually Ed ended up with two *B*+ grades in
> those courses, graduated from high school and
> entered college. I do not know what changed him,
> but I suspect that his own good sense was mobilized
> by being listened to—actively.

   Sometimes active listening merely helps a child accept a
situation that he knows he cannot change. Active listening

helps the child express his feelings about a situation, get them off his chest, and feel accepted by someone for having those feelings. It is probably the same phenomenon as griping in the Army; the griper usually knows he cannot change the situation but it does seem to help to be able to get negative feelings out in the presence of someone who accepts and understands. This is illustrated in the following exchange between Jane, aged twelve, and her mother:

JANE: Do I hate that Mrs. Adams, my new English teacher! She's just about the worst.

MOTHER: You really got a bad one this semester, huh.

JANE: Boy, did I! She stands up there yakking away about herself until I get so bored I can't stand it. I want to tell her to shut up.

MOTHER: You really get darned angry at her.

JANE: So does everyone else. Nobody likes her. Why do they let teachers like that teach in a public school? How do they keep their jobs, being so lousy?

MOTHER: Makes you wonder how anyone that bad is allowed to teach.

JANE: Yeah, but she's there and I'm going to have to face her everyday. Well, I've got to go make some posters for Margie's campaign. See you later.

Obviously, no clear solution was reached, nor can Jane do anything much to change her teacher. However, being permitted to express her feelings and have them accepted and understood frees Jane to move on to something else. This parent is also demonstrating to her daughter that *when she has difficulties she has an accepting person to share them with.*

WHEN DOES A PARENT DECIDE TO USE ACTIVE LISTENING?

To use active listening, do you have to wait until some rather serious problem comes up, such as in the case of

Danny, who was afraid to go to sleep? Quite the contrary. Your children send you messages every day that tell you they are experiencing troublesome feelings.

Little Johnny has just burned his finger on one of his mother's electric hair-curler heating rods.

JOHNNY: Oh, I burned my finger! Mommy, I burned my finger. Ow, it hurts, it hurts [crying now]! My finger got burned. Ow, ow!
  MOTHER: Oooo, it really hurts. It hurts terribly.
  JOHNNY: Yes, look how bad I burned it.
  MOTHER: It feels like it's burned real bad. It hurts *so* much.
  JOHNNY   (stops crying): Put something on it right away.
  MOTHER: Okay. I'll get some ice to make it cooler, then we can put some ointment on it.

Responding to this common little household incident, Mother avoided reassuring Johnny with "It's not so bad," or "It will feel better," or "You didn't burn it that badly." She respected Johnny's feelings that it *was* burned badly, it *did* hurt a lot. She also refrained from one of the most typical parental responses in situations like this:

"Now, Johnny, don't be a little baby. Stop that crying right now." [EVALUATION and COMMANDING.]

Mother's active listening reflects some important attitudes toward Johnny:

He has encountered a painful moment in *his* life—it is *his* problem and he has a right to *his own* unique reaction to it.

I don't want to deny *his own* feelings—they are real *to him.*

I can accept how bad *he* feels the burn is and how much *he* hurts.

I cannot risk making him feel wrong or guilty for *his own* feelings.

Parents in our classes report that active listening when a child is hurt and cries vigorously frequently brings about a dramatic and instantaneous cessation of the crying, *once the child is certain his parent knows and understands how badly he feels or how much he is afraid.* For the child, getting this understanding of his feelings is what he needs most.

Children can be very vexing to parents when they feel anxious, frightened or insecure as their parents leave for the evening or when they miss the favorite doll or their blanket or have to sleep in a strange bed, and so on. Reassurance seldom works in such situations, and parents get understandably impatient when the child won't stop whining or calling for what he is missing:

> "I want my blanket, I want my blanket, I want my blanket!"
>
> "I don't want you to go. I don't want you to go!"
>
> "I want my dolly. Where's my dolly? I want my dolly!"

Active listening can do wonders in such predicaments. The main thing the child wants is recognition from the parent of how deeply the child is feeling.

Mr. H. reported the following incident shortly after taking the P.E.T. class:

> Michele, aged three and a half, began to whine incessantly when Mother left her in the car with me while she shopped in the supermarket. "I want my Mommy," was repeated a dozen times, despite my telling her each time that Mommy would be back in a few minutes. Then she changed to loud crying: "I want my dolly. I want my dolly." After everything failed to pacify her, I remembered the active listening method. In desperation I said, "You miss your

Mommy when she leaves you." She nodded. "You don't like for Mommy to leave without you." She nodded again, still fearfully clutching her security blanket and looking like a frightened, lost kitten huddled in the corner of the back seat. I continued, "When you miss Mommy, you want to have your dolly." Vigorous nodding. "But you don't have your dolly here and you miss her, too." Then, as if by magic, she got out of her corner, dropped her blanket, stopped crying, crawled in the front seat with me and began to converse pleasantly about the people she saw in the parking lot.

The lesson for parents, as it was for Mr. H., is *to accept* the way your child feels rather than try the direct approach of trying *to get rid of* the whining and pestering by reassurance or threats. *Kids want to know that you know how badly they feel.*

Another situation where active listening can be put to work is that in which children send messages that are strangely coded, making it difficult for the parent to understand just what is going on inside their heads. Often, but not always, their messages are coded as questions:

"Will I ever get married?"
"What does it feel like to die?"
"Why do kids call me a kike?"
"Daddy, what did you like in girls when you were a boy?"

This last question came out of my own daughter's mouth one morning at breakfast before she left for junior high school. Like most fathers, I was immediately tempted to take the ball and run with it, once given such a chance to reminisce about my boyhood. Fortunately, I caught myself and came up with an active listening response:

FATHER: Sounds like you're wondering what you need in order to get boys to like you, is that right?

DAUGHTER: Yeah. For some reason they don't seem to like me and I don't know why...

FATHER: You're puzzled why they don't seem to like you.

DAUGHTER: Well, I know I don't talk much. I'm afraid to talk in front of boys.

FATHER: You just can't seem to open up and be relaxed with boys.

DAUGHTER: Yeah. I'm afraid I'll say something that will make me look silly to them.

FATHER: You don't want them to think you're silly.

DAUGHTER: Yeah. So if I'm quiet, I don't even take that risk.

FATHER: It seems safer to be quiet.

DAUGHTER: Yes, but that doesn't get me any place, because now they must think I'm dull.

FATHER: Being quiet doesn't get you what you want.

DAUGHTER: No. I guess you just have to take a chance.

How I would have muffed the chance to be helpful had I given in to the temptation to tell my daughter about my boyhood preferences in girls! Thanks to active listening, my daughter took a small step forward. She acquired a new insight, the type that often leads to constructive self-started behavior change.

Unusually coded messages that children send, particularly questions, often mean that the child is coping with a deeper problem. Active listening provides parents with a way of moving in and offering to help the child define the problem for himself, and starting up the process of problem-solving *within the child*. Giving direct answers to these feelings-coded-as-questions almost invariably results in the parent's muffing an opportunity to be an effective counselor on the real problem the child is grappling with.

When first trying it out, parents in our classes often forget that active listening is a skill that also has tremendous value in responding to children's intellectual problems. Children continually encounter problems as they strive to make sense out of what they read or hear about the world around them—student protests, riots, integration, police brutality, war, assassinations, air pollution, population control, divorce, crime, and so on.

What throws parents off so frequently is that kids generally state their views very strongly or in ways that make parents shudder at their apparent naïveté or immaturity. The temptation for Mom and Dad is to jump in and straighten the kid out or show him the broader picture. Parents' motivation here can be benign—to contribute to their children's intellectual development. Or it can be self-centered—to demonstrate their own superior intellectual abilities. Either way, parents jump in with one or more of the "Typical Twelve" responses, bringing on the inevitable effect of tuning the kids out or starting a verbal battle that ends up in hurt feelings and cutting remarks.

We have to ask our parts-in-training some rather penetrating questions to get them to start to use active listening when their kids are coping with ideas or current issues, as well as with the more personal problems. We ask:

> "Does your child have to think like you?"
> "Why do you have a need to teach him?"
> "Can't you tolerate an opinion very much different from your own?"
> "Can't you help him come to his own way of looking at this complex world?"
> "Can't you allow him to be where he is in his grappling with an issue?"
> "Can't you remember how you as a kid had some pretty kookie ideas about world problems?"

When parents in our classes begin to bite their tongues and open their ears, they report marked changes in dinner-table conversations. Their kids start bringing up problems that previously were never shared with the parents—drugs, sex, abortion, alcohol, morality, and so on. Active listening can work wonders in making the home a place where parents and their children can join in deep, penetrating discussions of the complex, critical problems kids are facing.

When parents in our P.E.T. classes complain that their kids never talk about serious problems at home, it usually turns out that such problems have been tentatively and hesitatingly tossed out on the table by their kids, but the parents went into the traditional routines: admonishing, preaching, moralizing, teaching, evaluating, judging, sarcasm, or diverting. Slowly, then, kids start pulling down the curtain that forever will separate their own minds from the parents' minds. No wonder there is a generation gap! It is prevalent in so many families because parents don't listen—they teach and correct and deprecate and ridicule the messages they hear from the developing minds of their children.

COMMON MISTAKES IN USING ACTIVE LISTENING

Parents seldom find it difficult to understand what active listening is and how it differs from the "Typical Twelve." Also, it is a rare parent who does not recognize the potential benefits to be derived from using active listening with children. However, some parents have more trouble than others in applying this skill successfully. As with any new skill one is trying to learn, mistakes can be made, either because of lack of competence or because the skill is used inappropriately. We point out some of these mistakes in the hope that it will help parents avoid them.

Manipulating Children Through "Guidance"

Some parents fail in starting to use active listening simply because their intentions are wrong. They want to use it to manipulate their children into behaving or thinking the way the parents think they should.

Mrs. J. walked into the fourth session of a P.E.T. class and could not wait to express her disappointment and resentment about her first experience with active listening. "Why, my son just stared at me and said nothing. You told us active listening would encourage kids to talk to you. Well, it didn't in my case."

When the instructor asked if she would like to tell the class what happened, Mrs. J. reported:

> James, aged sixteen, came home from school and announced that he had been told he was flunking two courses. Mrs. J. immediately tried to encourage him to talk by using her new-found skill. James clammed up and eventually walked away from his mother.

The instructor then suggested that he play the role of James and he and Mrs. J. would try to re-enact the scene. Mrs. J. agreed, although she warned the class that the instructor probably could never be as uncommunicative in the role as her son generally is at home. Here is how the instructor played the role of James. Note the mother's responses to him:

JAMES: Wow! I got the shaft today. Two failure notices—one in Math and the other in English.

MRS. J.:   You're upset [coldly].

JAMES: Course I'm upset.

MRS. J.:   You're disappointed [*still coldly*]

JAMES: That's putting it mildly. It means I won't graduate, that's all. Like, I've had it.

MRS. J.:   You feel there's nothing you can do about it now that you've been warned. [*Mother sends her own message here.*]

JAMES: You mean start studying more? [*James heard her message.*]

MRS. J.:   Yes, it's certainly not too late, is it? [*Now Mother is really pushing her solution.*]

JAMES: Study that junk? Why should I? It's a bunch of crap!

And so it went. James was backed into a corner by Mrs. J., who, under the guise of using active listening, was trying to manipulate James into a crash plan of intensive study. Feeling threatened by his mother, James wouldn't buy it and became defensive.

Mrs. J., like many parents at first, latched onto active listening because she saw it as a new technique for manipulating children—a subtle way of influencing them to do what the parent thinks they should do or *to guide the child's behavior or thinking.*

Shouldn't parents try to guide their children? Isn't guidance one of parents' principal responsibilities? While "parental guidance" is one of the most universally sanctioned functions for parents, it is also one that is most misunderstood. To guide means to steer in some direction. It also implies that the hand of the parent is on the steering wheel. Invariably, when parents grab the steering wheel and try to guide the child in some specific direction, they get resistance.

Children are quick to sense the parents' intentions. They immediately recognize that parental guidance usually means lack of acceptance of the child as he is. The child feels the parent is trying to do something to him. He is fearful of such indirect control. His independence is threatened.

Active listening is not a guidance technique toward parent-directed change. Parents who think that it is, will send indirect messages: the parent's biases, ideas, subtle pressures. Here are some examples of parents' messages creeping into responses to their children's communications:

GINNY: I'm mad at Sally and I don't want to play with her.

PARENT: You don't feel like playing with her today because you're temporarily mad at her.

GINNY: I don't ever want to play with her—never!

Note how the parent slipped in her own message: "I hope this is only temporary and tomorrow you won't be mad at her." Ginny sensed the parent's desire to change her, and in the second message strongly corrected her.

Another example:

BOB: What's so wrong about smoking marijuana? It doesn't harm you like cigarettes or alcohol. I think it's wrong to make it illegal. They ought to change the law.

PARENT: You feel that the law should be changed so more and more kids can get into trouble.

Obviously, the parent's feedback is an attempt to dissuade the child from thinking as he does about marijuana. No wonder his feedback turns out to be inaccurate, for it contains his own message to the child as opposed to reflecting accurately only what the child is communicating to him. An accurate feedback would have been something like: "You're convinced they ought to legalize marijuana, is that right?"

Opening the Door, Then Slamming It Shut

When they first try active listening, some parents start to use it to open the door for their children to communicate, but then they slam the door shut because they do not keep up the active listening long enough to hear the child out completely. It's like saying, "Come on, tell me what you feel, I'll understand." Then, when the parent hears what the child feels, he quickly shuts the door because he doesn't like what he hears.

Teddy, age ten, is looking down in the mouth and his mother moves in to help:

MOTHER: You look like you're unhappy. [ACTIVE LISTENING.]

TEDDY: Frankie pushed me.

MOTHER: You didn't like that. [ACTIVE LISTENING].

TEDDY: No. I'm going to bust him right in the mounth.

MOTHER: Now, that wouldn't be a nice thing to do, [EVALU-
ATING.]
TEDDY: I don't care. I'd like to punch him like this [swinging
hard].
MOTHER: Teddy, fighting is never a good way to solve conflicts
with your friends. [MORALIZING.] Why don't you go back and
tell him you'd like to make up? [ADVISING, OFFERING SOLU-
TIONS.]
TEDDY: Are you kidding? [Silence.]

The door was slammed shut in Teddy's face, so no more communicating. By evaluating, moralizing, and advising, this
parent has lost the chance to help Teddy work through his
feelings and arrive at some constructive solution to his problem *on his own.* Teddy also learned that his mother does not
trust him to solve such problems, that she cannot accept his
angry feelings, that she thinks he is not a nice boy, and that
parents just don't seem to understand.

There is no better way to insure the failure of active listening than to use it to encourage a child to express his true
feelings, after which the parent then moves in with evaluation, judgment, moralizing, and advice. Parents who do this
quickly discover that their children become suspicious and
learn that the parents only try to draw them out so they can
then turn around and use what they hear to evaluate them or
put them down.

The "Parroting Parent"

Mr. T. comes to class discouraged with his first efforts to
use active listening. "My son looked at me funny and told me
to stop repeating what he was saying." Mr. T. was reporting
an experience that many parents have when they simply
mirror back or "parrot" their children's facts, rather than
feelings. These parents need to be reminded that the child's
words (his particular *code*) are merely the vehicle for com-

municating feelings. *The code is not the message;* it must be decoded by the parent.

"You're a dirty, smelly stinkbug," says the child angrily to his father.

Obviously, the child knows the difference between a bug and his father, so his message is not, "Dad, you are a stinkbug." This particular code is merely the child's unique way of communicating his anger.

Were the father to respond with "You think I'm a stinkbug," the child would hardly feel that he had gotten his point across. If the father had said, "You're really angry at me!" the child would have said "I sure am!"—and would have felt understood.

The following examples show the contrasts between responses that merely parrot the code and those where the parent first decodes, then feeds back the child's inner feeling (the true message he is communicating):

1.

BILL: I never get a chance to get the ball when the bigger kids start playing catch.

(*a*) PARENT: You never get a chance to get the ball with big kids. [PARROTING THE CODE.]

(*b*) PARENT: You want to play too, and you feel it's not fair for them to leave you out. [FEEDING BACK THE MEANING.]

2.

BETTY: For a while I was doing good, but now I'm worse than ever. Nothing I do seems to help. What's the use of trying?

(*a*) PARENT: You're doing worse than ever now and nothing you do helps. [PARROTING THE CODE.]

(*b*) PARENT: You're sure discouraged and it makes you want to give up. [FEEDING BACK THE FEELING.]

3.

SAM: Look, Daddy, I made an airplane with my new tools!

(*a*) PARENT: You made an airplane with your tools. [PAR-ROTING THE CODE.]

(*b*) PARENT: You're really proud of the airplane you made. [FEEDING BACK THE FEELING.]

It takes practice for parents to learn accurate active listening. But in our P.E.T. classes we find that most parents who receive coaching and participate in skill-training exercises acquire a surprisingly high level of competence in this art.

Listening Without Empathy

A real danger for parents who try to learn active listening solely from a book's printed page is their inability to hear the warmth and empathy that must accompany their efforts. Empathy means a quality of communication that conveys to the sender of a message that the listener is feeling *with* him, putting himself in the shoes of the sender, living, for a moment, inside the sender.

Everyone wants others to understand how he feels when he talks, not just what he is saying. Children, especially, are feeling people. Therefore, much of what they communicate is accompanied by feelings: joy, hate, disappointment, fear, love, worry, anger, pride, frustration, sadness, and so on. When they communicate with parents, they expect empathy with such feelings. When parents don't empathize, children naturally feel that the essential part of them at that moment—their feeling—is not being understood.

Probably, the most common mistake parents make when they first try out active listening is to feed back a response devoid of the feeling component of the child's message.

Janet, aged eleven, runs into the kitchen where mother is working:

JANET: Jimmy [her nine-year-old brother] is a pest. He's mean! Mother, he pulls all my clothes out of the drawers. I hate him. I could kill him when he does that!

MOTHER: You don't like for him to do that.
JANET: Don't like it! I hate it! And I hate him!

Janet's mother hears her *words* but not her *feelings*. As of that particular moment, Janet is feeling angry and hateful. "You really are sore at Jimmy" would have caught her feelings. When Mother coldly feeds back only Janet's displeasure with having her bureau drawers emptied, Janet feels misunderstood and in her next message has to correct Mother with, "Don't like it! [That's putting it mildly]," and, "And I hate him [That's what's more important]."

Little Carey, aged six, pleads with his father who has been trying to encourage him to come into the water while the family is vacationing at the beach:

CAREY: I don't want to go in. It's too deep! And I'm afraid of
the waves.
FATHER: The water is too deep for you.
CAREY: I'm scared! Please don't make me go in!

This father is completely missing the child's feelings, and his attempt at feedback shows it. Carey is not sending an intellectual evaluation of the depth of the water. He is sending an urgent plea to his father: "Don't make me come in because I'm scared stiff!" The father should have acknowledged this with, "You're scared and don't want me to force you into the water."

Some parents who take our P.E.T. course find out they are very uncomfortable with feelings—their own as well as their child's. It is as if they are compelled to ignore a child's feelings because they cannot tolerate his having them. Or they want quickly to push his feelings out of the picture, and therefore deliberately avoid acknowledging them. Some parents are so frightened of feelings that they actually fail to detect them in their child's messages.

Such parents usually learn in our classes that children (and adults) inevitably do feel. Feelings are an essential part of living, not something pathological or dangerous. Our system also shows that feelings are generally transitory—they come and go, leaving no permanent damage to the child. The key to their going, however, is parental acceptance and acknowledgment, transmitted to the child by empathic active listening. When parents learn to do this, they report to us how quickly even intense negative feelings are dissipated.

Ralph and Sally, young parents of two daughters, brought back to class an incident that greatly reinforced their faith in the power of active listening. Both had been raised in strongly religious homes. Their parents had taught them in a hundred different ways that expressing feelings was a sign of weakness and not what a "Christian" ever does. Ralph and Sally learned: "It's a sin to hate!" "Love thy neighbor!" "Hold your tongue, young lady!" "When you can speak civilly to your mother, you may come back to the dinner table!"

Trained in childhood with such dictums, Ralph and Sally found it difficult as parents to accept their children's feelings and tune in to the frequent emotional communication from their two girls. P.E.T. was an eye-opener. At first, they began to accept the existence of feelings in their own relationship. Then, as many parents in P.E.T. do, they started communicating *their own feelings* to each other, helped by each active listening to the other.

Finding this new honesty and intimacy rewarding, Ralph and Sally had gained enough confidence to start listening to their two preadolescent girls. Within months, the two girls changed from being quiet, proper, introverted and repressed to being expressive, spontaneous, extroverted, communicative, and full of fun. Feelings became an accepted part of living in this liberated family environment.

"It's so much more fun now," Ralph reports. "We don't have to feel guilty about having feelings. And the kids are more open and honest with us now."

Active Listening at the Wrong Times

Unsuccessful experiences of parents who first try active listening often occur because parents use it at inappropriate times. As with any good thing, active listening can be overdone.

There are times when kids don't want to talk about their feelings, even to two empathic ears. They may want to live with their feelings for awhile. They may find it too painful at the moment to talk. They may not have the time to enter into a lengthy cathartic session with a parent. Parents should respect the child's need for privacy in his world of feelings and not try to push him to talk.

No matter how good a door-opener active listening is, kids often don't want to walk through. One mother told how her daughter found a way to tell her when she did not feel like talking: "Knock it off! I know it might help to talk, but I just don't feel like it now. So, please, no active listening right now, Mother."

Sometimes parents open the door with active listening when *they* lack time to stick around and hear all the feelings bottled up within the child. Such hit-and-run tactics are not only unfair to the child, but hurt the relationship. The child will come to feel his parents do not care enough to hear him out. We tell parents: "Don't start active listening unless you have the time to hear all of the feelings this technique so often releases."

Some parents have experienced resistance because they used active listening when a child needs different help. When a child is legitimately asking for information, for a helping hand, or for some special resource of the parent, he may have no need to talk out or work through something.

Parents sometimes grow so enamored of active listening that they employ it when the child does not need to be "drawn out" or encouraged to get in touch with his deeper feelings. It will be obvious how inappropriate active listening is in the following theoretical situations:

1.
CHILD: Hey, Mom, can either you or Dad give me a ride downtown Saturday? I've got to do some shopping.
PARENT: You'd like a ride downtown Saturday.

2.
CHILD: What time are you and Mom coming home?
PARENT: You are really puzzled as to when we are coming home?

3.
CHILD: How much will I have to pay for insurance if I bought my own car?
PARENT: You're worried about the cost of your insurance.

These children probably do not need to be encouraged to communicate more. They are asking for a specific kind of help that is quite different from the help that active listening provides. They are not transmitting feelings. They are asking for factual information. To respond to such requests with active listening will not only seem strange to the child; it will often produce frustration and irritation. These are times when a direct answer is what is wanted and called for.

Parents also discover that their children become perturbed when the parent continues to try active listening long after the child is finished sending messages. Parents need to know when to quit. Generally, clues will be forthcoming from the child—a facial expression, getting up to leave, silence, being fidgety, looking at his watch, and so on—or the child may say such things as:

> "Well, I guess that's about it."
> "I don't have time to go any further."
> "I see things kinda different now."

"Maybe that's enough for now."
"I got a lot of studying tonight."
"Well, I'm taking a lot of your time."

Wise parents back off when they get these clues or messages, even though it does not seem to them that the particular problem has been solved by the child. As professional therapists realize, active listening only starts children on the first step of problem-solving—getting the feelings out and the problem defined. Frequently, the children themselves take it from there, eventually winding up with a solution on their own.

5

How to Listen to Kids Too Young to Talk Much

Many parents ask: "While I see active listening can work wonders with children three and four years old and older, what can we do with infants and toddlers who don't talk?"

Or, "I see how we must rely much more on our children's inner capacities to work through their own problems helped by active listening. But younger children don't have problem-solving skills, so don't we have to solve most of their problems *for* them?"

It is a misperception that active listening is useful only for children old enough to talk. Using active listening with younger children does require some additional understanding about nonverbal communication and how parents can effectively respond to the nonverbal messages younger children send them. Furthermore, parents of very young children often think that just because these children are dependent on adults for many of their needs, infants and toddlers have very little capacity to work out their own solutions to problems they encounter early in life. This, too, just isn't so.

What Are Infants Like?

First, infants have needs like older children and adults. And they have their share of problems getting those needs met. They get cold, hungry, uncomfortably wet, tired, thirsty, frustrated, sick. Helping infants with such problems poses some special problems for parents.

Second, infants and very young children are extremely dependent upon their parents for the gratification of their needs or for providing them solutions to their problems. Their inner resources and capabilities *are* limited. A hungry infant has never been known to walk into the kitchen, open the refrigerator, and pour himself a glass of milk.

Third, infants and very young children do not have a well-developed capability of communicating their needs through verbal symbols. They do not yet have the language to share their problems and needs with others. Much of the time, parents are quite perplexed about what is going on inside pre-verbal children, because babies don't go around clearly announcing that they have a need for affection or for releasing gas from their stomach.

Fourth, infants and very young children frequently may not even "know" themselves what is bothering them. This is because so many of their needs are physiological—that is, problems caused by deprivation of their physical needs (hunger, thirst, pain, and so on). Also, because of their undeveloped cognitive and language skills, they may not be able to figure out what problems they are experiencing.

Helping very young children meet their needs and solve their problems is therefore somewhat different from helping older children. But not as different as most parents think.

Tuning In to Needs and Problems of Infants

Much as parents might wish that infants would resourcefully meet their own needs and solve their own problems, it is frequently up to a parent to see that little Nicky gets enough to eat, is dry, stays warm, gets affection, and the like. The problem is: how does the parent find out what is bothering a fussy, whining infant?

Most parents "go by the book"—what the parent has read about the needs of infants in general. No doubt Dr. Benjamin Spock has been a great boon to parents by providing them with information about infants and their needs and things parents can do to insure that these needs are gratified. Yet, as any parent knows, not everything is covered by Dr. Spock. To be effective in helping a particular child with his own unique needs and problems, a parent is obliged to acquire an understanding of that child. He does this chiefly through *accurate listening to his child's messages*, nonverbal though they may be.

A very young child's parent must *learn to listen accurately* just as much as parents of older children. It is a different kind of listening, principally because infants communicate nonverbally.

An infant starts crying at 5:30 A.M. Obviously, he has a problem—something is wrong, he has a need, he wants something. He cannot send a verbal message to the parent, "I feel very uncomfortable and upset." Therefore, the parent cannot use active listening as we have previously described it ("You feel uncomfortable, you are bothered by something"). The child obviously would not understand.

The parent does get a nonverbal message (crying) and he must go through the process of "decoding" it if he is to find out what is going on inside the child. Because the parent cannot utilize *verbal* feed back to check on the accuracy of his decoding, he must use a *nonverbal or behavioral* feedback method.

The parent might first throw a blanket over the child (decoding the child's crying as "He is feeling cold"). But the child keeps on crying ("You have not yet understood my message"). Then the parent picks the child up and rocks him (Now decoding, "He is scared by a dream"). The child continues to cry ("That's not what I am feeling"). Finally, the parent puts a bottle of milk in the infant's mouth ("He is feeling hungry") and after a few sucks the child stops crying. ("That's what I meant—I was feeling hungry—you finally understood me.")

Being an effective parent of a very young child, as with an older child, depends to a great extent upon *the accuracy of communication between parent and child*. And the principal responsibility for developing accurate communication in this relationship rests with the parent. He must learn to decode accurately the nonverbal behavior of the infant before making a determination of what is bothering him. He must also utilize the same feedback process for the purpose of checking on the accuracy of his decoding. This feedback process also can be called active listening; it is the same mechanism we described in the communication process with more verbal children. But with a child who sends a non-verbal message (crying), the parent must use a non-verbal feedback (bottle in the mouth).

This necessity for this kind of effective two-way communication partially explains why it is so critical in the first two years of a child's life for his parents to spend a lot of time with him. A parent gets to "know" his child better than anyone else—that is, the parent develops skill in decoding the infant's nonverbal behavior and hence becomes more able than anyone else to know what to do to satisfy the child's needs or provide solutions to his problems.

Everyone has had the experience of being unable to decode the behavior of a friend's child. We ask, "What does he mean when he rattles the slats of the playpen? He must want something." The mother replies, "Oh, he always does that when he is getting sleepy. Our first child tugged at his blanket when he got sleepy."

Using Active Listening to Help Infants

Too many parents of infants do not bother to use active listening to check on the accuracy of their decoding process. They jump in and take some kind of action to help the child without finding out what is really bothering him.

> Jimmy stands up in his crib and begins to whimper, then to cry loudly. Mother sets him back down and hands him his rattle. Jimmy stops crying for a moment, then knocks the rattle out of the crib and onto the floor, and begins to cry even more loudly. Mother picks up the rattle and firmly puts it into Jimmy's hand, saying harshly, "If you throw it out again, you won't get it back." Jimmy keeps crying and again knocks the rattle out of the crib. Mother slaps his hand. Jimmy really howls now.

This mother made an assumption that she knew what the baby needed, but she failed to "hear" the baby "tell" her that her decoding was inaccurate. As with many parents, this mother did not keep at it long enough to *complete the communication process.* She did not make certain that she understood what the child needed or wanted. The child remained frustrated and the mother became angry. In this way are sown the seeds of a deteriorating relationship and an emotionally unhealthy child.

Obviously, the younger the child, the less the parent can bank on the child's own resources or capabilities. This means that more parent intervention (or inputs) will be required in the problem-solving process of younger children. Everybody knows that parents have to prepare the formula, change the diapers, cover the child up, disentangle him from his blanket, move him, raise him, rock him, cuddle him, and the thousands of other things necessary to see to it that his needs are **not** being thwarted. Again, this means time with the child—and lots of it. Those early years require the almost constant presence of the parent. The infant *needs his parents,* and needs them desperately. This is why pediatricians so strongly insist on parents being around during those first few formative years when the child is so very helpless and dependent.

Yet being around is not enough in itself. *The critical factor is the parents' effectiveness in listening accurately* to the non-verbal communication of the child so that *she understands what is going on inside* and can effectively give the child *what he needs when he needs it.*

Failure of many child-rearing specialists to understand this has resulted in a great deal of poor research and some incorrect interpretations of research findings in the field of child development. Numerous research studies have been launched to demonstrate the superiority of one method versus another—bottle feeding versus breast, demand feeding versus scheduled, early toilet training versus late, early weaning versus late, strictness versus leniency. For the most part, these studies have failed to take into account the wide differences in the needs of various children and the extreme differences among mothers in their effectiveness in receiving their children's communications.

Whether a child is weaned early or late, for example, may not be the important factor in influencing his later personality or mental health. Rather it is whether his mother listens accurately to the messages *that particular child* is sending her every day about his particular eating needs, so that she can then have the flexibility to move in with solutions that truly satisfy his needs. Accurate listening, then, may result in a mother weaning one child late, another early, and perhaps a third child somewhere in between. I strongly believe the same principle applies to most of the child-rearing practices about which there has been so much controversy—feeding, amount of cuddling, degree of maternal separation, sleeping, toilet training, sucking, and so on. If this principle is valid, then we should say to parents:

> You will be the most effective parent by providing your infant with a home climate in which you will know how to gratify his needs appropriately by using active listening to understand the messages that announce specifically what his unique needs are.

Give the Child a Chance to Meet His Needs Himself

Certainly the ultimate goal of most parents should be to help the very young child gradually develop his own resources—to become weaned away from dependence on the parent's resources, more and more capable of meeting his own needs, solving his own problems. The parent who will be most effective in this is the one who can consistently follow the principle of first giving the child a chance to solve his problems himself before jumping in with a parental solution.

In the following illustration, the parent follows this principle quite effectively:

CHILD (Crying): Truck, truck—no truck.

PARENT: You want your truck, but you can't find it. [ACTIVE LISTENING.]

CHILD: (Looks under sofa, but doesn't find truck.)

PARENT: The truck's not there. [FEEDING BACK NON-VERBAL MESSAGE.]

CHILD: (Runs into his room, looks, can't find it.)

PARENT: The truck's not there. [FEEDING BACK NON-VERBAL MESSAGE.]

CHILD: (Thinks; moves to back door.)

PARENT: Maybe the truck's in the back yard. [FEEDING BACK NONVERBAL MESSAGE.]

CHILD   (runs out, finds truck in sandbox, looks proud):
Truck!

PARENT: You found your truck yourself. [ACTIVE LISTEN-
ING.]

This parent kept the responsibility for solving the problem
with the child at all times by avoiding direct intervention or
advice. By doing so, the parent is helping the child develop
and use his own resources.

Many parents are far too eager to take over their child's
problems. They are so anxious to help the child or so uncomfortable (nonaccepting) of his experiencing an unfulfilled
need that they are compelled to take over the problem-solving and *give the child a quick solution*. If this is done frequently, it is a sure way of retarding the child's learning how
to use his own resources and his developing independence
and resourcefulness.

6

How to Talk So Kids Will
Listen to You

Frequently when parents learn active listening in our classes, a parent becomes impatient and asks, "When do we learn how to get the kids to listen to us? That's the problem in our home."

Undoubtedly that is the problem in many homes, for children inevitably annoy, disturb, and frustrate parents at times; they can be thoughtless and inconsiderate as they go about trying to meet their own needs. Like small puppies, kids can be boisterous and destructive, noisy and demanding. As every parent knows, children can cause extra work, delay you when you are in a hurry, pester you when you are tired, talk when you want quiet, smear jam on you when you are dressed up, and so on ad infinitum.

Mothers and fathers need effective ways to deal with children's behavior that interferes with the parents' needs. After all, parents *do* have needs. They have their own lives to live, and the right to derive enjoyment and satisfaction from their existence. Yet, many of the parents who come to P.E.T. for training have allowed their children to be in a favored position in the family. These children demand that their needs are met but they are inconsiderate of the needs of their parents.

Much to their regret, many parents find that as their children get older, they act as if they are oblivious to their parents' needs. When parents permit this to happen, their children move through life as if it is a one-way street for the continuous gratification of their own needs. Parents of such children usually become embittered, and feel strong resentment toward their "ungrateful," "selfish" kids.

When Mrs. Lloyd enrolled in P.E.T., she was puzzled and hurt because her daughter, Jean, was becoming more and more selfish and inconsiderate. Indulged by both parents since infancy, Jean contributed very little to the family, yet expected her parents to do everything she requested. If she did not get her way, she would say abusive things about her parents, throw tantrums or walk out of the house and not return for hours.

Mrs. Lloyd, raised by her own mother to think of conflict or strong feelings as something cultured families are not supposed to let out, gave in to most of Jean's demands in order to avoid a scene or as she put it, "to keep peace and tranquility in the family." As Jean moved into adolescence, she became even more arrogant and self-centered, seldom helping around the house and rarely making adjustments out of consideration for the needs of her parents.

Often she told her parents that it was their responsibility that she was brought into the world and therefore their duty to take care of her needs. Mrs. Lloyd, a conscientious parent who wanted desperately to be a good mother, was beginning to develop deep feelings of resentment toward Jean. After all she had done for Jean, it hurt and angered her to see Jean's selfishness and lack of consideration for the needs of the parents.

"We do all the giving, she does all the taking," was the way this mother described the family situation.

Mrs. Lloyd was certain she was doing something wrong, but she did not dream that Jean's behavior was the direct result of the mother's fear of standing up for her own rights. P.E.T. first helped her accept the legitimacy of her own needs and then gave her specific skills for confronting Jean when her behavior was unacceptable to her parents.

What can parents do when they cannot genuinely accept a child's behavior? How can they get the child to consider the parents' needs? Now we will focus on how parents can talk to kids so they will listen to *their* feelings and be considerate of *their* needs.

Entirely different communication skills are required when the child causes the parent a problem as opposed to those needed when the child causes himself a problem. In the latter case, the child "owns" the problem; when the child causes the parent a problem, the parent "owns" it. This chapter will show parents what skills they need for effectiveness in solving problems that their children cause them.

WHEN THE PARENT OWNS THE PROBLEM

Many parents initially have difficulty understanding the concept of ownership of problems. Perhaps they are too accustomed to think in terms of having "problem children," which locates the problem within the child, rather than the parent. It is critical that parents understand the difference.

The best clue for parents comes when they begin to sense their own inner feelings of unacceptance, when they begin to have inner feelings of annoyance, frustration, resentment. They may find themselves becoming tense, experiencing discomfort, not liking what the child is doing, or monitoring his behavior.

Suppose:

A child is getting too close to a valued piece of china.

A child has his feet on the rungs of your new chair.

A child is interrupting your conversation with a friend.

A child is tugging at you to leave and break off your conversation with a neighbor.

A child has left his toys on the living-room floor.

A child appears about ready to tip his milk over onto the rug.

A child is demanding that you read him one more story, then another, then another.

A child won't feed his pet.

A child is not carrying his load of work around the house.

A child uses your tools and leaves them in the driveway.

A child drives your car too fast.

All these behaviors actually or potentially threaten legitimate needs of parents. The child's behavior *in some tangible* or direct way affects the parent: Mother does not want her vase broken, her chair scratched, her rug soiled, her discussion interrupted, and so on.

Confronted with such behaviors as these, a parent needs ways to help himself, not the child. The following chart helps to show the difference between the parent's role when he owns the problem, and when the child does.

When the Child Owns the Problem	When the Parent Owns the Problem
Child initiates communication	Parent initiates communication
Parent is a listener	Parent is a sender
Parent is a counselor	Parent is an influencer
Parent wants to help child	Parent wants to help himself
Parent is a "sounding board"	Parent wants to "sound off"
Parent facilitates child finding his own solution	Parent has to find his own solution
Parent accepts child's solution	Parent must be satisfied with solution himself
Parent primarily interested in child's needs	Parent primarily interested in his own needs
Parent is more passive	Parent is more aggressive

A parent has several alternatives when he owns the problem:

1. He can try to modify the child directly.
2. He can try to modify the environment.
3. He can try to modify himself.

Mr. Adam's son, Jimmy, takes his father's tools out of the tool box and usually leaves them scattered over the lawn. This is unacceptable to Mr. Adams, so *he* owns this problem.

He can confront Jimmy, say something, hoping this might modify Jimmy's behavior.

He can modify Jimmy's environment by buying him his own set of junior tools, hoping this will modify Jimmy's behavior.

He can try to modify his own attitudes about Jimmy's behavior, saying to himself that "boys will be boys" or "he'll learn proper care of tools in time."

In this chapter, we shall deal only with the first alternative, focusing on how parents can talk or confront their kids in order to modify behavior that is unacceptable to the parents.

In later chapters, we will deal with the other two alternatives.

INEFFECTIVE WAYS OF CONFRONTING CHILDREN

It is no exaggeration that ninety-nine out of a hundred parents in our classes use ineffective methods of communicating when their children's behavior is interfering with the parents' lives. In a typical class of twenty-five parents the instructor reads aloud a typical family situation of a child upsetting his parent:

> "You are very tired from a full day's work. You need to sit down and rest for awhile. You would like to take this time to read the evening paper. But, your five-year-old son keeps pestering you to play with him. He keeps pulling your arm, getting up on your lap, crumpling the newspaper. Playing with him is the last thing you feel like doing."

Then the instructor asks everybody to write on a slip of paper exactly what each would say to the child in this situation. (The reader may participate in this exercise by writing down his verbal response). Then the instructor reads another situation and then a third, and asks each to write his responses.

> "Your four-year-old has removed some pots and pans from the cupboard and is starting to play with them on the kitchen floor. This is interfering with your getting dinner for guests. You are already behind schedule."

> "Your twelve-year-old came home from school, fixed a sandwich for himself, and left the kitchen in a shambles after you had spent an hour cleaning it

up so that it would be clean when you started to get dinner."

We discover from this classroom experiment that parents, with rare exceptions, handle these rather typical situations ineffectively. They say things to the child that have a high probability of:

1. Causing the child to resist his parent's influence efforts by refusing to change the behavior that is unacceptable to the parent.
2. Making the child feel his parent does not think him very bright.
3. Making the child feel his parent has no consideration for his needs.
4. Making the child feel guilty.
5. Tearing down the child's self-esteem.
6. Causing the child to defend himself vigorously.
7. Provoking the child to attack the parent or get back at him in some way.

Parents are shocked at these findings, because it is a rare parent who consciously intends to do these things to his child. Most parents simply have never thought about the effects their words can produce on their children.

In our classes we then describe each of these ineffective ways of verbally confronting children and point out in greater detail why they are ineffective.

Sending a "Solution Message"

Have you ever been just about ready to do something considerate for a person (or initiate some change in your behavior to meet a person's needs) when all of a sudden that person directs you, exhorts you, or advises you to do exactly what you were going to do on your own?

Your reaction was probably, "I didn't need to be told" or "Darn it, if you had waited a minute, I would have done that without being told." Or you probably got irritated because you felt that the other person did not trust you enough or took away the chance for you to do something considerate for him on your own initiative.

When people do this to you, they are "sending a solution." This is precisely what parents often do with children. They do not wait for the child to initiate considerate behavior; they tell him what he *must* or *should* or *ought* to do. All the following types of messages "send a solution":

1. ORDERING, DIRECTING, COMMANDING
   "You go find something to play with."
   "You stop wrinkling the paper."
   "You put those pots and pans away."
   "You clean up that mess."

2. WARNING, ADMONISHING, THREATENING
   "If you don't stop, I'll scream."
   "Mother will get angry if you don't get from under my feet."
   "If you don't get out there and put that kitchen back where it was, you're going to be sorry."

3. EXHORTING, PREACHING, MORALIZING
   "Don't ever interrupt a person when he's reading."
   "Please play someplace else."
   "You shouldn't play when Mother is in a hurry."
   "Always clean up after yourself."

4. ADVISING, GIVING SUGGESTIONS OR SOLUTIONS
   "Why don't you go outside and play?"
   "Let me suggest something else for you to do."
   "Can't you put each thing away after you use it?"

These kinds of verbal responses communicate to the child *your* solution for him—precisely what *you* think he must do. You call the shots; you are in control; you are taking over;

you are cracking the whip. *You are leaving him out of it.* The first type of message orders him to employ *your* solution; the second threatens him; the third exhorts him; the fourth advises him.

Parents ask, "What's so wrong with sending your solution—after all, isn't he causing me a problem?" True, he is. But giving him the solution to your problem can have these effects:

1. Children resist being told what to do. They also may not like your solution. In any case, children resist having to modify their behavior when they are told just how they "must" or "should" or "better" change.

2. Sending the solution to the child also communicates another message, "I don't trust you to select your solution" or "I don't think you're sensitive enough to find a way to help me with my problem."

3. Sending the solution tells the child that your needs are more important than his, that he has to do just what you think he should, regardless of his needs ("You're doing something unacceptable to me, so the only solution is what I say").

If a friend is visiting in your home and happens to put his feet on the rungs of one of your new dining room chairs, you certainly would not say to him:

> "Get your feet off my chair this minute."
> "You should never put your feet on somebody's new chair."
> "If you know what's good for you, you'll take your feet off my chair."
> "I suggest you do not ever put your feet on my chair."

This sounds ridiculous in a situation involving a friend because most people treat friends with more respect. Adults want their friends to "save face." They also assume that a friend has brains enough to find his own solution to *your* problem once he is told what the problem is. An adult would simply tell the friend his feelings. He would leave it up to him to respond appropriately and assume he would be considerate enough to respect one's feelings. Most likely the chair owner would send some such messages as:

> "I am worried that my new chair might get scratched by your feet."
> "I'm sitting here on pins and needles because I hear your feet on my new chair."
> "I'm embarrassed to mention this, but we just got these new chairs and I'm anxious to keep them unscratched."

These messages do not "send a solution." People generally send this type of message to friends but seldom to their own children; they naturally refrain from ordering, exhorting, threatening, and advising friends to modify their behavior in some particular way, yet as parents they do this every day with their children.

No wonder children resist or respond with defensiveness and hostility. No wonder children feel "put down," squelched, controlled. No wonder they "lose face." No wonder some grow up submissively expecting to be handed solutions by everyone. Parents frequently complain that their children are not responsible in the family; they do not show consideration for the needs of parents. How are children ever going to learn responsibility when parents take away every chance for the child to do something responsible on his own out of consideration for his parents' needs?

Sending a "Put-Down Message"

Everyone knows what it feels like to be "put down" by a message that communicates blame, judgment, ridicule, criticism, or shame. In confronting children, parents rely heavily on such messages. "Put-down messages" may fall into any of these categories:

1. JUDGING, CRITICIZING, BLAMING
   "You ought to know better."
   "You are being very thoughtless."
   "You are being naughty."
   "You are the most inconsiderate child I know."
   "You'll be the death of me yet."

2. NAME-CALLING, RIDICULING, SHAMING
   "You're a spoiled brat."
   "All right, Mr. Busybody."
   "Do you like being a selfish free-loader here in the home?"
   "Shame on you."

3. INTERPRETING, DIAGNOSING, PSYCHOANALYZING
   "You just want to get some attention."
   "You're trying to get my goat."
   "You just love to see how far you can go before I get mad."
   "You always want to play just where I'm working."

4. TEACHING, INSTRUCTING
   "It's not good manners to interrupt someone."
   "Nice children don't do that."
   "How would you like it if I did that to you?"
   "Why don't you be good for a change."
   "Do unto others .. etc."
   "We don't leave our dishes dirty."

All these are put-downs—they impugn the child's character, deprecate him as a person, shatter his self-esteem, underline his inadequacies, cast a judgment on his personality. They point the finger of blame toward the child.

What effects are these messages likely to produce?

1. Children often feel guilty and remorseful when they are evaluated or blamed.
2. Children feel the parent is not being fair—they feel an injustice: "I didn't do anything wrong" or "I didn't mean to be bad."
3. Children often feel unloved, rejected: "She doesn't like me because I did something wrong."
4. Children often act very resistive to such messages—they dig in their heels. To give up the behavior that is bothering the parent would be an admission of the validity of the parent's blame or evaluation. A child's typical reaction would be: "I'm not bothering you" or "The dishes aren't in anybody's way."
5. Children often come back at the parent with a boomerang: "You're not always so neat yourself" or "You're always tired" or "You're a big grouch when company is coming" or "Why can't the house be a place we can live in?"
6. Put-downs make the child feel inadequate. They reduce his self-esteem.

Put-down messages can have devastating effects on a child's developing self-concept. The child who is bombarded with messages that deprecate him will learn to look at himself as no good, bad, worthless, lazy, thoughtless, inconsiderate, "dumb," inadequate, unacceptable, and so on. Because a poor self-concept formed in childhood has a tendency to persist into adulthood, put-down messages sow the seeds for handicapping a person throughout his lifetime.

These are the ways that parents, day after day, contribute to the destruction of their children's ego or self-esteem. Like drops of water falling on a rock, these daily messages gradually, imperceptibly leave a destructive effect on children.

EFFECTIVE WAYS OF CONFRONTING CHILDREN

Parents' talk can also build. Most parents, once they become aware of the destructive power of put-down messages, are eager to learn more effective ways of confronting children. In our classes we never encountered a parent who consciously wanted to destroy his child's self-esteem.

"You-messages" and "I-messages"

An easy way for parents to be shown the difference between ineffective and effective confrontation is to think of sending either "You-messages" or "I-messages." When we ask parents to examine the previously noted ineffective messages, they are surprised to discover that almost all begin with the word "You" or contain that word. All these messages are "You"-oriented:

> *You* stop that.
> *You* shouldn't do that.
> Don't *you* ever . . .
> If *you* don't stop that, then . . .
> Why don't *you* do this?
> *You* are naughty.
> *You* are acting like a baby.
> *You* want attention.
> Why don't *you* be good?
> *You* should know better.

But when a parent simply tells a child how some unacceptable behavior is making *the parent feel*, the message generally turns out to be an "I-message."

> "*I* cannot rest when someone is crawling on my lap."
> "*I* don't feel like playing when I'm tired."

"*I* can't cook when I have to walk around pots and pans on the floor."

"*I'm* worried about getting dinner ready on time."

"*I* sure get discouraged when I see my clean kitchen dirty again."

Parents readily understand the difference between "I-messages" and "You-messages," but its full significance is appreciated only after we return to the diagram of the communication process, first introduced to explain active listening. It helps parents appreciate the importance of "I-messages."

When a child's behavior is unacceptable to a parent because in some tangible way it interferes with the parent's enjoyment of life or his right to satisfy his own needs, the parent clearly "owns" the problem. He is upset, disappointed, tired, worried, harrassed, burdened, etc., and to let the child know what is inside him, the parent must select a suitable code. For the parent who is tired and does not feel like playing with his four-year-old child, our diagram would look like this:

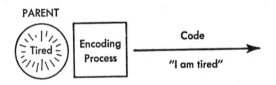

But if this parent selects a code that is "you"-oriented, he would not be coding his "feeling tired" accurately:

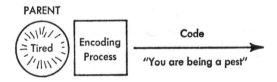

"You are being a pest" is a very poor code for the parent's tired feeling. A code that is clear and accurate would always be an "I-message": "I am tired," "I don't feel up to playing," "I want to rest." This communicates the feeling the parent is experiencing. A "You-message" code does not send the feeling. It refers much more to the child than to the parent. A "You-message" is child-oriented, not parent-oriented.

Consider these messages from the point of view of what the child hears:

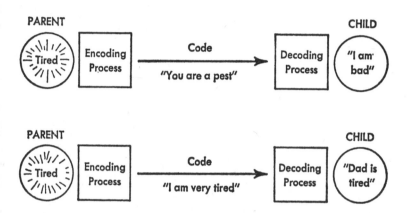

The first message is decoded by the child as an *evaluation* of him. The second is decoded as a *statement of fact* about the parent. "You-messages" are poor codes for communicating what a *parent* is feeling, because they will most often be decoded by the child in terms of either what *he* should do (sending a solution) or how bad *he* is (sending blame or evaluation).

Why "I-messages" Are More Effective

"I-messages" are more effective in influencing a child to modify behavior that is unacceptable to the parent as well as healthier for the child and the parent-child relationship.

The "I-message" is much less apt to provoke resistance and rebellion. To communicate to a child honestly the effect of his behavior on *you* is far less threatening than to suggest that there is something bad about *him* because he engaged in that behavior. Think of the significant difference in a child's reaction to these two messages, sent by a parent after a child kicks him in the shins:

> "Ouch! That really hurt me—I don't like to be kicked."
> "That's being a very bad boy. Don't you ever kick anybody like that!"

The first message only tells the child how his kick made you feel, a fact with which he can hardly argue. The second tells the child that he was "bad" and warns him not to do it again, both of which he can argue against and probably resist strongly.

"I-messages" are also infinitely more effective because they place responsibility within the child for modifying his behavior. "Ouch! That really hurt me" and "I don't like to be kicked" tell the child how you feel, yet leave him to be responsible for doing something about it.

Consequently, "I-messages" help a child grow, help him learn to assume responsibility for his own behavior. An "I-message" tells a child that you are leaving the responsibility with him, trusting him to handle the situation constructively, trusting him to respect your needs, giving him a chance to start behaving constructively.

Because "I-messages" are honest, they tend to influence a child to send similar honest messages *whenever he has a feeling.* "I-messages" from one person in a relationship promote "I-messages" from the other. This is why, in deteriorating relationships, conflicts often degenerate into mutual name-calling and reciprocal blaming:

PARENT: You're getting awfully irresponsible about doing your dishes after breakfast. ["You-message."]

CHILD: You don't always do yours every morning. ["You-message."]

PARENT: That's different—Mother has lots of other things to do around the house, picking up after a bunch of messy children. ["You-message."]

CHILD: I haven't been messy. [Defensive message.]

PARENT: You're just as bad as the others, and you know it. ["You-message."]

CHILD: You expect everyone to be perfect. ["You-message."]

PARENT: Well, you certainly have a long way to go to reach that when it comes to picking up. ["You-message."]

CHILD: You're so darned fussy about the house. ["You-message."]

This is typical of many conversations between parents and children when the parent starts his confrontation with a "You-message." Invariably, they end up in a struggle, with both alternately defending and attacking.

"I-messages" are much less likely to produce such a struggle. This is not to say that if parents send "I-messages" everything will be sweetness and light. Understandably, children do not like to hear that their behavior has caused a problem for their parents (just like adults, who are never exactly comfortable when someone confronts them with the fact that their behavior has caused pain). Nevertheless, telling someone how you feel is far less threatening than accusing him of *causing* a bad feeling.

It takes a certain amount of courage to send "I-messages," but the rewards are generally well worth the risks. It takes courage and inner security for a person to expose his inner feelings in a relationship. The sender of an honest "I-message" risks becoming known to the other *as he really is*. He is opening himself up—being "transparently real," revealing his "human-ness." He tells the other that he is a person *capable* of being hurt or embarrassed or frightened or disappointed or angry or discouraged, and so on.

For a person to reveal how he *feels* means opening himself to be viewed by the other. What will the other person think of me? Will I be rejected? Will the other person think less of me? Parents, particularly, find it difficult to be transparently real with children because they like to be seen as infallible—without weaknesses, vulnerabilities, inadequacies. For many parents, it is much easier to hide their feelings under a "You-message" that puts the blame on the child than to expose their own human-ness.

Probably the greatest reward that comes to a parent from being transparent is the relationship it promotes with the child. Honesty and openness foster intimacy—a truly inter-*personal* relationship. My child gets to know me as I am, which then encourages him to reveal to me what he is. Instead of being alienated from each other, we develop a relationship of closeness. Ours becomes an *authentic* relationship—two real persons, willing to be known in our realness to each other.

When parents and children learn to be open and honest with each other, they no longer are "strangers in the same house." The parents can have the joy of being parents to a real person—and the children are blessed by having real persons as parents.

7

Putting "I-Messages" to Work

Parents in the P.E.T. course warmly welcome being shown how to modify child behavior that is unacceptable to them. Some announce in class, "I can't wait to get home and try this out on something my child has been doing that's been irritating me for months."

Unfortunately, newly trained parents sometimes do not get the results that they hope for. At least, not at first. We therefore deal with the mistakes they frequently make when they try to put "I-messages" to work, and offer examples to increase their skill.

The Disguised "You-Message"

Mr. G., the father of two adolescent boys, came to class and reported that his first attempt to put "I-messages" to work had ended dismally.

"My son, Paul, contrary to what you told us, started sending his own 'You-messages' right back to me, like he always does."

"Did you send 'I-messages' yourself?" asked the instructor.

"Of course—or I think I did; I tried to anyway", Mr. G. replied.

The instructor suggested acting out the situation in class—he would play the part of Paul and Mr. G. would be himself. After explaining the situation to the class, Mr. G. began to recapture the situation:

MR. G.:   I feel very strongly that you have been neglectful of your chores.

PAUL: How's that?

MR. G.:   Well, take your job of mowing the lawn. I feel upset every time you goof off. Like last Saturday. I was angry at you because you sneaked off without mowing the backyard. I felt that was irresponsible and I was upset.

At this point, the instructor stopped the role-playing and said to Mr. G., "I did hear a lot of 'I feel's from you, but let's ask the class if they heard anything else."

One of the fathers in the class immediately chimed in with, "In a few seconds, you told Paul he was neglectful, he was a goof-off, he was sneaky, and he was irresponsible."

"Wow. Did I? I guess maybe I did", Mr. G. said sheepishly. "Those sound just like 'You-messages.' "

Mr. G. was correct. He had made the mistake many parents initially make—sending "You-messages" under the disguise of putting "I feel" in front of name-calling messages.

It sometimes takes this kind of re-enactment of a real situation for parents to see clearly that "*I feel* you are a slob" is just as much a "You-message" as "You are a slob." Parents are instructed to drop the "I feel" and state what they did feel specifically—such as, "I was disappointed," "I wanted the lawn to look nice Sunday," or "I was upset because I thought we had agreed the lawn would be mowed Saturday."

Don't Accentuate the Negative

Another mistake freshly trained parents sometimes make is to send "I-messages" to convey their negative feelings, and forget to send "I-messages" about their positive feelings.

Mrs. K. and her daughter, Linda, had an agreement that Linda would come home from a movie date no later than 12:00 A.M. Linda finally showed up at 1:30. Her mother had been kept from her sleep for an hour and a half and had worried herself sick that something terrible had happened to Linda.

In the classroom role-playing recapitulation of this incident, Mrs. K. sounded like this:

MRS. K. (as Linda walked in): I'm angry at you.
LINDA: I know I'm late.
MRS. K.: I'm really upset at you for keeping me awake.
LINDA: Why couldn't you sleep? I wish you'd go to sleep and not worry.
MRS. K.: How could I? I was mad at you and worried sick that you might have been in an accident. I'm really disappointed in you that you didn't stick to our agreement.

The instructor interrupted the role-playing and said to Mrs. K., "Not bad—you sent some pretty good "I-messages," but only the negative ones. How did you *actually* feel when Linda walked in the front door? What was your first feeling?"

Mrs. K. quickly answered, "I felt terribly relieved that Linda was home safe. I wanted to hug her and tell her how glad I was to see her in one piece."

"I believe you," said the instructor. "Now (I'll be Linda again) send me those real feelings as 'I-messages.' Let's try it again."

MRS. K.: Oh, Linda, thank God you're home safe. I'm so glad to see you. What a relief. [Hugs the instructor]. I was so afraid you'd been in an accident.
LINDA: Gosh, you *are* glad to see me, aren't you.

At this, the class actually applauded Mrs. K., expressing their amazement and delight at the entirely different quality of the second confrontation, starting out with her strongest "here-and-now" feelings. An exciting discussion ensued about the way parents miss so many chances of being honest with kids about their positive and loving feelings. Eager to "teach our kids a lesson," we miss golden opportunities to teach them far more fundamental lessons. For instance, that we love them so much, that it would pain us terribly if they were hurt or killed.

After sending the first honest expression of what was inside Mrs. K., there was plenty of time to confront Linda with her mother's disappointment that the agreement was not lived up to by her daughter. What a different kind of a discussion it would have been if the positive "I-message" had been sent first.

Sending a Boy to Do a Man's Job

Parents in P.E.T. hear a lot about "undershooting" their "I-messages". Many parents find it difficult at first to send an "I-message" that matches the intensity of their inner feelings. Usually, when a parent undershoots, the "I-message" loses its impact on the child and no behavior change occurs.

> Mrs. B. reported an incident in which her son, Bryant, did not change his unacceptable behavior even after she felt she sent a good "I-message." Bryant, age six, had hit his baby brother in the head with his father's old tennis racket, with which he was playing. Mother sent an "I-message," but Bryant went ahead and repeated his deadly assault on baby brother.

In the role-playing of this incident in class, it became apparent to the other parents that Mrs. B. was guilty of undershooting her feelings.

MRS. B: Bryant, I don't like for you to hit Sammy.

"I'm surprised, Mrs. B.," said the instructor," that you had such mild feelings about your smallest getting hit with a hard tennis racket."

"Oh, I was scared to death his little skull had been cracked open, I was sure I'd see blood on his head."

"Well, then," said the instructor, "let's put those very strong feelings into "I-messages" that match the intensity of how you really felt inside."

Thus encouraged and sanctioned to be honest with her real feelings, Mrs. B. then came out strongly with, "Bryant, I get *scared to death* when the baby is hit on the head! I would sure hate to see him hurt badly. And I get really mad when I see someone big hurting someone a lot smaller. Oooooh, I was so *afraid* his little head was going to bleed."

Mrs. B. and the other parents in the class agreed that this time she had not "sent a boy to do a man's job." The second "I-message," matching much more closely her true feelings, would have much more chance of having an impact on Bryant.

The Erupting Mt. Vesuvius

Some parents, when first introduced to "I-messages," rush home eager to begin confronting their kids and end up spewing and venting their pent-up emotions like a volcano. One mother returned to class and announced that she spent the entire week being angry at her two children. The only problem was that her children were scared out of their wits by her eruptions.

The discovery that a few parents were interpreting our encouragement for them to confront their children as license to vent their angry feelings forced me to re-examine the function of anger in the parent-child relationship. This critical re-examination of anger greatly clarified my own thinking and brought me to a new formulation about why parents vent their anger, why it is harmful to children, and how parents can be helped to avoid it.

Unlike other feelings, anger is almost invariably directed at another person. "I am angry" is a message that usually means "I am angry at *you*" or "*You* made me angry". It is really a "You-message," not an "I-message." A parent cannot disguise this "You-message" by stating it as "I feel angry." Consequently, such a message feels like a "You-message" to children. A child thinks he is being blamed as the one who *caused* his parent's anger. The predictable effect on the child is that he will feel put-down, blamed, and guilty, just as he is by other "You-messages".

I am convinced now that anger is something generated solely by the parent *after* he has experienced an earlier feeling. The parent manufactures the anger as a consequence of experiencing a primary feeling. Here is how it works:

> I am driving along on a freeway and another driver cuts in front of me precariously close to my right front fender. My primary feeling is fear, his behavior scared me. As a consequence of his scaring me, and some seconds later, I honk my horn and "act angry," perhaps even shouting something like "You sonuvabitch, why don't you learn how to drive," a message that no one could deny is a pure "You-message." The function of my "acting angry" is to punish the other driver or to make him feel guilty for scaring me so that he does not do it again.

The angry parent in most cases is similarly using his anger or his "acting angry" to teach his child a lesson.

> A mother loses her child in a department store. Her primary feeling is fear—she is afraid that something unpleasant may happen to him. If someone

asked her how she was feeling while she was searching for him, this mother would say "I'm scared to
death" or "I feel terribly worried or frightened."
When she finally finds the child, she experiences
great relief. To herself she says, "Thank God, you're
okay." But out loud she says something quite
different. Acting angry, she will send some such
message as, "You naughty boy" or "I'm mad at you!
How can you be so stupid and get separated from
me?" or "Didn't I tell you to stay close to me?"
Mother, in this situation, is acting angry (a *secondary* feeling), in order to teach the child a lesson or
punish him for causing her fear.

As a secondary feeling, anger almost always becomes a
"You-message" that communicates judgment and blame of
the child. I am almost convinced that anger is a posture
deliberately and consciously assumed by the parent for the
express purpose of blaming, punishing, or teaching a lesson to
a child because his behavior caused some other feeling (the
primary feeling). Whenever you get angry at another, you
are putting on an act, playing a role to affect the other, to
show him what he has done, teach him a lesson, try to convince him he shouldn't do it again. I'm not suggesting that
the anger isn't real. It is very real and makes people boil or
shake inside. I am suggesting that people *make* themselves
angry.

Here are some examples:

Child acts up in a restaurant. Parents' primary
feeling is *embarrassment*. Secondary feeling is
anger: "Stop acting like a two-year old."

Child forgets it is her father's birthday and fails to
say "Happy Birthday" or give him a present.

Father's primary feeling is *hurt*. Secondary feeling
is anger: "You're just like all the other thoughtless
kids today."

Child brings home her report card with *C*'s and
D's. Mother's primary feeling is *disappointment*.
Secondary feeling is anger: "I know you were
goofing off all semester. I hope you feel very proud
of yourself."

How can parents learn to avoid sending angry "You-messages" to children? The experience in our classes has been
rather encouraging. We help parents to comprehend the
difference between primary and secondary feelings. Then
they learn to become more aware of their primary feelings
when situations occur in the home. Finally they learn to send
their primary feelings to their children rather than venting
their secondary angry feelings. P.E.T. helps parents become
more aware of what is really going on inside them when they
are feeling angry—it helps them identify the primary feeling.

Mrs. C., an overly conscientious mother, told her
P.E.T. class how she discovered that her frequent
angry outbursts at her twelve-year-old daughter
were secondary reactions to her disappointment
that she was not turning out to be studious and
scholarly as her mother had been in childhood. Mrs.
C. began to realize how much her daughter's success in school meant to her and that whenever her
daughter disappointed her academically she would
blast her with angry "You-messages."

Mr. J., a professional counselor, admitted in class
that he now understood why he got so angry at his
eleven-year-old daughter when they were out in
public. His daughter was shy, unlike her socially

outgoing father. Whenever he introduced her to his friends, his daughter would not shake hands or say the accepted amenities, such as "How do you do" or "Pleased to meet you." Her muffled, almost inaudible little "Hello" embarrassed her father. He admitted that he was afraid his friends would judge him as a harsh, restrictive parent who had produced a submissive and fearful child. Once he recognized this, he found himself getting over his angry feelings at such times. He could now begin to accept the fact that his daughter simply did not have the same personality as he. And when he stopped getting angry, his daughter felt much less self-conscious.

Parents learn in P.E.T. that if they frequently vent angry "You-messages," they had better hold a mirror up to themselves and ask, "What is going on inside me?" "What needs of mine are being threatened by my child's behavior?" "What are my own primary feelings?" One mother courageously admitted in class that she had so often been angry at her children because she was deeply disappointed that having children had prevented her from going on to graduate school to become a school teacher. She discovered that her angry feelings were actually resentment because she was disappointed at having her own career plans interrupted.

What Effective "I-messages" Can Do

"I-messages" can produce startling outcomes. Parents frequently report that their children express surprise on learning how their parents really feel. They tell their parents:

> "I didn't know I was bugging you so much."
> "I didn't know it really upset you."
> "Why didn't you tell me how you felt before?"

"You really have strong feelings about this, don't you?"

Children, not unlike adults, often don't know how their behavior affects others. In the pursuit of their own goals they are often totally unaware of the impact their behavior might have. Once they are told, they usually want to be more considerate. Thoughtlessness frequently turns into thoughtfulness, once a child understands the impact of his behavior on others.

> Mrs. H. reported an incident during their family vacation. Their small children had been very loud and boisterous in the back of the station wagon. Mrs. H. and her husband had been resentfully enduring the racket, but finally Mr. H. could stand no more. He braked the car abruptly, pulled off the road and announced, "I just can't stand all this noise and jumping around in the back. I want to enjoy my vacation and I want to have fun when I'm driving. But, damn it, when there is noise back there, I get nervous and I hate to drive. I feel I have a right to enjoy this vacation, too."

The kids were startled by this pronouncement and said so. They hadn't realized that their carrying-on way back in the station wagon was in any way distressing their father. They apparently thought their father could take it. Mrs. H. reported that after this incident, the children were much more considerate and drastically reduced their horseplay.

> Mr. G., the principal of a continuation high school (name given to the type of school in which the most rebellious and troublesome students in the California public school system are placed), told this dramatic story:

For weeks I had been resentfully tolerating the behavior of a group of boys who were continually ignoring some of the school regulations. One morning I looked out my office window and saw them casually walking across the lawn carrying Coke bottles, which is against school regulations. That did it. Having just attended the session in the P.E.T. course that explained "I-messages," I ran out and started sending some of my feelings: "I feel so darned discouraged with you guys! I've tried everything I can to help you get through school. I've put my heart and soul into this job. And all you guys do is break the rules. I fought for a reasonable rule about hair length, but you guys won't even stick to that. Now, here you've got Coke bottles and that's against the rules, too. I feel like just quitting this job and going back to the regular high school, where I can feel I'm accomplishing something. I feel like an absolute failure in this job."

That afternoon, Mr. G. was surprised by a visit from the group. "Hey, Mr. G., we've been thinking about what happened this morning. We didn't know you could get mad. You never did before. We don't want another principal down here; he won't be as good as you've been. So we all agreed to let you take the electric clippers and cut our hair. We're also going to stick to the other rules."

Mr. G., after recovering from his shock, then went into another room with the boys, and each submitted to his barbering until their hair was short enough to conform to the regulation. Mr. G. told the P.E.T. class that the most significant thing about this incident was the amount of fun they all had during the volunteer hair-cutting session. "We all had a ball," he reported. The boys got close to him and to each other. They left the room friends, with warm feelings and the kind of closeness that so often results from mutual problem-solving.

When I head Mr. G. tell this story, I admit I was as amazed as the parents in the class at the dramatic impact of Mr. G's "I-messages." It reconfirmed my belief that adults often underestimate the willingness of kids to be considerate of adults' needs, once they are honestly and straightforwardly told how others feel. Kids can be responsive and responsible, if only grown-ups take a moment to level with them.

Here are more examples of effective "I-messages" that contain no blaming or shaming, and in which the parent is not "sending a solution":

> Father wants to read the paper and relax after arriving home from work. Child keeps climbing on his lap and crumpling the paper. *Father*: "I can't read the paper when you're on my lap. I don't feel like playing with you because I'm tired and want to rest awhile."
>
> Mother is using the vacuum cleaner. Child keeps pulling plug out of socket. Mother is in a hurry *Mother*: "I'm in a big rush and it really slows me down when I have to stop and replace the plug. I don't feel like playing when I have work to get done."
>
> Child comes to the table with very dirty hands and face. *Father*: "I can't enjoy my dinner when I see all that dirt. It makes me feel kind of sick and I lose my appetite."
>
> Mother and Dad want to talk about a private problem of concern to them. Child keeps hanging around, preventing them from talking. *Father:*

"Mother and I have something very important to discuss by ourselves. We can't talk about it when you're here."

Child keeps pleading to be taken to a movie but has not cleaned up his room for several days, a job he agreed to do. *Mother:* "I don't feel very much like doing something for you when you don't stick to your agreement about your room. I feel like I'm being taken advantage of."

Child is playing the record player so loud it is interfering with conversation of parents in next room. *Mother:* "We can't talk with the record player on so loud. And the noise is driving us mad."

Child promised to iron napkins to be used for dinner party. During the day she dawdled; now it's an hour before guests arrive and she hasn't started the job. *Mother:* "I really feel let down. I've worked all day to get ready for our party and now I still have to worry about the napkins."

Child forgot to show up at agreed time she was to be home so Mother could take her to buy shoes. Mother is in a hurry. *Mother:* "I sure don't like it when I carefully plan my day so we can shop for your new shoes and then you don't even show up."

Sending Nonverbal "I-Messages" to Very Young Kids

Parents of children who are under two years of age invariably ask how they can send "I-messages" to kids who are too young to comprehend the meaning of verbal "I-messages."

Our experience tells us that many parents underestimate the capacity of very young children to comprehend "I-messages." Most children by the age of two have learned to recognize when parents are accepting or nonaccepting, when they are feeling well or unwell, when they like something the child is doing or when they do not. By the time most children have reached their second birthday they are quite aware of the meaning of such parental messages as: "Ow, that hurts" or "I don't like that" or "Mommy doesn't want to play." Also, "That's not for Jimmy to play with," "That's hot," or "That will hurt Jimmy."

Very young children are also so sensitive to nonverbal messages that parents can use wordless signals to get across many of their feelings to a child.

> Rob is squirming while Mother is putting his clothes on. Mother gently but firmly restrains him and continues to dress him. (Message: "I can't dress you when you are squirming".)
>
> Mary is jumping up and down on the couch and Mother fears she will hit the lamp on the end table. Mother gently but firmly removes Mary from the couch and jumps up and down with her on the floor. (Message: "I don't like to have you jump on the couch, but I don't mind if you jump on the floor".)
>
> Johnny stalls and delays getting into the car when Mother is in a hurry. Mother puts her hand on Johnny's rear and gently but firmly guides him into the car. (Message: "I am in a hurry and I want you to get in the car now".)
>
> Randy tugs at the new dress Mother has just put on for a party. Mother removes his hand from the dress. (Message: "I don't want you to pull my dress".)
>
> While Dad is carrying Tim in the supermarket, he starts to kick Dad in the stomach. Dad immediately puts Tim down. (Message: "I don't like to carry you when you kick me".)

Sue leans over and takes food off Mother's plate. Mother retrieves her food and serves Sue a portion of her own from the serving dish. (Message: "I want my food and I don't like for you to take it from my plate".)

Such behavioral messages are understood by very young children. These messages tell the child what needs the parent has, yet they do not convey to the child that he is bad for having his own needs. Also, it is obvious that when the parent sends these nonverbal messages he is not punishing the child.

Three Problems With "I-messages"

Parents invariably encounter problems putting "I-messages" to work. None is insurmountable, but each requires additional skills.

Children frequently respond to "I-messages" by ignoring them, especially when parents first start using these messages. Nobody likes to learn that his behavior is interfering with the needs of another. The same is true of children. They sometimes prefer "not hearing" how their behavior is causing their parents to have feelings.

We advise parents to send another "I-message" when the first does not get a response. Perhaps the second "I-message" will come out stronger, more intense, louder, or with more feeling. The second message tells the child, "Look, I really mean it."

Some children walk away from an "I-message," shrugging their shoulders as if to say, "So what." A second message, this time stronger, may do the job. Or the parent may need to say something like:

"Hey, I'm telling you how I feel. This is important to me. And I don't like to be ignored. I hate it when you just walk away from me and don't even listen to

> my feelings. That doesn't sit well with me. I don't
> feel it's very fair to me when I really have a prob-
> lem."

This type of message sometimes brings the child back or gets
him to pay attention. It tells him "I'm really in earnest!"

Children also frequently respond to an "I-message" by
sending back an "I-message" of their own. Rather than
immediately modify their behavior, they want you to hear
what their feelings are, as in this incident:

MOTHER: I hate to see my clean living room all dirtied up as
soon as you come home from school. I feel very discouraged about
that after I've worked hard to clean it up.

SON: I think you're too fussy about keeping the house
clean.

At this point, parents untrained in P.E.T. often get defensive
and irritated, rebutting with, "Oh no I'm not," or "That's none
of your business," or "I don't care what you think about my
standards." To handle such situations effectively, parents
must be reminded of our first basic principle—when the child
has a feeling or a problem, use active listening. In the preced-
ing incident, Mother's "I-message" gave the child a problem
(as these messages usually do). So now is the time to show
understanding and acceptance, since your "I-message" has
caused him a problem:

MOTHER: You feel my standards are too high and that I'm too
fussy.

SON: Yeah.

MOTHER: Well, that may be true. I'll think about that. But
until I change, I sure feel darned discouraged about seeing all
my work go down the drain. I'm very upset right now about this
room.

Often, after the child can tell that his parent has understood his feeling, he will modify his behavior. Usually, all the child wants is understanding of *his* feelings—then he feels like doing something constructive about *your* feelings.

What also amazes most parents is the experience of seeing their active listening bring out feelings of a child which, now understood by the parent, have the effect of making the parent's original unaccepting feelings vanish or become modified. By encouraging the child to express the way he is feeling, the parent sees the whole situation in a brand new light. Earlier we presented the incident of a child afraid to go to sleep. The mother was upset with her son's bedtime stalling and told him so with an "I-message." The child responded by telling her that he was afraid to go to sleep for fear of closing his mouth and suffocating. This message immediately changed Mother's unaccepting attitude to one of understanding acceptance.

Another situation reported by a parent illustrates how subsequent active listening can modify a parent's "I" feeling.

FATHER: I'm upset about the supper dishes being left in the sink. Didn't we agree that you would get them done right after dinner?

JAN: I felt so tired after dinner because I stayed up until three A.M. doing that term paper.

FATHER: You just didn't feel like doing the dishes right after dinner.

JAN: No. So I took a nap until ten thirty. I plan to do them before I go to bed. Okay?

FATHER: Okay by me.

A problem that all parents encounter in putting "I-messages" to work is that sometimes the child refuses to modify his behavior even after he has understood the impact of that behavior on his parents. Sometimes even the clearest of "I-messages" does not work—the child does not change the behavior that is interfering with his parents' needs. The child's needs to behave in a particular way are in conflict with the needs of the parent for him not to behave that way.

In P.E.T., this is called a *conflict-of-needs* situation. When it occurs, as it inevitably does in *all* relationships between persons, this is the real moment of truth in that relationship.

How such conflict-of-needs situations are handled will be the heart of this book, beginning with Chapter 9.

8

Changing Unacceptable Behavior by Changing the Environment

Not enough parents try to change the behavior of their children by changing their children's surroundings.

Environmental modification is used more with infants and small children than with older children because, as kids get older, parents start relying more on verbal methods, especially those that "put down" a child or threaten him with parental power; they neglect environmental modification and try to talk the child out of unacceptable behavior. This is unfortunate, since environmental modification is often very simple and extremely effective with children of all ages.

Parents begin using this method more extensively, once they become aware of its wide range of possibilities:

1. Enriching the environment.
2. Impoverishing it.
3. Simplifying it.
4. Restricting it.
5. Child-proofing it.
6. Substituting one activity for another.
7. Preparing the child for changes in his environment.
8. Planning ahead with older children.

ENRICHING THE ENVIRONMENT

Every good nursery school teacher knows that one effective way of stopping or preventing unacceptable behavior is to provide children with a great many interesting things to do—enrich their environment with play materials, reading materials, games, clay, dolls, puzzles, and so on. Effective parents, too, make use of this principle: if children are involved in something interesting, they are less likely to "get into things" or pester parents.

Some of our parents in training have reported excellent results from setting up a special area in the garage or in a corner of the backyard and designating it as a place where the child is free to dig, pound, build, paint, mess, and create. The parents select a place where the child can do almost anything he wants to do without damaging anything.

Car trips are times when kids especially "bug" their parents. Some families make certain that their children have play materials, games and puzzles that will keep them from becoming bored or restless.

Most mothers know that their children are less likely to behave unacceptably if arrangements are made to have friends and playmates come over to the house. Frequently, two or three children will find it easier to find "acceptable" things to do than will a child alone.

Easels for painting, clay for modeling, puppet theaters for putting on shows, a doll family and a doll house, Tinker Toys, finger paints for smearing, Erector sets—all these can greatly reduce aggressive, restless, or troublesome behavior. Too often parents forget that children need interesting and challenging activities to keep them occupied, just as adults do.

IMPOVERISHING THE ENVIRONMENT

At times children need an environment with few stimuli —for example just before bedtime. Parents, especially fathers, sometimes overstimulate their children before bedtime or mealtime and then expect them suddenly to become quiet and controlled. These are times when the child's environment should be impoverished, not enriched. Much of the storm and stress that occur at these times could be avoided if parents made an effort to reduce the stimulation of the child's environment.

SIMPLIFYING THE ENVIRONMENT

Children often engage in "unacceptable" behavior because their environment is too difficult and complex for them; they pester the parent for help, give up an activity entirely, show aggression, throw things on the floor, whine, run away, cry.

The home environment needs to be modified in many ways to make it easier for a child to do things for himself, to manipulate objects safely, and to avoid frustration that comes when he cannot control his own environment. Many parents consciously make an effort to simplify the child's environment by:

> Buying clothes that are easy for the child to put on by himself.
>
> Building a stool or box the child can stand on to reach his clothes in the closet.
>
> Purchasing child-sized eating implements.
>
> Putting closet hooks at a low level
>
> Buying unbreakable cups and glasses.
>
> Nailing a door handle on screen doors low enough for the child to reach.

Putting washable paint or wall covering on the walls of the child's room.

LIMITING THE CHILD'S LIFE SPACE

When a mother places an unacceptably behaving child in a playpen, she is attempting to limit his "life space" so that his subsequent behaviors will be acceptable to her. Fenced-in backyards are effective in preventing such behavior as running out into the street, walking through the neighbor's flower garden, getting lost, and so on.

Some parents use a harness on their young children when they take them shopping. Others designate a special area in the house where the child is permitted to play with clay, to paint, to cut up paper, or to glue, limiting such messy activities to that special area. Special areas can also be designated as places for children to be noisy, roughhouse, dig in the mud, and so on.

Children generally accept such limitations of their life space, provided they seem reasonable and leave children considerable freedom to meet their own needs. Sometimes a child will resist the limitation and cause conflict with the parent. (In the next chapter, we discuss how such conflicts can be resolved.)

CHILD-PROOFING THE ENVIRONMENT

Although most parents remove medicines, sharp knives, and dangerous chemicals from the reach of children, a more thorough job of child-proofing might include such things as:

Turning pot handles to the back of stove when cooking.
Buying unbreakable cups and glasses.
Putting matches out of reach.
Repairing frayed electric cords and plugs.

Keeping the basement door locked.
Removing expensive breakable objects.
Locking up sharp tools.
Putting a rubber mat in the bath tub.
Making upstairs screens secure.
Storing slippery throw rugs.

Each family should conduct its own child-proofing inspection. With very little trouble most parents can find many ways to child-proof the home more thoroughly to prevent behaviors that would be unacceptable to them.

SUBSTITUTING ONE ACTIVITY FOR ANOTHER

If a child is playing with a sharp knife, offer him a dull one. If he is bent on examining the contents of your cosmetic drawer, give him some empty bottles or cartons to play with on the floor. If he is about to rip out pages in a magazine you wish to keep, give him one you can permit him to destroy. If he wants to draw with a crayon on your wall paper, get him a large piece of wrapping paper to draw on.

Failure to offer a child an alternative before taking something away from him will generally produce frustration and tears. But children frequently accept a substitute without fuss, provided the parent offers it gently and calmly.

PREPARING THE CHILD FOR CHANGES
IN THE ENVIRONMENT

Many unacceptable behaviors can be prevented by preparing the child ahead of time for changes in his environment. If his usual babysitter is unable to come on Friday, start talking with the child on Wednesday about the new babysitter who is going to come. If you are going to spend your vacation at the beach, prepare the child weeks ahead for some of the things he is going to encounter—sleeping in a strange bed, meeting new friends, not having his bicycle with him, the big waves, proper behavior in a boat, and so on.

Children have an amazing capacity to adjust comfortably to changes, if parents would only discuss these things ahead of time. This holds true even when the child may have to suffer some pain or discomfort, as in the case of going to the doctor to get his shots. Discussing this with him frankly, even telling him it will undoubtedly hurt for a second, can do wonders to help him cope with such a situation when it occurs.

PLANNING AHEAD WITH OLDER CHILDREN

Conflicts can be prevented by thoughtfully arranging the environment of teen-agers, too. They also need adequate space for their personal belongings, privacy, opportunity for independent activity. Here are suggestions for "enlarging your area of acceptance" for older children:

Provide the child with his own alarm clock.

Provide adequate closet space with numerous hooks.

Establish a message center in the home.

Provide a child with his own personal calendar for recording commitments.

Go over instructions on new appliances together.

Inform children ahead of time when you expect guests, so that they know when to clean up their rooms.

Provide a house key attached to cord sewn in a girl's handbag or worn around a boy's neck.

Give allowance monthly, instead of weekly, and agree ahead of time what things a child is not expected to purchase out of his allowance.

Explain how the phone company charges for

extra message units in various areas.

Discuss in advance such complicated legal matters as the curfew, auto liability insurance, responsibility in case of auto accidents, use of alcohol and drugs, and so on.

When a teen-ager is doing his own laundry, make the job easier by having all necessary equipment and supplies readily available.

Suggest that a child always carry a dime for an emergency telephone call.

Tell a child what foods in the refrigerator are earmarked for guests.

Have a child write out a list of friends and their telephone numbers, in case the child has to be located unexpectedly.

Give a child advance notice whenever special work needs to be done to prepare for guests.

Encourage a child to work out a personal list and time schedule for things to do to prepare for a family trip.

Encourage a child to read the morning forecast in the paper (or listen on TV or radio) as a guide for what to wear to school.

Tell a child ahead of time the names of your guests to avoid embarrassment when they arrive.

Tell children well in advance when you are going out of town so they can make their own plans for activities.

Teach a child how to take phone messages.

Always knock before entering a child's room.

Include children in discussions involving family plans that will affect them.

Arrive at mutually accepted "house rules" for party guests prior to party.

Most parents can think of many other examples in each of these categories. The more parents use environmental modification, the more enjoyable living with their children can be and the less parents need to confront the kids.

Parents who eventually learn in P.E.T. to rely heavily on environmental modification first go through some rather fundamental changes in their attitudes about children and their rights in the home. One of these changes has to do with the question: Whose home is it?

Most parents in our classes say they believe it is exclusively *their* home; that children, therefore, must be trained and conditioned to behave properly and appropriately. This means a child must be molded and scolded until he painfully learns what is expected of him in his parents' home. These parents seldom even consider making any major modifications in the home environment when a child is born into the home. They think in terms of leaving the home exactly as it was before the child arrived and expect the child to make all the adjustments.

We ask parents this question: "If you learned today that next week you will have to bring one of your own parents into your home because he has become partially paralyzed and sometimes has to use crutches and a wheelchair, what changes would you make in your home?"

Invariably this question generates a long list of changes that parents would readily make, such as:

Dispense with throw rugs.

Build a hand rail on the stairs.

Move furniture to provide room for the wheelchair to pass.

Place some frequently used articles in lower kitchen cupboards easy to reach.

Provide him with a loud bell to ring if he is in trouble.

Install a phone extension for him.

Remove tippy tables that he might accidentally hit and turn over.

Build a ramp on the back stairs so he can wheel himself out in the yard for sunning.

Purchase a rubber mat for the bathtub.

When parents see how much effort would go into modifying their home for their own handicapped parent, they become much more accepting of the idea of making modifications for a child.

Most parents are also shocked to recognize the contrast between their attitudes toward the paralyzed parent and toward the children when it comes to the question: "Whose home is it?"

Parents say they would make repeated efforts to convince their handicapped parent that their home was now *his* home, too. But not so with their children.

I am often amazed at how many parents show through their attitudes and behavior that they treat guests with far greater respect than they do their own children. Too many parents act as if children must do all the adjusting to their surroundings.

9

Inevitable Parent-Child Conflicts: Who Should Win?

All parents encounter situations when neither confrontations nor changes in the environment will change the behavior of their child; the child continues to behave in a way that interferes with the needs of the parent. These situations are inevitable in the parent-child relationship because the child "needs" to behave in a certain way even though he has been made aware that his behavior is interfering with his parent's needs.

> Johnny continues to play baseball in the lot next door even though his mother has repeatedly told him the family has to leave in a half-hour.
>
> Mrs. J. has told Mary how much of a hurry she is in to get to the department store, yet Mary continues to stop and gaze into store windows along the way.
>
> Sue refuses to give in to her parents' feelings about going to the beach with a group of her friends over the weekend. She desperately wants to go even though she hears how unacceptable this would be to her parents.

These conflicts between needs of the parent and needs of the child are not only *inevitable in every family* but are bound to *occur frequently.* They run all the way from rather unimportant differences to critical fights. They are problems in the *relationship*—not owned solely by the child nor solely by the parent. Both parent and child are involved in the problem—the needs of both are at stake. So THE RELA-TIONSHIP OWNS THE PROBLEM. These are the problems that come up when other methods have not modified behavior that is unacceptable to the parent.

A conflict is the moment of truth in a relationship—a test of its health, a crisis that can weaken or strengthen it, a critical event that may bring lasting resentment, smoldering hostility, psychological scars. Conflicts can push people away from each other or pull them into a closer and more intimate union; they contain the seeds of destruction and the seeds of greater unity; they may bring about armed warfare or deeper mutual understanding.

How conflicts are resolved is probably the most critical factor in parent-child relationships. Unfortunately, most parents try to resolve them by using only two basic approaches, both of which are ineffective and harmful to the child as well as the relationship.

Few parents accept the fact that conflict is part of life and not necessarily bad. Most parents look on conflict as something to avoid at all costs, whether between themselves and their children or between children. We often hear husbands and wives boast that they have never had a serious disagreement—as if that means theirs has been a good relationship.

Parents tell their children, "All right, there is to be no fighting tonight at the dinner table—we don't want to spoil our dinner hour." Or they yell, "Stop that bickering, right now!" Parents of teen-agers can be heard lamenting that now that their children are older there are many more disagreements and conflicts in the family: "We used to see eye to eye on most things." Or, "My daughter was always so cooperative and easy to handle, but now we don't see things her way and she can't see things our way."

Most parents hate to experience conflict, are deeply troubled when it occurs, and are quite confused about how to handle it constructively. Actually, it would be a rare relationship if over a period of time one person's needs did not conflict with the other's. When any two people (or groups) coexist, conflict is bound to occur just because people are different, think differently, have different needs and wants that sometimes do not match.

Conflict, therefore, is not necessarily bad—it exists as a reality of any relationship. As a matter of fact, a relationship with no apparent conflict may be unhealthier than one with frequent conflict. A good example is a marriage where the wife is always subservient to a dominating husband, or a parent-child relationship where the child is so deathly afraid of his parent that he does not dare cross him in any way.

Most people have known families, especially large families, where conflict crops up constantly and yet these families are wonderfully happy and healthy. Conversely, I often see newspaper accounts of youths who committed crimes and whose parents indicate complete astonishment that their boy could do such a thing. They never had any trouble with him; he had always been so cooperative.

Conflict in a family, openly expressed and accepted as a natural phenomenon, is far healthier for children than most parents think. In such families the child at least has an opportunity to experience conflict, learn how to cope with it, and be better prepared to deal with it in later life. As necessary preparation for the inevitable conflicts the child will encounter outside of the home, family conflict may actually be beneficial to the child, always provided that the conflict in the home gets resolved constructively.

This is the critical factor in any relationship: how the conflicts get resolved, not how many conflicts occur. I now believe it is the *most critical* factor in determining whether a relationship will be healthy or unhealthy, mutually satisfying or unsatisfying, friendly or unfriendly, deep or shallow, intimate or cold.

THE PARENT-CHILD POWER STRUGGLE

Rarely do we find a parent in our classes who does not think of conflict resolution in terms of someone winning and someone losing. This "win-lose" orientation is at the very root of the dilemma of today's parents—whether to be strict (parent wins) or to be lenient (child wins).

Most parents see the whole problem of discipline in child-rearing as a question of being either strict or lenient, tough or soft, authoritarian or permissive. Because they are locked into this either-or approach to discipline, they see their relationship with their children as a power struggle, a contest of wills, a fight to see who wins—*a war*. Today's parents and their children are literally at war, each thinking in terms of someone winning and someone losing. They even talk about their struggle in much the same way as two nations at war.

One father illustrated this clearly in a P.E.T. class when he forcefully stated:

> "You have to start early letting them know who's boss. Otherwise, they'll take advantage of you and dominate you. That's the trouble with my wife—she always ends up letting the kids win all the battles. She gives in all the time and the kids know it."

The mother of a teen-ager tells it in her words:

> "I try to let my child do what he wants, but then usually I suffer. I get walked on. You give him an inch and he takes a mile."

Another mother is convinced that she is not going to lose the "battle of the skirt length"!

> "I don't care how she feels about it, and it doesn't make any difference to me what the other parents do—no daughter of mine is going to wear those short skirts. Here's one thing I am not going to back down on. I am going to win this fight."

Children, too, see their relationship with parents as a win-lose power struggle. Cathy, a bright fifteen-year-old, who is worrying her parents because she won't talk to them, told me in one of our interviews:

> "What's the use of arguing? They always win. I know that before we ever get into an argument. They're always going to get their way. After all, they're the parents. They always know they're right. So, now I just don't get into arguments. I walk away and don't talk to them. 'Course it bugs them when I do that. But, I don't care."

Ken, a high-school senior, has learned to cope with the win-lose attitude of his parents in a different way:

> "If I really want to do something, I never go to my Mother, 'cause her immediate reaction is to say 'No.' I wait until Dad comes home. I can usually get him to take my side. He's a lot more lenient, and I generally get what I want with him."

When conflict arises between parents and children, most parents try to resolve it in their favor so that the *parent wins and the child loses*. Others, somewhat fewer in number than the "winners," consistently give in to their children out of fear of conflict or frustrating their children's needs. In these families the *child wins and the parent loses*. The major dilemma of parents today is that they see only these win-lose approaches.

The Two Win-Lose Approaches

In P.E.T. we refer to the two "win-lose" approaches to conflict resolution simply as Method I and Method II. Each involves one person winning and the other losing—one gets his way and the other does not. Here is how Method I operates in parent-child conflicts:

> Parent and child encounter a conflict-of-needs situation. The parent decides what the solution should be. Having selected the solution, the parent announces it and hopes the child will accept it. If the child does not like the solution, the parent may first use persuasion to try to influence the child to accept the solution. If this fails, the parent usually tries to get compliance by employing power and authority.

The following conflict between a father and his twelve-year-old daughter was resolved by Method I:

JANE: 'Bye. I'm off to school.
PARENT: Honey, it's raining and you don't have your raincoat on.
JANE: I don't need it.
PARENT: You don't need it! You'll get wet and ruin your clothes or catch a cold.
JANE: It's not raining that hard.
PARENT: It is too.
JANE: Well, I don't want to wear a raincoat. I hate to wear a raincoat.
PARENT: Now, honey, you know you'll be warmer and drier if you wear it. Please go get it.
JANE: I hate that raincoat—I won't wear it!
PARENT: You march right back to your room and get that rain-

coat! I will not let you go to school without your raincoat on a day like this.

JANE: But I don't like it . . .

PARENT: No "buts"—if you don't wear it your mother and I will have to ground you.

JANE   (angrily): All right, you win! I'll wear the stupid raincoat!

The father got his way. His solution—that Jane wear her raincoat—prevailed, although Jane did not want to. *The parent won and Jane lost.* Jane was not at all happy with the solution, but she surrendered in the face of her parent's threat to use power (punishment).

Here is how Method II operates in parent-child conflicts:

> Parent and child encounter a conflict-of-needs situation. The parent may or may not have a preconceived solution. If he does, he may try to persuade the child to accept it. It becomes obvious that the child has his own solution and is attempting to persuade the parent to accept it. If the parent resists, the child might then try to use his power to get compliance from the parent. In the end the parent gives in.

In the raincoat conflict, Method II would work like this:

JANE: 'Bye. I'm off to school.

PARENT: Honey, it's raining and you don't have your raincoat on.

JANE: I don't need it.

PARENT: You don't need it! You'll get wet and ruin your clothes or catch a cold.

JANE: It's not raining that hard.

PARENT: It is too.

JANE: Well, I don't want to wear a raincoat. I hate to wear a raincoat.

PARENT: I want you to.

JANE: I hate that raincoat—I won't wear it. If you make me wear it, I'll be mad at you.

PARENT: Oh, I give up! Go on to school without your raincoat, I don't want to argue with you anymore—you win.

Jane was able to get her own way—she won and her parent lost. The parent certainly was not happy with the solution, yet he surrendered in the face of Jane's threat to use her power (in this case, being mad at her father).

Method I and Method II have similarities even though the outcomes are totally different. In both, each person wants his own way and tries to persuade the other to accept it. The attitude of each person in both methods is "I want my way and I'm going to fight to get it." In Method I, the parent is inconsiderate and disrespectful of the needs of the child. In Method II, the child is inconsiderate and disrespectful of the needs of the parent. In both, one goes away feeling defeated, usually angry at the other for causing the defeat. Both methods involve a power struggle, and the adversaries are not loath to use their power if they feel it will be necessary in order to win.

Why Method I Is Ineffective

Parents who rely on Method I to resolve conflicts pay a severe price for "winning." The outcomes of Method I are quite predictable—low motivation for the child to carry out the solution, resentment toward his parents, difficulties for the parent in enforcement, no opportunity for the child to develop self-discipline.

When a parent imposes his solution to a conflict, the child will have very little motivation or desire to carry out that decision because he has no investment in it; he was given no voice in making it. Whatever motivation the child may have is extrinsic—outside himself. He may comply, but out of fear of parental punishment or disapproval. The child does not *want* to carry out the decision, he feels *compelled to*. This is why children so often look for ways to get out of carrying out a Method I solution. If they cannot get out of it, they usually "go through the motions" and carry it out with minimal effort, barely doing what was required and no more.

Children generally feel resentful toward their parents when Method I decisions have *made* them do something. It feels unfair to them, and their anger and resentment naturally are directed to the parents, whom they feel to be responsible. Parents who use Method I sometimes get compliance and obedience, but the price they pay is their children's hostility.

Observe children whose parents have just resolved a conflict by Method I; they almost invariably show resentment and anger in their faces or say something hostile, or they may even physically assault their parents. Method I sows the seeds for a continuously deteriorating relationship between the parent and child. Resentment and hate replace love and affection.

Parents pay another heavy price for using Method I: they generally have to spend a lot of time enforcing the decision, checking to see that the child is carrying it out, nagging, reminding, prodding.

Parents who come to P.E.T. often defend their use of Method I on the ground that it is a fast way to resolve conflict. This advantage is frequently more apparent than real, because it takes so much of the parent's time afterward to make certain the decision is carried out. Parents who say that they constantly have to nag their children are invariably the ones who use Method I. I could not count how many conversations I have had with parents that are similar to this one that occurred in my office:

PARENT: Our children are not cooperative around the house. It's like pulling teeth to get them to help. Every Saturday it's a battle getting them to do the work that has to be done. We literally have to stand over them to see that the work gets done.

COUNSELOR: How is it decided what work has to be done?

PARENT: Well, we decide, of course. We know what has to be done. We make a list on Saturday morning, and the kids see the list and know what has to be done.

COUNSELOR: Do the kids want to do the work?

PARENT: Heavens, no!

COUNSELOR: They feel they *have* to do it.

PARENT: That's right.

COUNSELOR: Have the kids ever been given a chance to participate in determining what has to be done? Do they have a voice in determining what work needs doing?

PARENT: No.

COUNSELOR: Have they ever been given a chance to decide who is to do what?

PARENT: No, we usually parcel out the different jobs as evenly as we can.

COUNSELOR: So you make the decision about what has to be done and who has to do it?

PARENT: That's right.

Few parents see the connection between their children's lack of motivation to help and the fact that decisions about chores are generally made by Method I. An "uncooperative" child is simply a child whose parents, through Method I decision-making, have in effect denied him a chance to cooperate. Cooperation is never fostered by *making* a child do something.

Another predictable outcome of Method I is that the child is denied the opportunity to develop self-discipline—inner-directed, self-initiated, responsible behavior. One of the most universally accepted myths about child-rearing is that if parents force their young children to do things, they will turn out to be self-disciplined and responsible persons. While it is true that *some* children cope with heavy parental authority by being obedient, conforming, and submissive, they usually turn out to be persons who depend upon *external* authority to control their behavior. As adolescents or adults, they show an absence of *inner* controls; they go through life jumping from one authority figure to the next to find answers to their lives or seek controls on their behavior. These people lack self-discipline, inner controls, or self-responsibility because they were never given a chance to acquire these traits.

If parents could learn only one thing from this book, I wish it were this: Each and every time they force a child to do something by using their power or authority, they deny that child a chance to learn self-discipline and self-responsibility.

> Charles, a seventeen-year-old son of two very strict parents who used their power constantly to get Charles to do his homework, made this admission; "Whenever my parents are not around, I find it impossible to pull myself out of the chair in front of the TV set. I am so used to their making me go do my homework, I cannot find *within myself* any power to make me go do it when they are not at home".

I am also reminded of the pathetic message scrawled in lipstick on the bathroom mirror by the child murderer, William Heirens of Chicago, after he had just killed still another of his victims: "FOR HEAVEN'S SAKE, CATCH ME BEFORE I KILL MORE."

Most parents in our P.E.T. classes have never had the opportunity to examine critically these outcomes of their "strictness." Most of them think they have been doing what parents are supposed to do—using their authority. Yet, once they are helped to see the effects of Method I, it is a rare parent who does not accept these truths. After all, parents were once children who themselves developed these same habits of coping with their own parents' power.

Why Method II Is Ineffective

What does it do to children to grow up in a home where *they* usually win and their parents lose? What are the effects on children of their generally getting their way? Obviously these children will be different from those in homes where Method I is the principal method of conflict resolution. Children who are allowed to get their way will not be as rebellious, hostile, dependent, aggressive, submissive, conforming, apple-polishing, withdrawing, and so on. They have not had to develop ways to cope with parental power. Method II encourages the child to use *his* power over his parents to win at their expense.

These children learn how to throw temper tantrums to control the parent; how to make the parent feel guilty; how to say nasty, deprecating things to their parents. Such children are often wild, uncontrolled, unmanageable, impulsive. They have learned that their needs are more important than anyone else's. They, too, often lack inner controls on their behavior and become very self-centered, selfish, demanding.

These children often do not respect other people's property or feelings. Life to them is get, get, get—take, take, take. "I" comes first. Such children are seldom cooperative or helpful around the house.

These children often have serious difficulties in their peer relationships. Other children dislike "spoiled kids"—they find them unpleasant to be around. Children from homes where Method II predominates are so accustomed to getting their way with their parents that they want to get their way with other children, too.

These children also frequently have difficulty adjusting to school, an institution whose philosophy is predominantly

Method I. Children accustomed to Method II are in for a rude shock when they enter the world of school and discover that most teachers and principals are trained to resolve conflicts by Method I, backed up with authority and power.

Probably the most serious effect of Method II is that children often develop deep feelings of insecurity about their parents' love. It is easy to understand this reaction when one considers how difficult it is for parents to feel loving and accepting toward a child who usually wins at the expense of the parent losing. In Method I homes resentment radiates from child to parent; in Method II homes from parent to child. The child of Method II senses that his parents are frequently resentful, irritated, and angry at him. When he later gets similar messages from his peers and probably other adults, it is no wonder he begins to *feel unloved*—because, of course, so often he *is* unloved by others.

While some studies have shown that children from Method II homes are likely to be more creative than children from Method I homes, parents pay a dear price for having creative children; they frequently cannot stand them.

Parents suffer greatly in the Method II home. These are the homes in which I have frequently heard parents say:

> "He gets his own way most of the time, and you just can't control him."

> "I'll be glad when the children are all in school so I can have some peace."

> "Parenthood is such a burden—I spend all my time doing things for them."

> "I must say, sometimes I just can't stand them—I just have to get away."

> "They seldom seem to realize that I've got a life, too."

> "Sometimes—and I feel guilty saying this—I wish

I could drown them or ship them off to someone else."

"I'm so ashamed to take them anywhere or even have friends come to our home and see those children."

Parenthood for Method II parents is seldom a joy—how unfortunate and sad it is to raise children you cannot love, or hate to associate with.

Some Additional Problems With Method I and Method II

Few parents use either Method I or Method II exclusively. In many homes one parent will rely heavily on Method I while the other parent leans toward Method II. There is some evidence that children brought up in this type of home have an even greater chance of developing serious emotional problems. Perhaps the inconsistency is more harmful than the extreme of one approach or the other.

Some parents start out using Method II, but as the child grows older and becomes more of an independent and self-directing person they gradually shift to Method I. Obviously, it can be harmful to the child to get used to having his own way most of the time and then start to experience a reversal. Other parents start out using mostly Method I and gradually shift to Method II. This is especially frequent when parents have a child who early in life resists and rebels against parental authority; gradually the parents give up and begin to give in to the child.

There are also parents who rely on Method I with their first child and switch to Method II with their second, hoping that this will work better. In these homes, one often hears the first child express strong resentment toward the second, who is allowed to get by with things that the first child was not. Sometimes the first child thinks this is evidence that the parents strongly favor the second child.

One of the most common patterns, particularly among parents who have been strongly influenced by the advocates of permissiveness and the opponents of punishment, is for parents to let a child win for long periods of time until his behavior becomes so obnoxious that the parents move in abruptly with Method I. Then they feel guilty and gradually move back to Method II, and then the cycle starts all over again. One parent expressed this clearly:

"I am permissive with my children until I can't stand them. Then I become strongly authoritarian until I can't stand myself"

Many parents, however, are locked in to either Method I or II. By conviction or tradition, a parent may be a strong Method I advocate. He discovers from his experience that this method does not work very well and may even feel guilty about being a Method I parent; he does not like himself when he is restrictive, dominating, and punishing. Yet the only alternative he knows is Method II—letting the child win. Intuitively this parent knows that would be no better or maybe even worse. So he stubbornly sticks with his Method I, even in the face of evidence that his children are suffering from this approach or that the relationship is deteriorating.

Most Method II parents are unwilling to switch to an authoritarian approach because they are philosophically opposed to using authority with children or because their own personalities will not permit them to exercise the necessary strength or to experience conflict. I have known many mothers, and even a few fathers, who find Method II more comfortable because they are afraid of conflict with their children (and usually with anyone else, too). Such parents, rather than run the risk of exercising their own will over their children, take the approach of "peace at any price"—giving up, appeasement, and surrender.

The dilemma of almost all parents who come to our P.E.T. classes, seems to be that they are locked in to either Method I or Method II, or oscillate between the two, *because they know of no other alternative to these two ineffective "win-lose" methods.* We find that most parents not only know which method they use most frequently; they also realize both methods are ineffective. It is as if they know they are in trouble, whichever method they use, but do not know where else they can turn. Most of them are grateful to be released from their self-imposed trap.

10

Parental Power: Necessary and Justified?

One of the most universally entrenched beliefs about child-rearing is that it is necessary and desirable for parents to use their authority to control, direct, and train children. Few parents, judging from the thousands in our classes, ever question this idea. Most parents are quick to justify their use of authority. They say that children need it and want it or that parents are wiser. "Father knows best" is a firmly rooted belief.

The stubborn persistence of the idea that parents must and should use authority in dealing with children has, in my opinion, prevented for centuries any significant change or improvement in the way children are raised by parents and treated by adults. Partly this idea persists because parents almost universally do not understand what authority actually is or what is does to children. All parents talk easily about authority, but few can define it or even identify the source of their authority.

WHAT IS AUTHORITY?

One of the basic characteristics of the parent-child relationship is this: parents have greater "psychological size" than the child. If we were to try to represent parent and child by drawing a circle for each, it would be inaccurate to draw the circles like this:

As the child sees it, the parent does not have equal "size," no matter what the age of the child. I am not referring to physical size (though a physical size differential is present until children reach adolescence), but rather to "psychological size." A more accurate representation of the parent-child relationship would look like this:

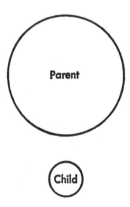

As seen by a child, the parent almost always has greater "psychological size" than he, which helps to explain such expressions as "Big Daddy," "The big boss," "My father loomed large in my life," "He was a big man to me," or "I didn't miss an opportunity to cut my parents *down to size*." To quote from a theme written by a troubled young man in his college composition class and later shared with me when I was his counselor:

> "Being but a small child, I looked toward my parents much as a grown man looks toward God . . . "

To all children, their parents are first seen as gods of a sort.

This "psychological size" differential exists not only because children see their parents as bigger and stronger, but also as more knowledgeable, more competent. To the young child there seems to be nothing his parents do not know, nothing they cannot do. He marvels at the breadth of their understanding, the accuracy of their predictions, the wisdom of their judgment.

While some of these perceptions may at times be accurate, others are not. Children attribute many traits, characteristics, and capabilities to their parents that are not based on reality at all. Few parents know as much as young children think they do. Experience is not always "the best teacher," as the child will later conclude when he becomes an adolescent and an adult and can judge his parents against a broader base of his own experience. And wisdom is not always related to age. Many parents find it difficult to admit, but those who are more honest with themselves recognize how exaggerated are children's evaluations of Mom and Dad.

While the cards are stacked in favor of the parents' far greater psychological size to begin with, many mothers and fathers foster the difference. They deliberately hide their limitations and mistakes in judgment from their children; or they promote such myths as "We know what's best for you" or "When you're older you'll realize how right we were."

I've always been intrigued to observe that when parents talk about their own mothers and fathers, they readily see in retrospect *their* mistakes and limitations; yet they will strongly resist the notion that they are subject to the same kinds of errors of judgment and lack of wisdom in relation to their own children.

However undeserved, parents do assume greater psychological size—and this is an important source of parental power over the child. Because the parent is seen as such an "authority," his attempts to influence the child carry a great deal of weight. It might be helpful to think of this as "assigned authority" because the child assigns it to the parent. Whether it is deserved or not is irrelevant—the fact is that "psychological size" gives the parent *influence and power over the child.*

An entirely different kind of power comes from the parent possessing certain things needed by his children. This also gives him authority over them. A parent has power over his children because they are so dependent upon him to satisfy their basic needs. Children come into the world almost completely dependent on others for nourishment and physical comfort. They do not possess the *means* for satisfying needs. The means are possessed and controlled by parents.

As the child grows older, and if he is permitted to become more independent of his parents, their power naturally diminishes. Yet at any age, up to the time the child moves into independent adulthood and is capable of satisfying his basic needs almost entirely through his own efforts, his parents have some degree of power over him.

Possessing the means for satisfying the basic needs of the child, a parent has the power of being "rewarding" to a child. Psychologists use the term "rewards" for whatever means are possessed by the parent to satisfy the needs of the child (being rewarding to him). If a child is hungry (has a need for food) and the parent provides a bottle of milk, we say the child is rewarded (his hunger need is satisfied).

The parent also possesses the means for causing pain or discomfort for the child, either through withholding what he needs (not feeding a child who is hungry) or doing something that produces pain or discomfort (slapping the child's hand when he reaches for his brother's glass of milk). Psychologists use the term "punishment" for the opposite of reward.

Any parent knows he can control a small child by using power. Through careful manipulation of rewards and punishment, the parent can encourage the child to behave in certain ways or discourage him from behaving in other ways.

Everyone knows from his own experience that humans (and animals) tend to repeat behavior that brings reward (satisfies a need), and to avoid or discard behavior that either is not rewarding or is actually punishing. So a parent can "reinforce" certain behavior by rewarding the child, and "extinguish" other behavior by punishing.

Suppose you want your child to play with his blocks and do not want him to play with the expensive glass ash trays on the coffee table. To reinforce playing-with-blocks behavior you might sit down with him when he is playing with the blocks, smile, and be pleasant or say, "That's a good boy." To extinguish his playing-with-ashtrays behavior you might slap his hand, smack his bottom, frown, look unpleasant, or say, "That's a bad boy." The child will quickly learn that playing with blocks will yield pleasant relations with the parent-power. Playing with ash trays will not.

This is what parents often do to modify the behavior of children. They usually call it "training the child." Actually, the parent is using his power to get the child to do something the parent wants him to do or to prevent the child from doing what the parent doesn't want. The same method is used by dog trainers to teach obedience and by circus people to teach bears to ride bicycles. If a trainer wants a dog to heel, he puts a rope around the animal's neck and starts walking, holding on to the other end of the rope. Then, he says, "Heel." If the dog doesn't stay close to the trainer he receives a painful jerk at his neck (punishment). If he does heel, he gets patted (reward). The dog soon learns to heel upon command.

No question about it: power works. Children can be trained this way to play with blocks rather than expensive ashtrays, dogs to heel on command, and bears to ride bicycles (even unicycles, amazingly).

At a very young age, after being rewarded and punished enough times, children can be controlled just by promising them they will be rewarded if they behave in a particular way, or threatening them with future punishment if they behave in an undesirable way. The potential advantages of this are obvious: the parent does not have to wait until the desired behavior occurs in order to reward it (reinforce it), nor wait until the undesired behavior occurs in order to punish it (extinguish it). He now can influence the child merely by saying in effect, "If you behave one way you'll get my reward; if you behave another way, you'll get my punishment.

SERIOUS LIMITATIONS OF PARENTAL POWER

If the reader is thinking that the parent's power to reward and punish (or to *promise* reward and *threaten* punishment) looks like an effective way of controlling children, he will be right in one sense, and very wrong in another: The use of parental authority (or power), seemingly effective under certain conditions, is quite ineffective under other conditions. (Later, I will examine actual dangers of parental power).

Many, if not most, of these side effects are unfortunate. Children often become cowed, fearful, and nervous as a result of "obedience training"; often turn on their trainers with hostility and vengeance; and often break down physically or emotionally under the stress of trying to learn behavior that is either difficult or unpleasant for them. The use of power can produce many harmful effects as well as risks for the trainer of animals—or children.

Parents Inevitably Run Out of Power

Using power to control children works only under special conditions. The parent must be sure to *possess the power*—his rewards have to be attractive enough to be wanted by the child and his punishments have to be potent enough to warrant avoidance. The child *must* be dependent upon the parent; the more the child depends on what the parent possesses (rewards), the more power the parent has.

This is true in all human relationships. If I need something very badly—say money to buy food for my children—and I must depend solely on another person for money—probably my employer, then obviously he will have a great deal of power over me. If I am dependent on this one employer, I will be inclined to do almost anything he wants in order to insure getting what I need so desperately. But a person has power over another only as long as the second is in a position of weakness, want, need, deprivation, helplessness, dependency.

As a child becomes less helpless, less dependent upon the parent for what he needs, the parent gradually loses power. This is why parents discover to their dismay that rewards and punishment that worked when their child was younger, become less effective as he grows older.

"We've lost our influence over our son," a parent complains. "He used to respect our authority, but now we just can't control him." Another says, "Our daughter has become so independent of us—we have no way of making her listen to us." A father of a fifteen-and-a-half year-old boy told his P.E.T. class how impotent he felt:

"We have nothing to use any more to back up our authority except the family car. Even that doesn't work too well, because he took our car key and had one made for himself. When we're not home, he sneaks off with the car any time he feels like it. Now that we don't have anything left that he really needs, I can't punish him anymore"

These parents expressed feelings that most parents experience as their children begin to grow out of their dependency. This inevitably occurs as the child approaches adolescence. Now he can acquire many rewards from his own activities (school, sports, friends, achievements). He also begins to figure out ways to avoid his parents' punishments. In those families where the parents have relied principally on power to control and direct their children throughout their early years, the parents inevitably come in for a rude shock when their power runs out and they are left with little or no influence.

The "Terrible Teens"

I am now convinced that most theories about the "stress and strain of adolescence" have focused incorrectly on such factors as the adolescent's physical changes, his emerging sexuality, his new social demands, his struggle between being a child and an adult, and so on. This period is difficult for children and parents largely because the adolescent becomes so independent of his parents that he can no longer be easily controlled by their rewards and punishments. And since most parents rely so heavily on rewards and punishment, adolescents react with much independent, resistive, rebellious, hostile behavior.

Parents assume that adolescent rebellion and hostility are inevitably a function of this stage of development. I think this is not valid—it is more that the *adolescent becomes more able to resist and rebel.* He is no longer controlled by his parents' rewards because he does not need them so much; and he is immune to threats of punishment because there is little they can do to give him pain or strong discomfort. The typical adolescent behaves as he does because he has acquired enough strength and resources to satisfy his own needs and enough of his own power so that he need not fear the power of his parents.

An adolescent, therefore, does not rebel against his *parents.* He rebels against their *power.* If parents would rely less on power and more on nonpower methods to influence their children *from infancy on,* there would be little for the child to rebel against when he becomes an adolescent. The use of power to change the behavior of children, then, has this severe limitation: parents inevitably run out of power, and sooner than they think.

Training by Power Requires Strict Conditions

Using reward and punishment to influence a child has another serious limitation: it requires very controlled conditions during the "training."

Psychologists who study the learning process by training animals in the laboratory have great difficulty with their "subjects" unless the most strict conditions prevail. Many of these requirements are exceedingly difficult to meet in training children through rewards and punishment. Most parents, every day, violate one or more of the "rules" for effective "training."

1. The "subject" must be highly motivated—he must have a strong need to "work for the reward." Rats must be quite hungry to learn how to get through a maze and reach the food at the end. Parents often try to influence a child by offering a reward that the child doesn't much need (promising a child you will sing to him if he goes to bed promptly and finding he doesn't buy it).

2. If punishment is too severe, the subject will avoid the situation entirely. When rats receive a shock to teach them not to go into a blind alley in a maze, they will "stop trying" to learn their way through the maze if the shock is too strong. If you severely punish a child for a mistake, he may "learn" to stop trying to do something well.

3. The reward has to be available to the subject soon enough to affect behavior. In training cats to push the correct lever that will bring them food, if you delay producing the food too long after they push the right lever, the cats will not learn which is the correct lever. Tell a child he can go to the beach three weeks from now if he does his chores today, and you may discover that such a far-off reward lacks strength to motivate the child to do those chores right now.

4. There must always be a great deal of *consistency* in giving reward for the desired behavior or punishment for the undesired behavior. If you give your dog food at the dining-room table when you don't have company and punish him if he begs when you do have company, the dog will become confused and frustrated (unless he learns the difference between having company and not having company, as our dog has). Parents are frequently inconsistent in using reward and punishment. Example: sometimes allowing the child to snack between meals but denying him this privilege on days when Mother has fixed something special for dinner and does not want him to spoil "his" dinner (or had we better call it *Mother's* dinner?).

5. Reward and punishment are seldom effective in teaching *complex* behaviors, except by using very complex and time-consuming "reinforcement" methods. True, psychologists have succeeded in teaching chickens to play ping-pong and pigeons to guide

missiles (believe it or not), yet such achievements require amazingly difficult and time-consuming training
conducted under the most controlled conditions.

Readers who have owned animals will appreciate how
difficult it would be to train a dog to play exclusively in his
own yard, to fetch his sweater whenever he sees it is raining
outside, or to be generous in sharing his dog biscuits with
other dogs. Yet these same people would not even question
the feasibility of trying to use reward and punishment to
teach their children the same behaviors.

Reward and punishment can work to teach a child to avoid
touching things on the coffee table or to say "please" when
asking for things at the dinner table, but parents will not find
this effective to produce good study habits, to be honest, to
be kind to other children, or to be cooperative as a member
of the family. Such complex behavior patterns are really
not *taught* children; children learn them from their own
experience in many situations, influenced by a variety of
factors.

I have pointed out only a few of the limitations of using
reward and punishment to train children. Psychologists who
specialize in learning and training could add many more.
Teaching animals or children to perform complex acts
through reward and punishment is not only a specialty of its
own, requiring extensive knowledge and an inordinate
amount of time and patience, but what is far more important
to us is this: *the skilled circus animal trainer and the
experimental psychologist are not very good models for
parents to copy in training their own children to behave as
mothers and fathers would like.*

THE EFFECTS OF PARENTAL POWER ON THE CHILD

Despite all the serious limitations of power, it strangely
enough remains the method of choice for most parents, no

matter what their education, social class, or economic level.

P.E.T. instructors invariably find that parents in their classes are surprisingly aware of the harmful effects of power. All we have to do is ask parents to draw from their own experience and tell us how they were affected when their parents used power over them. It is a strange paradox that parents remember how power felt to them as children but "forget" when they use power with their own children. We ask those in each class to list what they did as children to cope with their parents' use of power. Each class develops a list of coping mechanisms not too dissimilar from the following:

1. Resistance, defiance, rebellion, negativism.
2. Resentment, anger, hostility.
3. Aggression, retaliation, striking back.
4. Lying, hiding feelings.
5. Blaming others, tattling, cheating.
6. Dominating, bossing, bullying.
7. Needing to win, hating to lose.
8. Forming alliances, organizing against parents.
9. Submission, obedience, compliance.
10. Apple polishing, courting favor.
11. Conformity, lack of creativity, fear of trying something new, requiring prior assurance of success.
12. Withdrawing, escaping, fantasizing, regression.

Resistance, Defiance, Rebellion, Negativism

A parent recalled this typical incident with her father:

PARENT: If you don't stop talking, you're going to get my hand across your face.

CHILD: Go ahead, hit me!

PARENT: (Hits child).
CHILD: Hit me again, harder, I won't stop!

Some children rebel against parents' use of authority by doing exactly the opposite of what their parents desire them to do. One mother told us:

> "There were three main things we used our authority to try to get our daughter to do—be neat and orderly, go to church, and refrain from drinking. We were always strict about these things. Now we know that she is about the worst housekeeper I've ever seen, she doesn't set foot in church, and she has cocktails almost every night."

An adolescent revealed in one of his therapy sessions with me:

> "I won't even try to get grades in school, 'cause my parents have pushed me so hard to be a good student. If I got good grades it would make them feel pleased—like they were right or like they won. I'm not going to let them feel that way. So I don't study."

Another adolescent talked about his reaction to his parents' "hassling" him about his long hair:

> "I guess I might cut it if they didn't hassle me so much. But as long as they try to make me cut it, I'll be sure to keep it long."

Such reactions to adult authority are almost universal. Children have been defying and rebelling against adult authority for generations. History suggests little difference between today's youth and those at other times. Children, like adults, fight furiously when their freedom is threatened, and there have been threats to the freedom of children at all stages in history. One way for children to cope with threats to their freedom and independence is to fight against those who would take it away.

Resentment, Anger, Hostility

Children resent those who have power over them. It feels unfair and often unjust. They resent the fact that parents or teachers are bigger and stronger, if such advantage is used to control them or restrict their freedom.

"Pick on someone your own size" is a frequent feeling of children when an adult uses his power.

It seems to be a universal response of human beings *at any age* to feel deeply resentful and angry toward someone on whom they are, to a greater or lesser degree, dependent for providing gratification of their needs. Most people don't respond favorably to those who hold power to dispense or withhold rewards. They resent the fact that someone else controls the means for satisfying their needs. They wish they themselves were in control. Also, most people crave this independence because it is risky to depend on another. There is the risk that the person on whom one is dependent will turn out to be less than dependable—unfair, prejudiced, inconsistent, unreasonable; or the person with the power may demand conformity to his own values and standards as a price of his rewards. This is why employees of highly paternalistic employers—those who are generous in giving "benefits" and "bonuses" (on condition that the employees will gratefully accede to management's efforts to control by authority) are frequently resentful and hostile "to the hand that feeds them." Historians of industrial relations have pointed out that some of the most violent strikes hit companies where the management had been "benevolently paternalistic." This is also why the policy of a "have" nation giving handouts to a "have-not" nation so frequently results in the dependent nation's hostility toward the stronger one, much to the consternation of the "giver."

Aggression, Retaliation, Striking Back

Because parental domination by authority often frustrates the needs of the child, and frustration so often leads to aggression, parents who rely on authority can expect their children to show aggression in some way. Children retaliate, try to cut the parent down to size, are severely critical, talk back nastily, employ "the silent treatment," or do any one of the hundreds of aggressive things that they feel may get back at the parents or hurt them.

The formula for this way of coping seems to be "You hurt me, so I'll hurt you—then maybe you won't hurt me in the future." Its extreme manifestation are cases, frequently reported in newspapers, of children who kill their parents. No doubt many acts of aggression against school authorities (vandalism), against the police, or against political leaders are motivated by a desire to retaliate or get back at someone.

Lying, Hiding Feelings

Some children learn early in life that if they lie they can avoid a great deal of punishment. On occasion lying can even bring them rewards. Children invariably begin to learn their parents' values—they get to know accurately what their parents will approve or disapprove of. Without exception, every child I have seen in therapy whose parents used a heavy dose of rewards and punishment, revealed how much he lied to his parents. One adolescent girl told me:

> "My parents have forbidden me to go to drive-in theaters, so I just tell them I am going over to a girl friend's house. Then we go to the drive-in."

Another said:

> "My mother won't let me wear lipstick, so I wait until I get a few blocks from the house and then put it on. When I come home, I take it off before going into the house."

A 16 year old girl admitted:

> "My mother won't let me go out with this one boy, so I have my girl friend pick me up and tell Mother we're going to the show or something. Then I go meet my boy friend."

While children lie a lot because so many parents rely heavily on rewards and punishment, I firmly believe that the tendency to lie is not natural in youngsters. It is a learned response—a coping mechanism to handle the parents' attempts to control by manipulation of rewards and punishment. Children are not likely to lie in families where they are accepted and their freedom is respected.

Parents who complain that their children do not share their problems or talk about what is going on in their lives are also generally parents who have used a lot of punishment. Children learn how to play the game, and one way is to keep quiet.

Blaming Others, Tattling, Cheating

In families with more than one child, the children are obviously competing to get parental rewards and avoid punishment. They soon learn another coping mechanism: put the others at a disadvantage, discredit the other children, make them look bad, tattle, shift the blame. This formula is simple— "By making the other guy look bad, maybe I will look good."

How defeating for parents; they want cooperative behavior from their kids, but by using rewards and punishment they breed competitive behavior—sibling rivalry, fighting, ratting on brother or sister:

> "He got more ice cream than I did."
>
> "How come I have to work in the yard when Jimmy doesn't?"
>
> "He hit me first—he started it all."
>
> "You never punished John when he was my age and did the same things I'm doing now."
>
> "How come you let Tommy get by with everything?"

Much of the competitive bickering and mutual blaming among children can be attributed to the parents' use of rewards and punishment in child-rearing. Since no one has the time, temperament, or wisdom to dispense rewards or punishments fairly and equally at all times, parents are inevitably going to create competition. It is only natural that each child wants to get most of the rewards and see his brothers and sisters get most of the punishment.

Dominating, Bossiness, Bullying

Why does a child try to dominate or bully younger children? One reason is that his parents used their power to dominate him. Therefore, whenever he is in a power position over another child, he too tries to dominate and boss. This can be observed when children play with dolls. They generally treat their dolls (their own "children") as their parents treat them, and psychologists have known for some time that they can find out how a parent treats a child by watching that child play with dolls. If the child is dominating, bossy, and punitive to her doll when she plays the role of a mother, she has almost certainly been treated the same way by her own mother.

Parents, therefore, unwittingly run a high risk of rearing a child who will be authoritarian with other children if they use their own authority to direct and control their child.

Needing to Win, Hating to Lose

When children are reared in a climate full of rewards and punishment, they may develop strong needs to look "good" or to win, and strong needs to avoid looking "bad" or losing. This is particularly true in families with very reward-oriented parents who rely heavily on positive evaluation, money rewards, gold stars, bonuses, and the like.

Unfortunately, there are many such parents, particularly in middle- and upper-class families. While I do find some parents who philosophically reject punishment as a method of control, I seldom find parents who even question the value of using rewards. The American parent has been inundated by articles and books advising frequent praise and rewards. Most parents have bought this advice unquestioningly, with the result that a large percentage of children in America are daily manipulated by their parents through commendation, special privileges, awards, candy, ice cream, and the like. It is no wonder that this generation of "brownie point" children is so oriented to winning, looking good, coming out on top, and above all, avoiding losing.

Another negative effect of reward-oriented child-rearing is what generally happens to a child who is so limited in ability, intellectually or physically, that it is difficult for him to earn brownie points. I refer to the child whose siblings and peers are genetically better endowed, which makes him a "loser" in most of his endeavors at home, on the playground, or at school. Many families have one or more such children, who are destined to go through life experiencing the pain of frequent failure and the frustration of seeing others get the rewards. Such children acquire low self-esteem, and build up attitudes of hopelessnses and defeatism. The point is: a family climate heavy with rewards may be more harmful to children who cannot earn them than to those who can.

Forming Alliances, Organizing Against Parents

Children whose parents control and direct by authority and power learn, as they grow older, yet another way of coping with that power. This is the all-too-familiar pattern of forming alliances with other children, either in the family or out of it. Children discover that "in union there is strength"—they can "organize" much like workers in America have organized to cope with the power of employers and management.

Children frequently form alliances to present a common front to parents by:

Agreeing among themselves to tell the same story.

Telling their parents that all the other kids are permitted to do a certain thing, so why can't they?

Influencing other children to join them in some questionable activity, hoping that then their parents won't single them out for punishment.

Today's crop of adolescents feels the real power that comes from organizing and acting in union against parental or adult authority—witness the hippie movement, school strikes, sit ins, student demonstrations against dress codes, student demands for more voice in colleges and high schools, peace marchers, and so on.

Because authority has continued to be the preferred method of controlling and directing the behavior of children, parents and other adults bring about the very thing they most lament—adolescents forming alliances to pit their power against the power of adults. And so society is polarizing into two warring groups—young people organized against adults and the Establishment, or, if you will, the "have nots" against the "haves." Instead of children identifying with the family, they are increasingly identifying with their own peer group to combat the combined power of all adults.

Submission, Obedience, Compliance

Some children choose to submit to the authority of their parents for reasons that are not usually well understood. They cope through submission, obedience, and compliance. This response to parental authority often occurs when the parents have been very severe in their use of power. Particularly when punishment has been strong, children learn to submit out of a strong fear of the punishment. Children may react to parental power just as dogs become cowed and fearful from severe punishment. When children are quite young, severe punishment is more likely to cause submission because a reaction such as rebelling or resisting may seem too risky. They almost have to respond to parental power by becoming obedient and compliant. As children approach adolescence, this response might change abruptly because they have acquired more strength and courage to try resistance and rebellion.

Some children continue to be submissive and compliant through adolescence and often into adulthood. These children suffer the most from early parental power, for they are the ones who retain a deep fear of people in power positions wherever they encounter them. These are the adults who remain children throughout their lives, passively submitting to authority, denying their own needs, fearing to be themselves, frightened of conflict, too compliant to stand up for their own convictions. These are adults who fill the offices of psychologists and psychiatrists.

Apple Polishing, Courting Favor

One way of coping with a person who has power to reward or punish is to "get on his good side," to win him over by special efforts to make him like you. Some children adopt this approach with parents and other adults. The formula: "If I can do something nice for you and get you to favor me, then perhaps you will give me your rewards and withhold your punishment." Children learn early that rewards and punishments are not meted out equitably by adults. Adults can be won over; they can have "favorites." Some children learn how to take advantage of this and resort to behavior known as "apple polishing," "buttering someone up," "getting to be teacher's pet," and other terms less acceptable in polite society.

Unfortunately, while children may become quite skillful in winning adults over, this is usually strongly resented by other children; the apple polisher is often ridiculed or rejected by his peers, who suspect his motives and envy his favored position.

Conformity, Lack of Creativity, Fear of Trying Something New, Requiring Prior Assurance of Success

Parental authority fosters conformity rather than creativity in children, much as an authoritarian work climate in an organization stifles innovation. Creativity comes from freedom to experiment, to try new things and new combinations. Children reared in a climate of strong rewards and punishment are not as likely to feel such freedom as children reared in a more accepting climate. Power produces fear and fear stifles creativity and fosters conformity. The formula is simple: "In order to get rewards I will keep my nose clean and conform to what is considered proper behavior. I dare not do anything out of the ordinary—this would risk my getting punished."

Withdrawing, Escaping, Fantasizing, Regression

When it becomes too difficult for children to cope with parental authority, they may try to escape or withdraw. The power of parents may cause withdrawal if punishment is too severe for the child, if parents are inconsistent in administering rewards, if rewards are too difficult to earn, or if it is too difficult to learn behaviors required to avoid punishment. Any of these conditions may cause a child to give up trying to learn "the rules of the game." He simply quits trying to cope with reality—it has become too painful or too complex to figure out. This child cannot find suitable adjustment to the forces in his environment. He can't win. So his organism somehow tells him it is safer to escape.

The forms of withdrawal and escape may range from almost total to only occasional withdrawal from reality, including:

> Daydreaming and fantasizing.
> Inactivity, passivity, apathy.
> Regressing to infantile behavior.
> Excessive TV watching.
> Excessive reading of novels.
> Solitary play (often with imaginary playmates).
> Getting sick.
> Running away.
> Using drugs.
> Excessive and compulsive eating.
> Depression.

SOME DEEPER ISSUES ABOUT PARENTAL AUTHORITY

Even after parents in our classes are reminded of their own coping mechanisms as children and even after they use our list to identify specific coping methods being used by their own children, some remain convinced that authority and power are justified in raising children. Consequently, in most P.E.T. classes additional attitudes and feelings about parental authority are brought into the open for discussion.

Don't Children Want Authority and Limits?

A belief commonly held by laymen and professionals (and one that parents always bring up in P.E.T. classes) is that children actually want authority—they like parents to restrict their behavior by setting limits. When parents use their authority, so the argument goes, children feel more secure. Without limits, they not only will be wild and undisciplined but also insecure. An extension of this belief is that if parents do not use authority to set limits, their children will feel the parents do not care and will feel unloved.

While I suspect this belief is embraced by many because it gives them a neat justification for using power, I do not want to discredit the belief as a mere rationalization. There is some truth in the belief and so it must be examined rather carefully.

Common sense and experience strongly support the idea that children do want limits in their relationship with parents. They need to know how far they can go before their behavior will be unacceptable. Only then can they choose not to engage in such behaviors. This applies to all human relationships.

For example, I am much more secure when I know which of my behaviors are unacceptable to my wife. One that comes to mind is playing golf or going to my office to work on a day when we entertain guests. By knowing ahead of time that my absence will be unacceptable because my wife needs my help, I can choose not to play golf or go to the office and avoid her displeasure or anger and probably a conflict.

However, it is one thing for a child to want to know the "limits of his parents' acceptance" and an entirely different thing to say that he wants his parent *to set those limits* on his behavior. To return to the example involving my wife and me: I am helped when I know her feelings about my playing golf or going to the office on days we entertain. But I certainly will bristle and be resentful if she tries *to set a limit on my behavior* by some such statement as, "I cannot permit you to play golf or go to the office on days we are having guests. That's a limit. You are not to do those things."

I would not appreciate this power approach at all. It is ridiculous to suppose that my wife would even try to control and direct my behavior this way. Children respond no differently to *limit setting* on the part of the parent. Equally strong is their bristling and resentment when a parent unilaterally tries to set a limit on their behavior. I have never known a child who wants a parent *to set a limit* on his behavior like this:

> "You must be in by midnight—that's my limit."
> "I cannot permit you to take the car."
> "You cannot play with your truck in the living room."
> "We must demand that you not smoke pot."
> "We have to restrict you from going with those two boys."

The reader will recognize all these communications as our familiar "sending the solution" (also, all are "you"-messages).

A much sounder principle than "children want their parents to use their authority and set limits" is the following:

> Children want and need information from their parents that will tell them the parents' feelings

about their behavior, so that they themselves can
modify behavior that might be unacceptable to the
parents. However, children do not want the parent
to try to limit or modify their behavior by using or
threatening to use their authority. In short, children
want to limit their behavior *themselves* if it becomes apparent to them that their behavior must be
limited or modified. Children, like adults, prefer to
be their own authority over their behavior.

One further point: children actually would *prefer* that *all*
their behavior were acceptable to their parents, so that it
would be unnecessary to limit or modify any of their
behavior. I, too, would prefer that my wife would find *all* my
behavior unconditionally acceptable. That's what I would
prefer, but I know it is not only unrealistic, but impossible.
So parents should not expect, nor will their children expect
of them, that they will be accepting of all behavior. What
children have a right to expect, however, is that they always
be told when their parents *are not feeling accepting* of a
certain behavior ("I don't like to be tugged and pulled when
I'm talking to a friend"). This is quite different from wanting
parents to use authority to set limits on their behavior.

Isn't Authority All Right If Parents Are Consistent?

Some parents justify the use of power by their belief that
it's effective and not harmful as long as parents are consistent
in using it. In our classes, these parents are surprised to learn
that they are absolutely correct about the need for
consistency. Our instructors assure them that consistency *is*
essential, *if they choose to use power and authority*. Furthermore, children prefer parents to be consistent, *if those parents
choose to use power and authority*.

The "ifs" are critical. Not that the use of power and

authority is not harmful; the use of power and authority will be even more harmful when parents are inconsistent. Not that children want their parents to use authority; rather, if it is to be used they would prefer it to be used consistently. If parents feel they have to use authority, consistency in applying it will give the child much more chance of knowing for certain what behaviors will be consistently punished and what others will be rewarded.

Considerable experimental evidence shows the harmful effects of inconsistency in using rewards and punishment to modify the behavior of animals. A classic experiment by a psychologist, Norman Maier, is one example. Maier rewarded rats for jumping from a platform and through a hinged door on which was painted a particular design, like a square. The door opened to food and the rat was rewarded. Then Maier punished rats who jumped from the platform toward a door that was painted with a different design, a triangle. This door did not open, causing the rats to hit their noses and fall a considerable distance into a net. This "taught" rats to discriminate between a square and a triangle—a simple conditioning experiment.

Now Maier decided to be "inconsistent" in using rewards and punishment. He deliberately changed the conditions by randomly alternating the designs. Sometimes the square was on the door that led to food, sometimes it was on the door that did not open and made the rats fall. Like many parents, the psychologist was inconsistent in applying reward and punishment.

What did this do to the rats? It made them "neurotic"; some developed skin disorders, some went into catatonic states, some ran around their cages frantically and aimlessly, some refused to associate with the other rats, some would not eat. Maier created "experimental neuroses" in rats by being inconsistent.

The effect of inconsistency in the use of rewards and

punishment can be similarly harmful to children. Inconsistency gives them no chance to learn the "proper" (rewarded) behavior and to avoid the "undesirable" behavior. They cannot win. They may become frustrated, confused, angry, and even "neurotic."

But Isn't It the Parents' Responsibility to Influence Children?

Probably the most frequent attitude about power and authority expressed by parents in the P.E.T. classes is that it is justified because of parents' "responsibility" to influence their children to behave in certain ways considered desirable by parents or "society"(whatever that means). This is the age-old issue of whether power in human relationships is justified as long as it is used benevolently and wisely—"for the other person's welfare or best interests" or "for the good of society."

The problem is *who is to decide* what is in the best interest of society. The child? The parent? Who knows best? These are difficult questions, and there are dangers in leaving the determination of "best interest" with the parent.

He may not be wise enough to make this determination. All men are fallible—and that includes parents and others who possess power. And whoever is using power may falsely claim that it is for the other's welfare. The history of civilization has recorded the lives of many who claimed to use their power for the welfare of the person on whom the power is used. "I'm only doing this for your own good" is not a very convincing justification for power.

"Power corrupts and absolute power corrupts absolutely" wrote Lord Acton. And from Shelley, "Power, like a desolating pestilence, pollutes whate'er it touches." Edmund Burke maintained that "The greater the power, the more dangerous the abuse."

The dangers of power, perceived by statesmen and poets alike, are still present. The use of power is seriously questioned today in relations between nations. World government with a world court may someday come to pass out of the necessity for mutual survival in the atomic age. The use of the power of whites over blacks is no longer considered justified by the nation's highest court. In industry and business, management by authority is already considered by many an outmoded philosophy. The power differential that has existed for years between husband and wife has been gradually but surely reduced. Finally, the absolute power and authority of the church has recently been attacked both from without and from within that institution.

One of the last strongholds for the sanction of power in human relationships is in the home—in the parent-child relationship. A similar pocket of resistance is in the schools—in the teacher-student relationship, where authority still remains the principal method for controlling and directing the behavior of students.

Why are children the last ones to be protected against the potential evils of power and authority? Is it because they are smaller or because adults find it so much easier to rationalize the use of power with such notions as "Father knows best" or "It's for their own good"?

My own conviction is that as more people begin to understand power and authority more completely and accept its use as unethical, more parents will apply those understandings to adult-child relationships; will begin to feel that it is just as immoral in those relationships; and then will be forced to search for creative new nonpower methods that all adults can use with children and youth.

But quite apart from the moral and ethical issue of using power over another, when parents ask, "Isn't it my responsibility to use my power to influence my child?" they reveal a common misunderstanding about the effectiveness of power as a way of influencing their children. Parental power does not really "influence" children; it *forces* them to behave in prescribed ways. Power does not "influence" in the sense of persuading, convincing, educating, or motivating a child to behave in a particular way. Rather, power *compels* or *prevents* behavior. Compelled or prevented by someone with superior power, a child is not really persuaded. As a matter of fact, he will generally return to his former ways as soon as the authority or power is removed because *his own needs and desires remain unchanged.* Frequently he will also be determined to get back at his parent for the frustration of those needs as well as the humiliation inflicted on him. Therefore, power actually empowers its own victims, creates its own opposition, fosters its own destruction.

Parents who use power actually lessen their influence on children because power so often triggers rebellious behavior (children coping with power by doing the opposite of what the parent desires). I have heard parents say, "We would have more influence over our child if we had used our authority to make him do just the opposite of what we want him to do. Then he might end up doing what we wanted him to do."

It is paradoxical but true that parents lose influence by using power and will have more influence on their children by giving up their power or refusing to use it.

Parents obviously will have more influence on their children if their methods of influence *do not* produce rebellion or reactive behavior. Nonpower methods of influence make it much more likely that children might seriously consider their parents' ideas or their feelings and as a result modify their own behavior in the direction desired by the parent. They won't always modify their behavior, but then again sometimes they will. But the rebellious child will seldom feel like modifying his behavior out of consideration for his parent's needs.

Why Has Power Persisted in Child-Rearing?

This question, raised so often by parents in P.E.T. classes, has puzzled and challenged me. It is difficult to understand how anyone can justify the use of power in child-rearing, or in any human relationship, in the face of what is known about power and its effects on others. Working with parents, I am now convinced that all but a small handful hate to use power over their children. It makes them feel uneasy and often downright guilty. Frequently, parents even apologize to their children after using power. Or they try to assuage their guilt with the usual rationalizations: "We did it only because we have your own welfare in mind," "Someday you'll thank us for this," "When you are a parent, you'll understand why we have to keep you from doing these things."

In addition to having guilt feelings, many parents admit that their power methods are not very effective, especially parents whose children are old enough to have begun rebelling, lying, sneaking, or passively resisting.

I have come to the conclusion that parents over the years have continued to use power because they have had very little, if any, experience in their own lives with people who use nonpower methods of influence. Most people, from childhood on, have been controlled by power—power exercised by parents, school teachers, school principals, coaches, Sunday school teachers, uncles, aunts, grandparents, Scout leaders, camp directors, military officers, and bosses. Parents therefore persist in using power out of a lack of knowledge and experience with any other method of resolving conflicts in human relations.

11

The "No-Lose" Method for Resolving Conflicts

It comes as a revelation to parents, locked in by tradition to either of the "win-lose" power methods of resolving conflicts, that they do have an alternative. Almost without exception, parents are relieved to learn that there is a third method. While this method is easy to understand, parents usually need training, practice and coaching to become competent in using it.

The alternative is the "no-lose" method of resolving conflicts—where nobody loses. In P.E.T. we call it Method III. Although Method III strikes almost all parents as a new idea for resolving parent-child conflicts, they immediately recognize this method from seeing it used elsewhere. Husbands and wives often employ Method III to resolve their differences through mutual agreement. Partners in business rely on it to achieve agreement out of their frequent conflicts. Labor unions and managers of companies use it to negotiate contracts by which both organizations agree to abide. And countless legal conflicts are resolved in out-of-court settlements arrived at by Method III and agreed upon by both parties.

Method III is frequently employed to resolve conflicts between individuals *who possess equal or relatively equal power*. When there is little or no power differential between two people, there are cogent and obvious reasons why neither attempts to use power to resolve conflicts. To use a method that depends upon power when no power advantage exists, is plainly foolish; it only invites ridicule.

I can imagine my wife's reaction if I attempted to use Method I to resolve a conflict we sometimes get into—the number of people we should invite when we decide to entertain. I generally prefer a larger number of people than she feels up to entertaining. Suppose I said to her, "I have decided we will invite ten couples, no less." After recovering from her initial surprise and disbelief, she would probably come back with something like:

> "*You* have decided!"
>
> "Well, *I* have just decided we won't invite anyone!"
>
> "Isn't that nice! I hope you have fun cooking the dinner and washing the dishes!"

I have enough wisdom to realize how utterly ridiculous my attempt at Method I in this situation would be. And she has enough strength (power) in our relationship *to resist* such a foolish attempt on my part to win at the expense of her losing.

Perhaps it is a principle that people who have equal or relatively equal power (an equalitarian relationship) seldom try to use Method I. If on occasion they do try, the other person will not permit the conflict to be resolved in this way, in any event. But when one person thinks he has (or is sure he has) more power than the other, he may be tempted to use Method I. If, then, the other thinks the first has more power, he has little choice but to submit, unless he chooses to resist or fight with whatever power he thinks he possesses.

It is clear by now that Method III is a no-power method—or more accurately a "no-lose" method; conflicts are resolved with no one winning and no one losing. Both win because *the solution must be acceptable to both.* It is conflict-resolution by mutual agreement on the ultimate solution. In this chapter, I will describe how it works.* First, a brief description of Method III:

> Parent and child encounter a conflict-of-needs situation. The parent asks the child to participate with him in a joint search for some solution acceptable to both. One or both may offer possible solutions. They critically evaluate them and eventually make a decision on a final solution acceptable to both. No selling of the other is required after the solution has been selected, because both have already accepted it. No power is required to force compliance, because neither is resisting the decision.

Bringing back our familiar raincoat problem, here is how it was resolved by Method III, as reported by the parent involved:

JANE: 'Bye, I'm off to school.
PARENT: Honey, it's raining outside and you don't have your raincoat on.
JANE: I don't need it.
PARENT: I think it's raining quite hard and I'm concerned that you'll ruin your clothes or get a cold, and that will affect us.
JANE: Well, I don't want to wear my raincoat.
PARENT: You sure sound like you definitely don't want to wear that raincoat.
JANE: That's right, I hate it.

---

* The following two chapters discuss parents' problems in accepting this method and in putting it to work at home.

PARENT: You really hate your raincoat.

JANE: Yeah, it's plaid.

PARENT: Something about plaid raincoats you hate, huh?

JANE: Yes, nobody at school wears plaid raincoats.

PARENT: You don't want to be the only one wearing something different.

JANE: I sure don't. Everybody wears plain-colored raincoats—either white or blue or green.

PARENT: I see. Well, we really have a conflict here. You don't want to wear your raincoat cause it's plaid, but I sure don't want to pay a cleaning bill, and I will not feel comfortable with you getting a cold. Can you think of a solution that we both could accept? How could we solve this so we're both happy?

JANE: (Pause) Maybe I could borrow Mom's car coat today.

PARENT: What does that look like? Is it plain-colored?

JANE: Yeah, it's white.

PARENT: Think she'll let you wear it today?

JANE: I'll ask her. [Comes back in a few minutes with car coat on; sleeves are too long, but she rolls them back.] It's okay by Mom.

PARENT: You're happy with that thing?

JANE: Sure, it's fine.

PARENT: Well, I'm convinced it will keep you dry. So if you're happy with that solution, I am too.

JANE: Well, so long.

PARENT: So long. Have a good day at school.

What happened here? Obviously, Jane and her father resolved their conflict to the mutual satisfaction of both. It was resolved rather quickly, too. The father did not have to waste time being an imploring salesman, trying to sell his solution, as is necessary in Method I. No power was involved—either on the part of the father or of Jane. Finally, both walked away from the problem-solving feeling warmly toward each other. The father could say, "Have a good day at school" and really mean it, and Jane could go to school free of the fear of embarrassment over a plaid raincoat.

Below is another kind of conflict familiar to most parents, solved by a family using Method III. It is unnecessary to illustrate how it could be tackled by Method I or II; most parents are only too familiar with unsuccessful win-lose battles over the cleanliness and neatness of their child's room. As reported by one of the mothers who had completed the P.E.T. course, this is what happened:

MOTHER: Cindy, I'm sick and tired of nagging you about your room, and I'm sure you're tired of my getting on your back about it. Every once in a while you clean it up, but mostly it's a mess and I'm mad. Let's try a new method I've learned in class. Let's see if we can find a solution we both will accept—one that will make us both happy. I don't want to make you clean your room and have you be unhappy with that, but I don't want to be embarrassed and uncomfortable and be mad at you either. How could we solve this problem once and for all? Will you try?

CINDY: Well, I'll try but I know I'll just end up having to keep it clean.

MOTHER: No. I am suggesting we find a solution that would definitely be acceptable to both, not just to me.

CINDY: Well, I've got an idea. You hate to cook-but like cleaning and I hate cleaning and love to cook. And besides I want to learn more about cooking. What if I cook two dinners a week for you and Dad and me if you clean up my room once or twice a week.

MOTHER: Do you think that would work out—really?

CINDY: Yes, I'd really love it.

MOTHER: Okay, then let's give it a try. Are you also offering to do the dishes?

CINDY: Sure.

MOTHER: Okay. Maybe now your room will get cleaned according to my own standards. After all, I'll be doing it myself.

These two examples of conflict-resolution by Method III bring out a very important aspect that at first is not always understood by parents. Using Method III, different families will generally come up with different solutions to the same problem. It is a way of arriving at *some* solution acceptable to both parent and child, not a method for obtaining a single stock solution "best" for all families. In trying to resolve the raincoat problem another family using Method III might have come up with the idea for Jane to take an umbrella. In still another family they might have agreed that the father would drive Jane to school that day. In a fourth family, they might have agreed that Jane wear the plaid raincoat that day and that a new one would be bought later.

Much of the literature in parent education has been "solution-oriented"; parents are advised to solve a particular problem in child rearing by some standard "cook book" solution considered best by experts. Parents have been offered "best solutions" for the bedtime problem, for a child dawdling at the table, for the TV problem, the messy room problem, the chores problem, and so on, ad infinitum.

My thesis is that parents need only learn a *single method for resolving conflicts*, a method usable with children of all ages. With this approach, there are no "best" solutions applicable to all or even most families. A solution best for one family—that is, one that is acceptable to that particular parent and child—might not be "best" for another family.

Here is how one family resolved a conflict about the use of the son's new mini-bike. The father reported:

> "Rob, aged thirteen and a half, was allowed to buy a mini-bike. One neighbor complained because Rob drives his mini-bike in the street, which is against the law. Another neighbor complained that Rob has driven onto their yard, spun his wheels, and dug up their lawn. He also has torn up his mother's flower beds. We problem-solved this and came up with several possible solutions:

1. No bike-riding except on camping expeditions.
2. No bike-riding except on our property.
3. No jumping the bike in Mother's flower beds.
4. Mom hauls Rob to the park for a couple of hours each week.
5. Rob can ride in fields, if he walks bike there.
6. Rob can build a jump on neighbor's lot.
7. No driving on anyone else's lawn.
8. No wheel stands on Mom's lawn.
9. Sell the mini-bike.

We threw out solutions 1, 2, 4, and 9. But we reached agreement on all the others. Two weeks later: so far, so good. Everyone is happy."

Method III, then, is a method by which each unique parent and his unique child can solve each of their unique conflicts by finding their own unique solutions acceptable to both.

Not only does this seem to be a more realistic approach in parent education, but it greatly simplifies the job of training parents to be more effective in child-rearing. If we have discovered a single method by which most parents can learn to solve conflicts, then we can afford to be far more hopeful about increasing the effectiveness of future parents. Learning parent effectiveness may not be quite as complex a task as parents and professionals have been led to believe.

WHY METHOD III IS SO EFFECTIVE

The Child Is Motivated to Carry Out the Solution

Method III conflict-resolution brings about a higher degree of motivation on the part of the child to carry out the decision because it utilizes the *principle of participation*:

A person is more motivated to carry out a decision that he has participated in making than he is a decision that has been imposed upon him by another.

The validity of this principle has been proven time and time again by experiments in industry. When employees have had a hand in making a decision, they carry it out with more motivation than a decision their superiors made unilaterally. And supervisors who permit a high degree of participation by subordinates in matters that affect them maintain high productivity, high job satisfaction, high morale, and low turnover.

While Method III carries no guarantee that children will always eagerly carry out the agreed-upon solutions to conflicts, it greatly increases the probability that they will. Children get a feeling that a Method III decision has been *their* decision, too. They have made a commitment to a solution and feel a responsibility to carry it out. They also respond favorably to the fact that their parents have refused to try to win at the expense of their losing.

Solutions produced by Method III are frequently the child's own idea. Naturally, this increases his desire to see that it will work. A P.E.T. parent submitted this example of Method III conflict-resolution:

Jean, a four-year-old, wanted her Daddy to play with her immediately after he arrived home from work every night. Daddy, however, generally felt tired from driving the crowded freeways after work and needed relaxation. Usually he wanted to read the paper and have a drink when he first got home. Jean would frequently climb on his lap, muss the paper, and persistently interrupt him with coaxing and begging. Daddy tried Method I and Method II.

He was dissatisfied with disappointing the child when he used Method I and refused to play, and resentful for giving in when he used Method II. He stated the conflict to Jean and suggested they try to find a solution agreeable to both. In just a few minutes they agreed on a solution: Daddy promised to play with Jean provided she waited until he had finished reading the paper and had one drink. They both kept to their agreement, and later Jean told her Mother, "Now don't you interrupt Daddy during his rest period." Several days later when a playmate of hers approached Daddy to talk or play, Jean emphatically told her that Daddy should not be interrupted during his rest period.

This incident illustrates how strong the motivation of a child can be to enforce and carry out a decision if the child participated in making it. In Method III decision-making, it seems that children feel they are making a commitment—they have invested part of themselves in the problem-solving process. Also, the parent reveals an attitude of trusting the child to hold up his end of the bargain. When children feel they are trusted, they are more likely to behave in a trustworthy manner.

More Chance of Finding a High-Quality Solution

In addition to producing solutions that have a higher probability of being accepted and implemented, Method III is more likely than Method I or II to yield solutions of a higher quality—more creative, more effective in solving the conflict; solutions that meet the needs of both parent and child, and that neither would have thought of alone. The way the room-cleaning conflict was resolved by the family whose daughter took on some of the cooking chores is a good illustration of how highly creative a solution can be. Both the mother and daughter admitted that the final solution was surprising to them.

Another high-quality solution emerged from a family using Method III to solve a conflict between the parents and their two small daughters about the noise of the TV, which the girls liked to watch around dinner time. One of the daughters suggested that they would enjoy the program just as much with the sound off—just seeing the picture. All agreed to this solution—a novel one, indeed, although perhaps unacceptable to children in another family.

Method III Develops Children's Thinking Skills

Method III encourages—actually requires—children to think. The parent is signaling the child: "We have a conflict, let's put our heads together and think—let's figure out a good solution." Method III is an intellectual exercise in reasoning for both parent and child. It is almost like a challenging puzzle and requires the same kind of "thinking through" or "figuring out." I would not be surprised if future research demonstrates that children in homes using Method III develop mental capacities superior to children in homes using Method I or II.

Less Hostility—More Love

Parents who consistently use Method III generally report a drastic reduction in hostility from their children. This is not surprising; when any two people *agree* on a solution, resentments and hostility are rare. In fact, when a parent and child "work through" a conflict and arrive at a mutually satisfying solution, they often experience feelings of deep love and tenderness. Conflict, if resolved by a solution acceptable to both, brings parent and child closer. They not only feel good that the conflict has been cleared away, but each feels good that he has not lost. Finally, each warmly appreciates the other's willingness to consider his needs and respect his rights. In this way Method III strengthens and deepens relationships.

Many parents have reported that immediately following a resolution of a conflict, everyone feels a special kind of joy. They often laugh, express warm feelings toward the other members of the family, and often hug and kiss each other. Such joy and love are apparent in the following excerpt from a tape recording of a session with a mother, two teen-aged daughters, and a teen-aged son. The family had just spent a week resolving several conflicts with Method III.

ANN: We get along much better now; we all like each other.

COUNSELOR: You really feel a difference in your whole attitude, the way you feel about each other.

KATHY: Yes, I really love them now. I respect Mom and I now like Ted, so I feel better about this whole thing.

COUNSELOR: You're really kind of glad you belong to this family.

TED: Yeah, I think we're great.

A parent wrote the following to me, a year or so after she had taken P.E.T.:

"The changes in our family relationships have been subtle but real. The older children especially appreciate these changes. At one time our home had 'emotional smog'—critical, resentful, hostile feelings that were held in check until some would trigger an explosion. Since P.E.T. and our sharing our new skills with all the children, the 'emotional smog' is gone. The air is clear and stays clear. We have no tension in our home except that necessary for coping with everyday schedules. We deal with problems as they arise, and we all tune in to the feelings of others as well as ourselves. My eighteen-year old son says he can feel tension in the homes of his friends, and he expresses appreciation for the lack of tension in our home. P.E.T. has closed the 'generation gap' for us. And since we can communicate freely, my children are open to the teaching of my own value system and my perspective on life. But their views are enriching to me."

Requires Less Enforcement

Method III requires very little enforcement, for once children agree to an acceptable solution, they usually carry it out, in part because of their appreciation for not being pressured to accept a solution in which they lose.

With Method I, enforcement is generally required, because the parent's solution is often not acceptable to the child. The less acceptable a solution is to those who have to carry it out, the greater the need for enforcement—nagging, cajoling, reminding, harassing, checking up, and so on. A father in P.E.T. became aware of this reduced need for enforcement:

> "In our family Saturday morning has always been a big hassle. Every Saturday I had to fight with the kids about doing their jobs around the house. It was the same thing each time—a big struggle, angriness and bitterness. After we used Method III to work out the chore problem, the kids just seemed to go about doing their jobs on their own. They didn't need reminding and prodding."

Method III Eliminates the Need for Power

The no-lose Method III makes it unnecessary for either the parent or the child to use power. While Method I and

Method II breed power struggles, Method III calls for an entirely different posture. Parent and child are not struggling against each other but, rather, *working with each other* on a common task, so children do not need to develop any of the ubiquitous methods of coping with parental power.

In Method III, the parent's attitude is one of respect for the needs of the child. But he also has respect for his own needs. The method conveys to the child, "I respect your needs and your right to have your needs met, but I also respect my own needs and my right to have them met. Let's try to find a solution that will be acceptable to both of us. In this way your needs will be met, but so will mine. No one will lose—both will win."

A sixteen-year-old girl came home one night and told her parents:

> "You know I really feel funny with my friends when they all talk and gripe about how unfair their parents are. They talk all the time about getting mad at them and hating them. I just stand around quietly because I don't have any of those feelings. I'm really out of it. Somebody asked me why I didn't feel hostile toward my parents—what the difference was in our family. I didn't know what to say at first, but after thinking about it, I said that in our family you always know that you won't be made to do something by your parents. There's no fear of their making you do something or punishing you. You always feel you'll have a chance."

Parents in P.E.T. quickly grasp the significance of having a home where power can be thrown out the window. They see the exciting implications—a chance to raise kids who have less need to acquire harmful, defensive, coping mechanisms.

Their children will have much less need to develop habit

patterns of resisting and rebelling (there will be nothing for them to resist or rebel against); much less need to develop habits of submissiveness and passive surrendering (there will be no authority to submit or surrender to); much less need to withdraw and escape (there will be nothing to withdraw or escape from); much less need to counterattack and cut the parents down to size (the parents won't be trying to win by employing their greater psychological size).

Method III Gets to the Real Problems

When parents use Method I, they often miss the chance to discover what is really bothering their child. Parents who jump quickly to *their solutions* and then apply their power to enforce those quick solutions block the child from communicating feelings that lie much deeper and are much more significant determiners of his behavior at the time. Thus Method I prevents parents from getting to the more basic problem, and it won't let them contribute something far more significant toward their child's long range growth and development.

Method III, on the other hand, usually starts a chain reaction. The child is allowed to get down to the real nitty-gritty problem that causes him to behave in a particular way. Once the *real* problem is revealed, an appropriate solution to the conflict often becomes almost obvious. Method III actually is a *problem-solving process*: it generally enables parent and child first to define what the real problem is, which increases the chances that they will end up with a solution that solves the real problem, not the initial "presenting" problem, which so often is a superficial or symptomatic one. A good illustration is the "raincoat problem," which turned out to be caused by the child's fear of being embarrassed by a *plaid* raincoat. And here are some other examples.

Freddy, aged five, began balking about going to nursery

school several months after he started. His mother at first pushed him out of the house against his will a couple of mornings. Then she went into problem-solving. She reported that it took only ten minutes to get to the real cause: Freddy was afraid his mother might not pick him up and the time between clean-up at school and mother's arrival seemed interminable to him. He also wondered if mother was trying to get rid of him by sending him off to school.

Mother told Freddy what her feelings were: she wasn't trying to get rid of him and she enjoyed having him home. But she also valued his school. In the Method III problem-solving process, several solutions emerged and they chose one: his mother would be there to pick him up before clean-up time. The mother reported that Freddy thereafter departed happily for school and that he mentioned the arrangement frequently, indicating how important it was to him.

An identical conflict in another family was resolved in a different way because the Method III process unearthed a different basic problem. In this family Bonnie, aged five, had also been resisting getting up and dressing for kindergarten, causing the whole family a problem each morning.

Here is a rather lengthy but beautiful and moving word-for-word transcript of a tape-recorded session where Bonnie and her mother work through to a creative solution. This session not only illustrates how the process helps a parent discover an underlying problem but also how essential active listening is in Method III conflict-resolution and how this method brings about whole-hearted acceptance of the solution. Finally, it poignantly illustrates how, in Method III, children as well as parents are very much concerned that, once a mutually acceptable solution has been reached, it will be carried out.

The mother had just completed solving a problem involving all four of her children. Now she directs her conversation to Bonnie and shares a problem she is having only with her.

MOTHER: Bonnie, I have a problem that I'd like to bring up, and that is that Bonnie is so slow getting dressed in the morning that she makes the rest of us late and sometimes keeps Terri from getting to the bus on time, and I have to go up there and help her get dressed, and then I don't have time to get breakfast for everyone else, and I have to rush, rush, rush, and yell at Terri to hurry up and get off on the bus. It's just a big problem.

BONNIE   (Strongly): But I don't *like* to get dressed in the morning!

MOTHER: You don't like to get dressed for school.

BONNIE: I don't feel like going to school—I like to stay home and look at books when you're wide awake and you're all in your clothes.

MOTHER: You'd rather stay home than go to school?

BONNIE: Yes.

MOTHER: You'd rather stay home and play with Mommy?

BONNIE: Yes . . . like play games and look at books.

MOTHER: You don't get much chance to do that . . .

BONNIE: No—I don't even get to play games like we do at birthdays—but we don't do it at school—we do different kinds of games at school.

MOTHER: You like the games you have at school.

BONNIE: Not too much because we always play them.

MOTHER: You liked them once, but you don't like them all the time.

BONNIE: Yeah, that's why I like to play some games at home.

MOTHER: Because they're different from the games you play at school, and you don't like to keep doing the same thing every day.

BONNIE: Yeah, I don't like to keep on doing the same things every day.

MOTHER: It's fun to have a little something different to do.

BONNIE: Yeah—like do art work at home.

MOTHER: You do art work at school?

BONNIE: No, we only do coloring and painting and flannel board.

MOTHER: Sounds like the main thing you don't like about school is that you keep doing the same things over and over again—is that right?

BONNIE: Not every day—we don't do the same games.

MOTHER: You don't do the same games every day?

BONNIE   (frustrated): I do the same games every day, but sometimes we learn new games—but *I just don't like it.* I like to stay *home.*

MOTHER: You don't like to learn new games.

BONNIE   (very irritated): Yes, I do . . .

MOTHER: But you'd rather stay home.

BONNIE   (relieved): Yes, I really like to stay home and play games and look at books and stay at home and sleep—when *you* are home.

MOTHER: Only when I'm home.

BONNIE: When you are staying home all day, I want to stay home. When you are gone, I'll go to school.

MOTHER: Sounds like you think Mommy doesn't stay home enough.

BONNIE: You don't. You always have to go to school to teach a class in the mornings or in the night time.

MOTHER: And you would rather I didn't go out so much.

BONNIE: Yes.

MOTHER: You don't really see enough of me.

BONNIE: But every night I see a babysitter named Susan—when you're gone.

MOTHER: And you'd rather see me.

BONNIE   (positively): Yes.

MOTHER: And you think maybe in the mornings when I'm home . . .

BONNIE: I stay home.

MOTHER: You'd like to stay home so you could see Mommy.

BONNIE: Yes.

MOTHER: Well, let me see. I do have my classes that I have to teach. I wonder if we could work this problem out somehow. **Do you** have any ideas?

BONNIE   (hesitantly): No.

MOTHER: I was thinking about maybe having some time when we could be together more in the afternoons when Ricky is taking his nap.

BONNIE   (joyfully): That's what I would like!

MOTHER: You would like that.

BONNIE: Yes.

MOTHER: You'd like to have time with just Mommy.

BONNIE: Yes, without Randy, without Terri, without Ricky—just with you and me playing games and reading stories. But I wouldn't like you to read stories because then you'd get sleepy—when you read stories—you always do that....

MOTHER: Yes, that's right. Then you'd like maybe instead of taking a nap—that's another problem, too. You haven't been taking your naps lately and I'm thinking maybe that you don't really need them.

BONNIE: I don't like naps—anyway we aren't talking about naps.

MOTHER: That's right, we aren't talking about naps, but I was thinking instead of taking naps maybe we could set aside that time when you would usually take a nap—we could have that time for ourselves.

BONNIE: For ourselves....

MOTHER: Uh huh. Then maybe you wouldn't feel that you wanted to stay home in the mornings so much. Think that would solve that problem?

BONNIE: I didn't even know what you said.

MOTHER: I said that maybe if we have several hours in the afternoon where we could just be together and do only the things that you wanted to do, and Mommy wouldn't even keep working—just do the things that you want to do—then maybe you would want to go to school in the mornings, if you knew that we were going to have time in the afternoons.

BONNIE: Yeah, that's what I want to do. I want to go to school in the mornings and when it's nap time—because we do have rest time at school—you don't even work. You stay home and do what I want to do.

MOTHER: Only what you want Mommy to do and no housework.

BONNIE   (firmly): No—no housework.

MOTHER: Okay, then, shall we try that? Starting right away—like tomorrow?

BONNIE: Okay, but we'll have to have a sign because *you don't remember*.

MOTHER: Then if I don't remember, we'll have to solve our problem over again.

BONNIE: Yeah. But Mommy, you should draw that sign and put it over the door of your room so you'll remember, and put it in the kitchen so you'll remember, and when I come home from school, you'll remember because you'll look at that sign, and when you get out of bed, you'll remember 'cause you'll look at that sign.

MOTHER: And I won't accidentally forget and start taking a nap myself or doing housework.

BONNIE: Yeah.

MOTHER: Okay, that's a good idea. I'll make a sign then.

BONNIE: And make it tonight when I'm sleeping.

MOTHER: Okay.

BONNIE: And then you can go out to your meeting.

MOTHER: Okay, I guess we solved that problem didn't we?

BONNIE   (happily): Yeah.

This mother, who so effectively used Method III to solve this rather common and sticky family problem, reported afterward that Bonnie stopped her stalling and complaining behavior in the morning. Several weeks later Bonnie announced that she would rather go out and play than spend so much time with her Mother. The lesson here is that once the real needs of the child were discovered through problem-solving, and a solution found that was *appropriate* to those needs, the problem disappeared as soon as the child's temporary needs had been met.

Treating Kids Like Adults

The No-lose, Method III approach communicates to kids that parents think *their* needs are important, too, and that the kids can be trusted to be considerate of parental needs in return. This is treating kids much as we treat friends or a spouse. The method feels so good to children because they like so much to feel trusted and to be treated as an equal. (Method I treats kids as if they are immature, irresponsible, and without a brain in their heads).

The following was submitted by a P.E.T. graduate:

DAD: I have a need for us to work out something about bedtime. Each night Mother or I or both of us have to nag you and worry you and sometimes force you to get you into bed at your regular time, eight o'clock. I don't feel very good about me when I do that and I wonder how you are feeling about it.

LAURA: I don't like for you to nag me . . . and I don't like to go to bed so early. I'm a big girl now and I should be able to stay up later than Greg [brother, two years younger].

MOTHER: You feel we treat you the same as Greg and that to do that isn't fair.

LAURA: Yeah, I'm two years older than Greg.

DAD: And you feel we should treat you like you're older.

LAURA: Yes!

MOTHER: You have a good point. But, if we let you stay up later and then you fool around about going to bed, I'm afraid you'll really be very late getting to sleep.

LAURA: But I won't fool around—if I can just stay up a little longer.

DAD: I wonder if you might show us how well you can cooperate for a few days and then we might change the time.

LAURA: That's not fair either!

DAD: It wouldn't be fair to make you "earn" the later time, huh?

LAURA: I think I should be able to stay up later because I'm older. [Silence.] Maybe if I went to bed at eight and *read in bed* until eight-thirty?

MOTHER: You would be in bed at the regular time but the lights could stay on for a while and you could read?

LAURA: Yeah—I like to read in bed.

DAD: That sounds pretty good to me—but who is going to watch the clock?

LAURA: Oh, I'll do that. I'll turn the light off right at eight-thirty!

MOTHER: Sounds like a pretty good idea, Laura. Shall we try that for a while?

The outcome was reported by this father as follows:

> "We had very little bedtime problem thereafter. On the occasions when Laura's light was not out at eight-thirty, one of us would confront her with something like, 'It's eight-thirty now, Laura, and we do have an agreement about lights out.' She always responded acceptably to these reminders. This solution allowed Laura to be a 'big girl' and read in bed like Mother and Dad."

Method III as "Therapy" for the Child

Frequently, Method III brings about changes in children's behavior not unlike the changes that take place when children are seen in therapy by a professional therapist. There is something potentially therapeutic in this method of resolving conflicts or solving problems.

A P.E.T. father submitted two examples where the use of Method III produced immediate "therapeutic" changes in his five-year-old son:

> "He had developed a strong interest in money and frequently would take loose change from my dresser. We had a Method III conflict-resolution

session which resulted in our agreeing to give him a penny a day for an allowance. As a result, he has ceased taking money from the dresser, and has been very consistent in saving money to buy special things he wants."

"We were quite concerned about our five-year-old's interest in a science fiction TV program, which seemed to be causing nightmares. Another TV program on at the same time was quite educational and not scary. He like this program too, but seldom selected it. In our Method III session we all decided on the solution that he would see each program on alternate days. As a result, his nightmares subsided, and he eventually began watching the educational program more often than the science fiction one."

Other parents have reported marked changes in their children after the parents used Method III over a period of time—improved grades in school, better relationships with peers, more openness in expressing feelings, fewer temper tantrums, less hostility toward school, more responsibility about homework, more independence, greater self-confidence, happier disposition, better eating habits, and other improvements that the parents welcomed.

12

Parents' Fears and Concerns About the No-Lose Method

The no-lose method of conflict-resolution is easily understood and immediately perceived as a promising new alternative by almost all parents in our classes. However, as they progress from discussing this new method *in theory* in the classroom to *putting it to work* at home, many parents experience legitimate fears and express understandable concerns about the method.

"It sounds great in theory," we hear many parents say, "But will it really work in practice?" It is human nature to be apprehensive about something new and to want to be rather thoroughly sold on it before giving up what one is accustomed to. Also, parents are reluctant to "experiment" with the youngsters who are so dear to them.

Here, as a starter, are some of the most important concerns and fears of parents, and what we tell them in the hope that they will give the no-lose method a real try.

JUST THE OLD FAMILY CONFERENCE UNDER A NEW NAME?

Some parents at first resist Method III because they think it sounds like the "family conference" method their own parents tried with them. When we ask these parents to describe how their family conferences operated, almost universally they describe something that fits this picture:

> Every Sunday Mom and Dad would make us sit around the dining room table for the purpose of having a family conference to discuss problems. Usually they brought up most of the problems, but occasionally we kids would throw out something. Dad and Mom did most of the talking and Dad ran the meeting. Often they would give us a kind of lecture or sermon. Usually we got a chance to express our opinions, but they almost always decided what the solution would be. At first, we thought it was kinda fun, but then it got boring. We didn't keep it up very long, as I recall. The things we talked about were chores and bedtime and how we should be more considerate of our mother during the day.

While this does not represent all family conferences, these meetings were quite parent-centered, Dad was clearly the chairman, solutions invariably came from the parents, kids were "teached at" or "preached to," the problems were generally rather abstract and noncontroversial, and the atmosphere was usually quite pleasant and amiable.

Method III is not a meeting but a *method* for resolving conflicts, preferably as soon as they occur. Not all conflicts involve the entire family; most involve one parent and one child. Others need not and should not be present. Method III is also not an excuse for mothers and fathers to sermonize or "educate," which usually implies that the teacher or preacher already has the answer. In Method III, parent and child search for their own unique answer and there is generally no preconceived answer to problems that come up for a no-lose solution. Also, there is no "chairman" or "leader"; parent and child are equal participants, hard at work to find a solution to their common problem.

Generally, Method III is applied in a brief, on-the-spot, here-and-now way. We call them "stand-up" problems, because the participants are tackling conflicts right when they occur, rather than waiting to bring them up in the abstract at some family sit-down conference.

Finally, the atmosphere during Method conflict-resolution is not always pleasant and amiable. Conflicts between parent and child frequently get rather emotional and feelings often run pretty high.

Dad needs the car to go to a meeting, but Joe was counting on having it for an important date.

Sally insists on going on her date with her mother's new sweater.

Little Timmy wants to go swimming when he has a cold.

Chuck has to play his guitar with top volume on his amplifier.

Such conflicts may involve very strong feelings. When parents begin to understand these differences between the old-style family conference and conflict-resolution, it becomes clear that we are not reviving an ancient tradition under a new name.

METHOD III SEEN AS PARENTAL WEAKNESS

Some parents, fathers particularly, at first equate Method III with "giving in" to the child, "being a weak parent," "compromising one's own convictions." One father, after hearing in class the tape-recorded session with Bonnie and her mother working out the going-to-school conflict, rather angrily protested, "Why, that mother simply gave in to the child! Now she has to spend an hour with her spoiled kid every afternoon. The kid won, didn't she?" Of course the child "won," but so did her mother. She doesn't have to go through an emotional hassle five mornings per week.

P.E.T. instructors understand this reaction; they hear it in almost every class because people are so accustomed to thinking about conflicts in *win-lose terms*. They think that if one person gets his way, the other must fail to get his. Somebody has to lose.

It is at first difficult for parents to understand that there is a possibility for *both* persons to get their way. Method III is not Method II, where the child gets his way at the expense of the parents not getting theirs. It is so natural at first for some parents to reason, "If I give up Method I, I'm left with Method II." "If I don't get my way, the kid will get his way." This is the familiar "either-or" thinking about conflicts.

Parents have to be helped to grasp the fundamental difference between Method II and Method III. They need repeated reminders that in Method III, they *too* must get their needs met; they *too* must accept the ultimate solution. If they *feel* they have given in to a child, then they have used Method II, not Method III. For example, in the conflict between Bonnie and her mother (Bonnie not wanting to go to school), that mother must genuinely accept giving her child that hour of exclusive attention as she actually did in this case. Otherwise, she would be giving in to Bonnie (Method II).

Some parents initially fail to see not only how Bonnie's mother, too, gained by no longer having to put up with hassles and nagging in the morning, but that she also felt no more guilt about Bonnie's going off to school, and had the satisfaction of discovering Bonnie's unfulfilled need and finding a way to meet it.

A few parents nevertheless perceive Method III as necessarily a "compromise," and to them compromise means backing down or getting less than they wanted, being "weak." When I hear them voice such a feeling, I am often reminded of the phrase in the late John F. Kennedy's inaugural address, "Fear not to negotiate, but never negotiate out of fear." Method III means negotiating, but not negotiation without courage to persist in problem-solving until a solution meets the parent's needs as well as the child's.

We do not equate Method III with the term "compromise" in the sense of accepting less than you want, because it is our experience that its solutions almost always bring more to both parent and child than either expected. These solutions are frequently what psychologists call an "elegant solution"—good, or often best, for both. Method III, then, does not mean that parents back down or roll over dead. Quite the contrary. Consider the following conflict involving an entire family and note how rewarding it was to the parents as well as the children. As reported by the Mother:

> Thanksgiving planning time was at hand. As usual, I felt the need to prepare a family dinner with turkey and to have a formal family gathering. My three sons and my husband voiced some other desires, so we went into problem-solving. Father wanted to paint the house and resented having to take time out for an elaborate dinner and entertaining company. My son in college wanted to bring home a friend who had never had a real Thanksgiving family gathering in his own home. My high-school boy wanted to go to the family cabin for the entire four days. The youngest boy complained about having to get all dressed up and going through the ordeal of a "formal" dinner. I, of course, put a lot of value on the family feeling the unity of togetherness, plus having needs to be a good mother by preparing an elegant turkey dinner. The plan that resulted from the problem-solving was that I would prepare a token turkey dinner that

we would take up to the cabin after father painted the house. My college son would bring home his friend, and all of them would help Father paint so we could get up to the cabin sooner. The results: for a change there was no door-slamming, no anger. Everybody had a great time—the best Thanksgiving the family ever spent together. Even my son's guest helped with the painting. It was the first time our sons helped their Father do any of the work on the house without a major hassle. Dad was ecstatic, the boys were enthused, and I felt good about my role for Thanksgiving. Yet I didn't have all the work usually required of me to prepare a huge dinner. It worked out better than our fondest dreams. Never again will I dictate family decisions!

In my own family, a very serious conflict arose about the Easter vacation, and Method III produced a novel solution unexpectedly acceptable to all of us. My wife and I felt in no way weak at the end; we felt lucky to have avoided the Newport Beach nightmare.

Our daughter, fifteen years old, wanted to accept an invitation to spend Easter vacation with several girl friends at Newport Beach ("where the boys are" in California, as well as the beer, the pot, and the cops). My wife and I had real fears about exposing our daughter to what we had heard so often goes on at these yearly gatherings of thousands of high-school kids. We expressed our fears, which our daughter heard but discounted in view of her strong wish to be with her friends at the beach. We knew we would lose sleep and feared we would be called out in the middle of the night to haul her out of real trouble. Active Listening uncovered something surprising—her principal needs were to be with a particular girl friend, to be someplace where there would be boys, and to be at the beach so she could return to school with a deep tan. Two days after the conflict arose, and was still unresolved, our daughter came up with a novel solution. Would we consider a golfing weekend ("You haven't taken one for a long time, you know")? She could take her friend and we would all stay at the motel on the grounds of one of my favorite golf courses, which also happened to be close to the beach—not Newport Beach, but another where boys were also likely to be found. We literally pounced on her solution, greatly relieved to find a way to avoid all the anxieties we would have had about her being at Newport Beach without supervision. She was delighted, too, because she would get all her needs met. We carried out the plan. We all had fun together at night after my wife and I had golfed and the girls had spent the day on the beach. It so happened that few boys were on this particular beach, which disappointed the girls. Still, neither complained to us or expressed any feelings indicating resentment toward us for the decision we had reached.

This situation also illustrates how some Method III solutions do not turn out to be perfect. Sometimes, unpredictably, what appears to be a solution meeting everyone's needs, ends up being disappointing to someone. Yet, in families using Method III, this does not seem to cause resentment and bitterness, possibly because it is clear that it was not the parents who caused the kids' disappointment (as with Method I) but, rather, chance or fate or the weather or luck. They can blame external or unpredictable forces, yes, but not the parents. Another factor, of course, is that Method III makes kids feel that the solution was as much theirs as the parents'.

"GROUPS CANNOT MAKE DECISIONS"

It is a commonly believed myth that only individuals, not groups, are capable of making decisions. "A camel is the result of a committee that made a group decision about how to design a horse". This humorous quotation is often quoted by parents to support their belief that groups either cannot end up with a solution or the solution will be inferior. Another statement that parents often bring up in class is, "Some*one* eventually has to decide for the group."

This myth persists because so few people have been given the opportunity to be in an effective decision-making group. Throughout their lives, most adults have been denied this experience by those who have had power over them and have consistently used Method I to solve problems or resolve conflicts—parents, teachers, aunts, uncles, Scout leaders, coaches, babysitters, military leaders, bosses, and so on. Most adults in our "democratic" society have seldom been given the chance to experience seeing a group solve problems and conflicts democratically. No wonder that parents are skeptical of the decision-making capabilities of groups: they have never had a chance to see one! The implications are frightening in view of how frequently leaders proclaim the importance of bringing up kids to be responsible citizens.

Perhaps this is why some parents in our classes require a great deal of evidence that a family group can and will make high quality decisions to resolve problems—even those that are frequently rather sticky and complex, such as conflicts about:

Allowances and money.
Care of the home.
Chores.
Family purchases.
Use of the car.
Use of the TV.
Vacations.
Conduct of kids at parties in the home.
Use of the phone.
Bedtime hours.
Meal times.
Who sits where in the car.
Use of the swimming pool.
Kinds of food available.
Allocation of rooms or closets.
Condition of rooms.

The list is interminable—families *can* make decision as a group, and the proof will come every day when they use the no-lose method. Of course, parents must make a commitment to use Method III and give themselves and their children the opportunity to experience how much a group can be trusted to arrive at creative and mutually acceptable solutions.

"METHOD III TAKES TOO MUCH TIME"

The idea of having to spend much time problem-solving worries many parents. Mr. W., a busy executive, already over-extended in meeting the demands of his job, declares, "I can't possibly find the time to sit down and spend an hour with each of my kids every time a conflict comes up—it's ridiculous!" Mrs. B., mother of five youngsters, says, "Why, I'd never get any housework done if I had to use Method III with each of my five—they're a handful now!"

There is no denying that Method III takes time. How much time depends on the problem and the willingness of parent and child to search for a no-lose solution. Here are some findings from the experiences of parents who made a genuine effort with Method III:

1. Many conflicts are "quickies" or "stand-up" problems requiring from a few minutes to ten minutes.
2. Some problems take longer—such as allowances, chores, use of the TV set, bedtime hours. However, once they are solved by Method III, they generally stay solved. Unlike Method I decisions, Method III decisions don't continually come up again and again.
3. Parents save time in the long run because they don't have to spend countless hours reminding, enforcing, checking up, hassling.
4. When Method III is first introduced in a family, the initial Method III sessions usually take longer because the kids (and the parents) are inexperienced with the new process, because kids may distrust their parents' good intentions ("What's this new technique you've got to control us?"); or because they have residual resentments or a habitual win-lose posture ("I've got to get my way").

Probably the most significant outcome of families' using the no-lose way, and one that I had not expected, is the greatest time-saver of all: after a period of time conflicts simply do not come up very often.

"We seem to have run out of things to problem-solve," one mother reported to us less than a year after taking P.E.T.

Another mother, in response to my request for examples of

Method III in her family, wrote, "We want to respond to your appeal for case material, but we don't seem to have had many conflicts lately to give us further Method III practice."

In the last year in my own family, so few serious parent-child conflicts have occurred that I frankly cannot at this time recall one, simply because things got worked out easily without turning into full-fledged "conflicts."

I expected conflicts would keep cropping up, year after year, and I'm sure most parents in P.E.T. did, too. Why the decrease? It makes sense to me, now that I have thought about it: Method III brings about a radically different posture of kids and parents toward each other. Knowing that parents have given up using power to get their way—to win at the expense of not respecting the needs of the kids—these kids have no reason to press hard to get their way or to defend vigorously against the parents' power. Consequently, strong clashes of needs disappear almost totally. Instead, a youngster becomes accommodating—as respectful of his parents' needs as he is his own. When he has a need, he expresses it and his parents look for ways of accommodating; when the parents have needs, they express them and the youngster looks for ways of accommodating. When either has any difficulty in accommodating, they see it as more of a problem to be worked out rather than a fight to be fought.

One other thing happens: parents and kids start to use methods *to avoid* conflict. An adolescent daughter makes a point of leaving a note for her father at the front door, reminding him of her need to have the car that night. Or she asks ahead of time if it would interfere with her parents if she invites her girl friend for dinner next Friday. Note that she does not ask for *permission*; getting parents' permission is a pattern born out of a Method I home, and implies that parents might *deny* permission. In a Method III climate, the child says, "I want to do my thing, unless I learn it might interfere with you doing your thing."

"AREN'T PARENTS JUSTIFIED IN USING METHOD I BECAUSE THEY ARE WISER?"

The notion that a parent is justified in using power over his children because he is wiser or more experienced has firm roots. We listed many of the usual rationalizations earlier: "We know best from our experience," "We're denying you only for your own good," "When you're older, you'll thank us for making you do these things," "We just want to prevent you from making the same mistakes we made," "We just can't let you do something that we know you'll be sorry for later," etc., etc.

Many parents who convey these or similar messages to their children sincerely believe what they say. No other attitude is more difficult to modify in our classes than the one that parents are justified in using power—even have a responsibility to use power—because they know more, are brighter, wiser, more mature, or more experienced.

This is not an attitude held exclusively by parents. Throughout history tyrants have used this argument to justify their use of power over those whom they have oppressed. Most had a very low opinion of their subjects—whether slaves, peasants, barbarians, backwoodsmen, blacks, wetbacks, Christians, heretics, rabble, commoners, the workingman, Jews, Latins, Orientals, or women. It seems almost universal that those who exercise power over others must somehow rationalize and justify their oppression and inhumanity by judging those on whom they use their power to be inferior.

How can anyone refute the idea that parents are wiser and more experienced than children? It seems to be such a self-evident truth. Yet, when we ask parents in our classes, whether their own parents made unwise Method I decisions, they all say, "Yes." How easy it is for parents to forget their own experience as children! How easy to forget that children sometimes know better than parents when they are sleepy or hungry; know better the qualities of their friends, their own aspirations and goals, how their various teachers treat them; know better the urges and needs within their bodies, whom they love and whom they don't, what they value and what they don't.

Parents have superior wisdom? No, not about many things concerning their children. Parents do have much valuable wisdom and experience, and that wisdom and experience need never be buried.

Many parents in P.E.T. overlook at first the point that the *wisdom of both the parent and the child* is mobilized by the no-lose method. Neither is left out of problem-solving (in contrast to Method I, which ignores a child's wisdom, or Method II, which ignores the wisdom of parents).

A mother of two lovely, exceptionally bright twin girls reported a successful problem-solving session about whether the twins should be advanced one grade in school, so their school work would be more interesting and challenging, or remain in their present class with their friends. This is the type of problem that is traditionally solved by "experts" exclusively—teachers and parents. In this case the mother had ideas, but she also trusted the wisdom of her daughters' feelings, their own assessment of their intellectual potential, their own judgment of what would be best for them. After several days of weighing pros and cons, including listening to ideas and contributions from the mother as well as information given to them by their teacher, the twins accepted the solution that they should be advanced. The outcome of this family decision turned out to be favorable without exception, both in terms of the twins' happiness and their school performance.

CAN METHOD III WORK WITH YOUNG CHILDREN?

"I can see how Method III might work with older kids who are more verbal, more mature and capable of reasoning, but not with youngsters aged two to six. They're just too young to know what's best for them, so don't you have to use Method I?"

This question is asked in every P.E.T. class. However, evidence from families who have tried Method III with very young children proves it can work. Here is a brief session between a three-year-old girl and her mother, who submitted the situation:

CATHY: I don't want to go to my babysitter's anymore.

MOTHER: You don't like going to Mrs. Crockett's house when I go to work.

CATHY: No, I don't want to go.

MOTHER: I need to go to work and you can't stay at home, but you are sure unhappy about staying there. Is there something we could do to make it easier for you to stay there?

CATHY (silence): I could stay on the sidewalk until you drive away.

MOTHER: But Mrs. Crockett needs you to be inside with the other children so she knows where you are.

CATHY: I could watch you from the window when you drive away.

MOTHER: Will that make you feel better?

CATHY: Yes.

MOTHER: Okay. Let's try that next time.

A two year old girl responded to the nonpower method in this incident described by her mother:

"I was cooking dinner one night and my daughter was gurgling happily on her rocking horse. Then she took the straps used to buckle the child on and began to try to buckle the straps herself. Her face reddened and she began to scream in a high-pitched voice as her frustration mounted. I found myself getting angry at her screaming, so in my usual fashion I knelt down to do it for her. But she fought me and kept screaming. Now I was ready to pick up her and the rocking horse and deposit them both in her room, slamming the door to shut out the noise. Then something clicked in me. So I knelt down, placed my hands on top of hers and said, 'You're really mad because you can't do that yourself.' She shook her head, 'Yes,' stopped the screaming, and a few belated sobs later was again happily rocking away. And I thought, 'You mean it really is that simple?' "

To this somewhat surprised mother, I would have to say, "No, it isn't always that simple," but Method III does work surprisingly well with preschool children—and even infants. I remember well this incident in our family:

When our daughter was only five months old, we went on a month's vacation during which we lived in a cabin beside our fishing lake. Before this the trip we had felt lucky because the youngster had never needed a feeding from 11:00 P.M. until 7:00 A.M. The change in surroundings brought a change in our luck. She started waking up at 4:00 A.M. for a feeding. At that hour of the morning, getting up to feed her was painful. In northern Wisconsin in September, it was freezing in the cabin and all we had was a wood-burning stove. This meant we either had to go to the trouble of building a fire or, equally bad, wrap up in blankets and try to stay warm for the hour it took to prepare the formula, warm the bottle, and feed her. We truly felt this was a "conflict-of-needs situation," needing some joint problem-solving. Putting our heads together, my wife and I decided to offer the infant an alternative solution in the hope that she would find it acceptable to her. Instead of waking her up and feeding her at 11:00, the next night we let her sleep until 12:00, then fed her. That morning she slept until 5:00 A.M. So far, pretty good. The next night we made a special effort to see to it that she drank more than her usual amount of milk and then put her to bed around 12:30. It worked—she bought it. That morning, and subsequent mornings, she did not waken until 7:00, when we wanted to get up anyway to get out on the lake when the fish were biting best. Nobody lost, we all won.

Not only is it possible to use Method III with infants; it is important to begin using it early in the child's life. The earlier it is started, the sooner the child will learn how to relate to others democratically, to respect others' needs, and to recognize it when his own needs are respected.

Parents who have taken P.E.T. after their kids are older and introduce them to Method III after they have become accustomed to the two power-struggle methods invariably have a more difficult time of it than parents who start using Method III from the very start.

One father told his P.E.T. class that the first few times he and his wife tried Method III their older boy said, "What's this new psychological technique you're using to try and make us do what you want?" This perceptive son, accustomed to win-lose conflict-resolution (with the kids usually losing), was finding it hard to trust his parents' good intentions and their genuine desire to try the no-lose method. In the next chapter I will show how to handle such resistance from teen-agers.

AREN'T THERE TIMES WHEN METHOD I
HAS TO BE USED?

It has become a joke with those of us who are teaching P.E.T. that in almost every new class some parent will challenge the validity or limits of Method III by one of two questions:

> "But what if your kid runs into the street in front of a car? Don't you *have* to use Method I?"
> "But what if your kid gets severe appendicitis? Don't you *have* to use Method I to make him go to the hospital."

Our answer to both these questions is "Yes, of course." These are crisis situations that demand immediate and firm action. Yet, prior to the crisis of the child running in front of a car or needing to be taken to the hospital, nonpower methods can be used.

If a child develops a habit of running into the street, a parent might first try to talk to the child about the dangers of cars, walk him around the edge of the yard, and tell him that anything beyond is not safe, show him a picture of a child hit by a car, build a fence around the yard, or watch him when he is playing in the front yard for a couple of days, reminding him each time when he goes beyond the limits. Even if I took the punishment approach, I would never risk my child's life on the assumption that punishment alone would keep him from going into the street. I would want to employ more certain methods in any event.

With children who get sick and require surgery or shots or medicine, nonpower methods also can be extremely effective. In the following situation with a nine-year old, she and her mother were driving to the allergy clinic to start a regimen of twice-weekly injections for her hay fever. The mother used only active listening.

BETTY　　　(in a lengthy monologue): I don't want to take those shots—Who wants shots? . . . Shots hurt. . . . I suppose I'll have to have them forever. . . . Twice every week . . . I'd rather sniffle and sneeze. . . . What did you get me into this for?

MOTHER:　Hm—mmmm.

BETTY:　Mommy, do you remember when I had a whole lot of splinters in my knee and I had a shot afterwards?

MOTHER:　Yes, I remember. You had a tetanus shot after the doctor took out the splinters.

BETTY:　That nurse talked to me and told me to look at a picture on the wall, so I didn't even know it when the needle went in.

MOTHER:　Some nurses can give shots so you don't even know you're getting them.

BETTY　　　(upon arriving): I'm not going in there.

MOTHER　　(over her shoulder while walking in): You would really rather not come.

BETTY:　(Walks in with exaggerated slowness).

This mother then described the outcome—Betty eventually went in, kept the appointment as planned, had her shots, and received a compliment from the nurse on her cooperation. Betty's mother also added the following:

> Prior to P.E.T. I would have lectured her about the necessity of carrying out a doctor's treatment plan, or I would have told her how much my own allergy shots were helping, or said that shots really didn't hurt much, or moralized about how lucky she was to have no other health problem, or else I would have become exasperated and told her outright to quit complaining. I certainly wouldn't have given her a chance to remember the nurse who gives shots so you don't "even know it when the needle goes in."

"WON'T I LOSE MY KIDS' RESPECT?"

Some parents, particularly fathers, fear that using Method III will cause their kids to lose respect for them. They tell us:

> "I'm afraid my kids will run all over me."
>
> "Shouldn't kids look up to their parents?"
>
> "I think kids should respect the authority of their parents?"
>
> "Are you suggesting that parents treat their kids as equals?"

Many parents are confused about the term "respect." Sometimes when they use the term, as in "respect my authority", they really mean "fear." They are concerned about their kids losing their fear of the parents and then not obeying or resisting efforts to control them. When confronted by this definition, some parents have said, "No, I don't mean that—I want them to respect me for my abilities, my knowledge, and so on. I guess I really wouldn't want them to fear me."

We then ask such parents, "How do *you* get to respect another adult for *his* abilities and his knowledge?" Usually, the answer is, "Well, he would have demonstrated his abilities—he would somehow have *earned my respect.*" Generally, it becomes obvious to these parents that they, too, must *earn* their kids' respect by demonstrating their competence or their knowledge.

Most parents, when they think clearly about it, know that they cannot *demand* someone's respect—they have to earn it. If their abilities and knowledge are worthy of respect, their kids will respect them. If they are not, they won't.

Parents who have made a genuine effort to substitute Method III for the win-lose methods generally discover their kids have developed a new kind of respect for them—not one based on fear, but one based on a change in their perception of the *parent as a person*. A school principal wrote this moving letter to me:

> "I can best tell you what P.E.T. has meant in my life by telling you that my stepdaughter didn't like me from the time I came on the scene when she was two and one-half years old. This really got to me—her disdain. Kids generally like me—but not Sally. I began to dislike her—even loathe her. So much so that one early morning I had a dream in which my feelings about her were so antagonistic, so distasteful that the intensity of the negative feelings awakened me with a shock. I knew then I needed help. I got into therapy. The therapy helped me relax a bit, but Sally still didn't like me. Six months after my therapy—Sally was ten years old by now—I took P.E.T. and later began teaching it. Within a year, Sally and I had as rich a relationship as I would desire and dream of. She is thirteen now. We respect one another, we like one another, we laugh, we argue, play, work, and occasionally cry with one another. I received my 'graduation certificate' from Sally about a month ago. Our family was eating in a Chinese restaurant. While we were all opening our fortune cookies, Sally silently read hers and then handed it to me saying, 'This should be for you, Dad.' It read, 'You will be happy in your children and they in you.' You see, I have reason to thank you for giving me P.E.T."

Sally's respect for her stepfather, most parents would readily agree, is the kind of respect they *really* want from their kids. Method III does cause children to lose fear-based "respect," but what has a parent lost when in its place he has earned a far better kind of respect?

13

Putting the "No-Lose" Method to Work

Even after parents in P.E.T. become convinced they want to begin using the no-lose method, they pose questions about how to get started. Also, some parents run into difficulties when they first begin. Here are some pointers on getting started, on handling some of the most common problems parents encounter, and on resolving irritating conflicts that develop *between* children.

HOW DO YOU START?

Parents who have had the most success getting started with the no-loose method take seriously our advice to sit down with their kids and explain what the method is all about. Remember, most kids are as unfamiliar with this method as the parents. Accustomed to having conflicts with parents resolved by Method I or Method II, they need to be told how Method III differs.

Some parents have used the same diagrams as their P.E.T. instructors used in class. They draw all three methods and describe the differences. They admit that often they have won at the expense of the kids losing, and vice versa. Then they freely express their eagerness to get away from the win-lose methods and try the no-lose method.

Kids usually get turned on by such an introduction. They are curious to learn about Method III and are anxious to try it. Some parents first explain that they have been taking a course in how to be more effective parents and that this new method is one of the things they would now like to try out. Of course, this approach is not appropriate for youngsters under three. With them, you just start out with no explanation.

THE SIX STEPS OF THE NO-LOSE METHOD

It has been helpful for parents to understand that the no-lose method really involves six separate steps. When parents follow these steps, they are much more likely to have successful experiences:

Step 1: Identifying and defining the conflict.
Step 2: Generating possible alternative solutions.
Step 3: Evaluating the alternative solutions.
Step 4: Deciding on the best acceptable solution.
Step 5: Working out ways of implementing the solution.
Step 6: Following up to evaluate how it worked.

There are some key points to be understood about each of these six steps. When parents understand and apply these key points, they avoid many difficulties and pitfalls. Even though some "quickie" conflicts get worked out without going through all the steps, parents do better when they understand what is involved at each stage.

Step 1: Identifying and Defining the Conflict

This is the critical phase when parents want the child to become involved. They have to get his attention and then secure his willingness to enter into problem-solving. Their chances of doing this are much greater if they remember to:

1. Select a time when the child is not busy or occupied or going someplace, so he won't resist or resent being interrupted or delayed.

2. Tell him clearly and concisely that there is a problem that must be solved. Don't pussyfoot or be tentative with such ineffective statements as, "Would you like to problem-solve?" or "I think it might be a good idea if we tried to work this out."

3. Tell the child clearly, and as strongly as you feel, exactly what feelings you have or what needs of yours are not being met or what is bothering you. Here it is critical to send "I-messages": "*I* have been upset when *I* see the kitchen *I* have worked hard to clean get all messed up after you have your after-school snack"; or "*I* am worried about *my* car getting smashed up and you getting hurt if you continue to drive faster than the speed limits"; or "*I* feel it is unfair to *me* to do so much of the work around the house when you kids might help out."

4. Avoid messages that put-down or blame the child, such as "You kids have been sloppy about the kitchen," "You're being reckless with my car," "You kids are a bunch of free-loaders around this house."

5. Be very clear that you want them to join with you in finding a solution *acceptable to both,* a solution "we both can live with," in which nobody loses and both of your needs will be met. It is critical that children believe that you are sincere in wanting to find a no-lose solution. They must know that the "name of the game" is Method III, no-lose, not more win-lose in a new disguise.

Step 2: Generating Possible Solutions

In this phase, the key is to generate a *variety of solutions*. The parent can suggest: "What are some of the things we might do?" "Let's think of possible solutions," "Let's put our heads to work and come up with some possible solutions," "There must be a lot of different ways we can solve this problem." These additional key points will help:

1. Try first to get the kids' solutions—you can add your own later. (Younger children may not come up with solutions initially).

2. Most important, do not evaluate, judge, or belittle any of the solutions offered. There will be time for that in the next phase. Accept *all* ideas for solutions. For complex problems you may want to write them down. Don't even evaluate or judge solutions as being "good," because that may imply that others on the list are not so good.

3. At this point try not to make any statements conveying that any of the offered solutions would be unacceptable to you.

4. When using the no-lose method on a problem involving several children, if one doesn't offer a solution, you might have to encourage him to contribute.

5. Keep pressing for alternative solutions until it looks as though no more are going to be suggested.

Step 3: Evaluating the Alternative Solutions

In this phase, it is legitimate to start evaluating the various solutions. The parent may say, "All right, which of these solutions look best?" or "Now, let's see which solution we feel is the one we want?" or "What do we think of these variouss solutions we have come up with?" or "Are any of these better than the others?"

Generally, the solutions get narrowed down to one or two that seem best by eliminating those that are not acceptable to either parent or the kids (for whatever reason). At this stage parents must remember to be honest in stating their own feelings—"I wouldn't be happy with that," or "That wouldn't meet my need," or "I don't think that one would seem fair to me."

Step 4: Deciding on the Best Solution

This step is not as difficult to work through as parents often think. When the other steps have been followed and the exchange of ideas and reactions has been open and honest, a clearly superior solution often emerges naturally from the discussion. Sometimes either the parent or a child has suggested a very creative solution that obviously is the best one—and is also acceptable to everyone.

Some tips for arriving at a final decision are:

1. Keep testing out the remaining solutions against the feelings of the kids with such questions as, "Would this solution be okay, now?" "Are we all satisfied with this solution?" "Do you think this one would solve our problem?" "Is this going to work?"

2. Don't think of a decision as necessarily final and impossible to change. You might say, "Okay, let's try this one out and see if it works," or "We seem to agree on this solution—let's start carrying it out and see if it really solves our problems," or "I'm willing to accept this one; would you be willing to give it a try?"

3. If the solution involves a number of points, it is a good idea to write them down so they won't be forgotten.

4. Make certain it is clearly understood that each one is making a commitment to carry out the decision: "Okay, now, this is what we are agreeing to do," or "We

understand, now, this is to be our agreement and we're saying we're going to keep to our part of the bargain."

Step 5: Implementing the Decision

Frequently, after a decision is reached there is a need to spell out in some detail exactly how the decision will be implemented. Parent and kids may need to address themselves to "*Who* is to do *what*, by *when*?" or "Now what do we need to do to carry this out?" or "When do we start?"

In conflicts about chores and work duties, for example, "How often?" "On what days?" and "What are to be the standards of performance required?" are questions that often must be discussed.

In conflicts about bedtime, a family may want to discuss who is going to watch the clock and call time.

In conflicts about the neatness of the children's rooms, the issue of "how neat" may have to be explored.

Sometimes decisions may require purchases, such as a blackboard for a message center, a clothes hamper for the child, a new iron for daughter, and so on. In such cases it may be necessary to determine who is to shop for these, or even who is to pay for them.

Questions of implementation are best delayed until after there is a clear agreement on the final decision. Our experience is that once the final decision has been reached, the implementation issues are usually worked out rather easily.

Step 6: Follow-Up Evaluation

Not all initial decisions from the no-lose method turn out to be good ones. Consequently, parents sometimes need to check back with a child to ask if he is still happy with the decision. Kids often commit themselves to a decision that later proves difficult to carry out. Or a parent may find it difficult to keep his bargain, for a variety of reasons. Parents may want to check back after a while with, "How is our decision working out?" "Are you still satisfied with our decision?" This communicates to kids your concern about their needs.

Sometimes the follow-up turns up information that requires the initial decision to be modified. Taking out the trash once every day might turn out to be impossible or unnecessary. Or, coming in at 11:00 P.M. on weekend nights proves to be impossible when the kids go to a double-feature movie. One family discovered that their no-lose resolution of the chore problem required their younger daughter, who agreed to wash the evening dishes, to work on an average of five to six hours a week, while the older daughter, whose job it was to do a weekly clean up of their common bathroom and playroom, needed only to work three hours a week. This seemed unfair to the youngest, so the decision was modified after a couple of weeks' trial.

Of course, not all no-lose conflict-resolution sessions proceed in an orderly fashion through all six steps. Sometimes conflicts are resolved after only one solution has been proposed. Sometimes the final solution pops out of someone's mouth during Step 3, when they are evaluating previously proposed solutions. Nevertheless, it pays to keep the six steps in mind.

The Need for Active Listening and "I-Messages"

Because the no-lose method requires the involved parties to join together in problem-solving, effective communication is a prerequisite. Consequently, parents must do a great deal of active listening, and must send clear "I-messages." Parents who have not learned these skills seldom have success with the no-lose method.

Active listening is required, first, because parents need to understand the feelings or needs of the kids. What do they want? Why do they persist in wanting to do something even after they know it is not acceptable to their parents? What needs are causing them to behave in a certain way?

Why is Bonnie resisting going to nursery school? Why does Jane not want to wear the plaid raincoat? Why does Freddy cry and fight his mother when she drops him off at the babysitter's? What are my daughter's needs that make it so important for her to go to the beach during the Easter vacation?

Active listening is a potent tool for helping a youngster to open up and reveal his real needs and true feelings. When these become understood by the parent, it is often an easy next step to think of another way of meeting those needs that will not involve behavior unacceptable to the parent.

Since strong feelings may come out during problem-solving—from parents as well as youngsters, active listening is critically important in helping to release feelings and dissipate them, so that effective problem-solving can continue.

Finally, active listening is an important way to let kids know that their proposed solutions are understood and accepted as proposals made in good faith; and that their thoughts and evaluations concerning all proposed solutions are wanted and accepted.

"I-messages" are critical in the no-lose process so kids will know how the parent feels, without impugning the character of the child or putting him down with blame and shame. "You-messages" in conflict-resolution usually provoke counter "You-messages" and cause the discussion to degenerate into a nonproductive verbal battle with the contestants vying to see who can best clobber the other with insults.

"I-messages" also must be used to let kids know that *parents* have needs and are serious about seeing that those needs are not going to be ignored just because the youngster has his needs. "I-messages" communicate the parent's own limits—what he cannot tolerate and what he does not want to sacrifice. "I-messages" convey, "I am a person with needs and feelings," "I have a right to enjoy life," "I have rights in our home."

The First No-Lose Attempt

Parents in P.E.T. are advised that their first no-lose problem-solving session probably should take up some long-standing conflicts rather than a more immediate and incendiary one. It is also wise at this first session to give kids a chance to identify some problems that are bothering them. Thus, a first attempt at no-lose conflict-resolution might be presented by a parent in some such fashion as this:

> "Now that we all understand what no-lose problem-solving (or Method III) is, let's start listing some conflicts we are having in our family. First, what problems do you kids see we have? What problems would you like to see us resolve? What situations cause you kids to get upset?"

The advantages of starting with problems identified by the kids are rather obvious. First, kids are delighted to see that this new method can work to *their* benefit. Second, it keeps them from the incorrect notion that their parents have picked up some new device to get just their own needs met. One family that started out this way ended up with a list of grievances against their Mother's behavior:

> Mom doesn't shop often enough to keep food in the house.
>
> Mom leaves her underclothes and stockings

hanging out to dry in the bathroom, leaving no room for the kids.

Mom frequently doesn't tell the kids when she is coming home to cook dinner after work.

Mom makes the son (the oldest) chauffeur his two sisters too much.

After they got their grievances listed, these teen-agers were much more receptive to hearing some of the problems Mom was having with their behavior.

Sometimes it is wise for a family to start out by talking about the ground rules they might need to conduct an effective no-lose conflict-resolution session. Parents might suggest that all agree to let one person talk without being interrupted. It should be clearly stated that voting is not to be used—you are after a solution acceptable to everyone. Agree to go out of the room when two people are resolving a conflict not involving the others. Agree on no physical horseplay during the problem-solving. One family even agreed that during their problem-solving conferences they would not answer the telephone. Many families have found it very useful to use a blackboard or a chart pad to assist with complex problems.

PROBLEMS PARENTS WILL ENCOUNTER

Parents often make mistakes trying to put the new method to work and it also takes time for kids to learn how to resolve conflicts without power, especially adolescents who have had years of experience with win-lose methods. Both parents and their offspring have to undo some old patterns of behavior and learn some new ones, and this naturally doesn't always work without a hitch. From parents in our P.E.T. classes we have learned what mistakes are most frequently made and what the common problems are.

Initial Distrust and Resistance

Some parents encounter resistance to the no-lose method—invariably when the kids are teen-agers accustomed to years of continuous power struggle with parents. They report:

> "Jan simply refused to sit down with us."
>
> "Billy got angry and left the problem-solving session because he didn't get his way."
>
> "Pam just sat there in sullen silence."
>
> "Jimmy said that we would get our way like we usually do."

The best way to handle such distrust and resistance is for the parents temporarily to put aside the problem-solving and try to understand with empathy what the child is really saying. Active listening is the best tool for finding out. It may encourage kids to express more of their feelings. If they do, that is progress because, after their feelings get ventilated, these youngsters will often enter into problem-solving. If they remain withdrawn and unwilling to participate, parents will want to send their own feelings—as "I-messages," of course:

> "I don't want to use my power anymore in this family, but I also don't want to surrender to yours."
>
> "We are really serious about finding a solution that you can accept."
>
> "We are not trying to make you give in—nor do *we* want to give in."
>
> "We are tired of having fights in this family. We think we can resolve our conflicts this new way."
>
> "I sure wish you would give it a try. We know it'll work."

Usually these messages are effective in dispelling distrust and resistance. If not, parents can simply leave the problem unresolved for a day or two and try the no-lose method again.

We tell parents, "Just remember how skeptical and distrustful you were when you heard us talk about the no-lose method the first time in class. That may help you understand your kids' first skeptical reactions."

"What If We Can't Find an Acceptable Solution?"

This is one of the most frequent fears of parents. While it is justifiable in some cases, surprisingly few no-lose conflict-resolution sessions fail to come up with an acceptable solution. When a family encounters such a stalemate or deadlock, it is usually because parents and children are still in a win-lose, power-struggle frame of mind.

Our advice to parents is: try everything you can think of in such cases. For instance:

1. Keep talking.
2. Go back to Step 2 and generate more solutions.
3. Hold over the conflict until a second session tomorrow.
4. Make strong appeals, such as, "Come on, there must be a way to resolve this," "Let's really try hard to find an acceptable solution," "Have we explored all of the possible solutions?" "Let's try harder."
5. Bring the difficulty out in the open and try to find out whether some underlying problem or "hidden agenda" is obstructing progress. You might say, "I wonder what's going on here that prevents us from finding a solution," "Are there other things bugging us that we haven't brought out?"

Usually, one or several of these approaches works and problem-solving gets started again.

Reverting to Method I When Method III Bogs Down

"We tried the no-lose method and got nowhere. So my wife and I had to put our foot down and make the decision."

Some parents are tempted to revert to Method I. Usually this has rather severe consequences. The kids are angry; they feel they were duped into believing that their parents were trying a new method; and the next time the no-lose method is tried they will be even more distrustful and disbelieving.

Parents are strongly urged to avoid reverting to Method I. Also, it is just as disastrous to revert to Method II and let the kids win, for the next time the no-lose method is tried, they'll be primed to keep fighting until they again get their own way.

Should Punishment Be Built into the Decision?

Parents have reported back in class that they (or the kids) found themselves, after a no-lose decision had been reached, building into the agreement the penalties or punishments to be administered if the kids did not keep to their agreement.

My earlier reaction to these reports was to suggest that mutually-set penalties and punishments might be all right, *if they also applied to the parents*, should *they* not uphold their end of the bargain. I now think differently about this issue.

It is far better for parents to avoid bringing up penalties or punishments for failure to stick to an agreement or carry out a Method III decision. In the first place, parents will want to communicate to the youngsters that punishment is not to be used at all any more, even if it is suggested by the kids, as it often will be. Secondly, more is gained by an attitude of trust—trust in the kids' good intentions and integrity. Youngsters tell us, "When I feel trusted, I'm less likely to betray that trust. But when I feel my parent or a teacher is not trusting me, I might as well go ahead and do what they already think I've done. I'm already bad in their opinion. I've already lost, so why not go and do it anyway."

In the no-lose method, parents should simply *assume that the kids will carry out the decision.* That is part of the new method—trust in each other, trust in keeping to commitments, sticking to promises, holding up one's end of the bargain. Any talk about penalties and punishments is bound to communicate distrust, doubt, suspicion, pessimism. This is not to say that kids will *always* stick to their agreement. They won't. It says merely that parents should *assume* that they will. "Innocent until proven guilty" or "responsible until proven irresponsible" is the philosophy we recommend.

When Agreements Are Broken

It is almost inevitable that kids sometimes will not keep their commitment. Here are some of the reasons:

1. They may discover they committed themselves to something too hard to carry out.
2. They simply have not had much experience in being self-disciplined and self-directed.
3. They previously depended on parental power for their discipline and control.
4. They may forget.
5. They may be testing the no-lose method—testing whether Mom and Dad really mean what they say, whether the kids can get by with breaking their promise.
6. They may have expressed acceptance of the decision at the time just because they got tired of the uncomfortable problem-solving session.

Our parents have reported all of these reasons for kids failing to keep to their commitments.

We teach parents to confront, directly and honestly, any youngster who has not stuck to an agreement. The key is to send the child an "I-message"—no blame, no put-down, no threat. Also the confrontation should come as soon as possible, perhaps like this:

> "I'm disappointed that you didn't keep to your agreement."
>
> "I'm surprised that you didn't keep your end of the bargain."
>
> "Hey, Jimmy, I don't feel it's fair to me that I stuck to my end of bargain but you didn't."
>
> "I thought we had agreed to _____, and now I find you didn't do your part. I don't like that."
>
> "I'd hoped we had our problem solved, and I'm irritated that we apparently didn't solve it."

Such "I-messages" will invoke some response from the youngster that may give you more information and help you to understand the reason. Again this is a time to listen actively. But always, in the end, the parent must make it clear that in the no-lose method each person is *expected* to be self-responsible and trustworthy. The commitments are *expected* to be met: "This is no game we're playing—we're seriously trying to consider the needs of one another."

That may take real discipline, real integrity, real *work*. Depending on the reasons why a child did not keep his word, parents may (1) find the "I-messages" are effective; (2) find they need to reopen the problem and find a better solution; or (3) want to help the child look for ways to help him remember.

If a youngster forgets, parents can raise the problem of what he might do to remember the next time. Does he need a clock, a timer, a note to himself, a message on the bulletin board, a string around his finger, a calendar, a sign in his room?

Should the parents remind the youngster? Should they take on the responsibility of telling him when he is to do what he agreed to do? In P.E.T. we say *definitely not.* Apart from the inconvenience to the parent, it has the effect of keeping the child dependent, slowing down the development of his self-discipline and self-responsibility. Reminding children to do what they committed themselves to do is coddling them—it treats them as if they are immature and irresponsible. And that is what they will continue to be, unless parents start right away to *shift the seat of responsibility to the child, where it belongs.* Then, if the child slips, send him an "I-message."

When Children Have Been Accustomed to Winning

Frequently parents who have relied heavily on Method II report difficulties in switching over to Method III because their children, accustomed to getting their way most of the time, strongly resist becoming involved in a problem-solving method that might require them to give a little, cooperate, or compromise. Such children are so used to winning at the expense of their parents' losing that they are naturally reluctant to give up this advantageous competitive position. In such families, when the parents initially encounter strong resistance to the no-lose method, they sometimes get scared off and give up trying to make it work. Often they are parents who gravitated to Method II because of fear of their children's anger or tears.

A change to Method III for previously permissive parents will therefore require of them much more strength and firmness than they have been accustomed to exhibiting with their children. These parents need somehow to find a new source of strength in order to move away from their previous "peace at any price" posture. It often helps to remind them of the terrible price they will have to pay in the future if their kids always win. They have to be convinced that they as parents have rights, too. Or they must be reminded that their usual giving in to the child has made him selfish and inconsiderate. Parents like this need some convincing that parenthood can be a joy when their needs are met, too. They must *want* to change, and they must be prepared to get a lot of static from the child when they change over to Method III. During the period of changing over, the parents must also be ready to handle feelings with the skill of active listening and send their own feelings, using good, clear "I-messages."

In one family the parents had difficulties with a thirteen-year-old daughter accustomed to getting her own way. On their first attempt to use Method III, when it appeared to the girl that she was not getting her way, she threw a temper tantrum and ran back to her room in tears. Instead of either consoling her or ignoring her, as they usually had done, the father ran after her and said, "I'm darned angry at you right now! Here we bring up something that is bothering your Mother and me and you run away! That really feels to me like you don't give a darn about our needs. I don't like that! I think it's unfair. We want this problem solved now. We don't want you to lose, but we sure are not going to be the ones to lose while you win. I think we can find a solution so we'll both win, but we can't for sure unless you come back to the table. Now will you join me back at the table so we can find a good solution?"

After drying her tears, the daughter came back with her father and in a few minutes they arrived at a solution that was satisfactory to the child and the parents. Never again did the daughter run out on a problem-solving session. She stopped trying to exercise control with her anger when it was clear that her parents were through letting her control them in this way.

THE NO-LOSE METHOD
FOR CHILD-CHILD CONFLICTS

Most parents approach the inevitable and all-too-frequent child-child conflicts with the same win-lose orientation they use in parent-child conflicts. Parents feel they have to play the role of judge, referee, or umpire—*they* assume the responsibility for getting facts, determining who is right and who is wrong, and deciding what the solution should be. This orientation has some serious drawbacks and generally results in unhappy consequences for all concerned. The no-lose method is generally more effective in resolving such conflicts and much easier on parents. It also plays an important part in influencing children to become more mature, more responsible, more independent, more self-disciplined.

When parents approach child-child conflicts as judges or referees, they are making the mistake of assuming *ownership* of the problem. By moving in as problem-solvers, they deny children the opportunity to assume the responsibility for owning their own conflicts and to learn how to resolve them through their own efforts. This prevents their children from growing and maturing and may leave them forever dependent on some authority to resolve their conflicts *for* them. From the standpoint of parents, the worst effect of the win-lose approach is that their kids will continue to bring all their conflicts to the parents. Instead of solving their conflicts themselves, they run to the parent to settle their fights and their disagreements:

"Mommy, Jimmy is teasing me—make him stop."

"Daddy, Maggie won't let me play with the clay."

"I want to sleep but Frankie keeps talking. Tell him to be quiet."

"He hit me first, it's his fault. I didn't do anything to him."

Such "appeals to authority" are common in most families because parents allow themselves to be sucked into *their children's* fights.

In P.E.T. it takes some convincing to get parents to accept these fights as their children's fights, and that *the kids own the problem.* Most fights and conflicts between children belong in the area of PROBLEMS OWNED BY THE CHILD, the upper area of our diagram:

Problems Owned by the Child
No problems
Problems Owned by the Parent

If parents can remember to locate these conflicts where they belong, then they can handle them with the appropriate methods:

1. Staying out of the conflict completely.
2. Door-openers, invitations to talk.
3. Active listening.

Jimmy and Tommy, who are brothers, are both tugging on the toy truck, one on the front, the other on the back. Both are shouting and screaming; one is crying. *Each is trying to use his power to get his way.* If parents stay out of this conflict, the boys may find some way of resolving it themselves. If so, well and good; they have been given the chance to learn how to solve their problems independently. By staying out of the conflict, the parents have helped both boys grow up a little.

If the boys continue to fight and the parent feels it would be helpful to move in to facilitate *their* problem-solving, a door-opener or invitation is often helpful. Here is how:

JIMMY: I want the truck! Gimme the truck! Let go! Let go!

TOMMY: I had it first! He came in and took it away. I want it back!

PARENT: I see you really have a conflict about the truck. Do you want to come here and talk about it? I'd like to help if you want to discuss it.

Sometimes, just such a door-opener brings an end to the conflict immediately. It is as if children sometimes would rather find some solution *themselves* rather than go through the process of working it out through discussion in the presence of a parent. They think, "Oh, it really isn't that big a deal."

Some conflicts may require a more active role on the part of the parent. In such cases, the parent can encourage problem-solving by using active listening and turning into a transmission belt, not a referee. It works like this:

JIMMY: I want the truck! Gimme the truck! Let go! Let go!

PARENT: Jimmy, you really want that truck.

TOMMY: But I had it first! He came in and took it away. I want it back!

PARENT: Tommy, you feel you should have the truck because

you had it first. You're mad at Jimmy because he took it away from you. I can see you really have a conflict here. Is there any way you can see of solving this problem? Got any ideas?

TOMMY: He should let me have it.

PARENT: Jimmy, Tommy is suggesting that solution.

JIMMY: Yeah, he would, 'cause then he'd get his way.

PARENT: Tommy, Jimmy is saying he doesn't like that solution 'cause you'd win and he'd lose.

TOMMY: Well, I'd let him play with my cars until I get through with the truck.

PARENT: Jimmy, Tommy is suggesting another solution—you can play with his cars while he plays with the truck.

JIMMY: Do I get to play with the truck when he's through, Mom?

PARENT: Tommy, Jimmy wants to make sure you'll let him play with the truck when you're through.

TOMMY: Okay. I'll be through pretty soon.

PARENT: Jimmy, Tommy is saying that's okay with him.

JIMMY: Okay, then.

PARENT: I guess you've both solved this problem, then, right?

Parents have reported many such successful resolutions of conflicts between children, with the parent first suggesting the no-lose method and then facilitating communication between the combatants by active listening. Those parents who have difficulty believing that they can involve their children in the no-lose approach need to be reminded that in the absence of adults children often resolve their conflicts with the no-lose method—at school, on the playground, in games and sports, and elsewhere. When an adult is present, and lets himself be drawn in as judge or referee, kids are inclined to use that adult—each appealing to the adult's authority to try to win at the expense of the other child losing.

Usually parents welcome the no-lose method for resolving child-child conflicts, because almost all have had bad experiences trying to solve their children's fights. Invariably, when a parent tries to resolve a conflict, one kid feels the parent's decision is unfair and reacts with resentment and hostility toward the parent. Sometimes parents incur the wrath of both children, perhaps by denying both children what they were fighting for ("Now neither one of you can play with the truck!")

Many parents, after they try the no-lose approach and keep responsibility with the kids for working out their own solution, tell us how terribly relieved they are to find a way of staying out of the role of judge or referee. They tell us: "It's such a relief to feel I don't have to settle their arguments. I always used to end up being the bad guy no matter how I decided."

Another predictable outcome of getting kids to resolve their own conflicts with the no-lose method is that they gradually stop bringing their fights and disagreements to their parents. They learn after awhile that going to the parent only means they are going to end up finding their own solution anyway. Consequently, they drop this old habit and start resolving their conflicts independently. Few parents can resist the appeal of this outcome.

WHEN BOTH PARENTS ARE
INVOLVED IN PARENT-CHILD CONFLICTS

Sticky problems are sometimes encountered in families when they come up against conflicts with kids in which both parents have a stake.

Everyone on His Own

It is essential that each parent enters into no-lose problem-solving as a "free agent." They should not expect to have a "united front" or to be on the same side of every conflict, although on occasion this might happen. The essential ingredient in no-lose problem-solving is that each parent be real—each must represent accurately his or her own feelings and needs. Each parent is a separate and unique participant in conflict-resolution and should think of problem-solving as a process involving three or more separate persons, not parents aligned against children.

Some solutions under consideration during problem-solving may be acceptable to Mom and unacceptable to Dad. Sometimes Dad and his teen-age son may be together on a particular issue and Mom may take an opposing point of view. Sometimes Mom may be aligned closer to her son while Dad is pushing for a different solution. Sometimes Mom and Dad will be close in their positions and the teen-ager's point of view is at variance with theirs. Sometimes each participant will find himself at odds with the others. Families that practice the no-lose method discover that all these combinations occur, depending on the nature of the conflict. The key to no-lose conflict-resolution is that these differences get worked through until a solution is reached that is acceptable to everyone.

In our classes we have learned from parents what types of conflicts most commonly bring out marked differences between fathers and mothers:

1. Fathers most frequently side with kids on conflicts involving possible physical injury to kids. Fathers seem to accept more than mothers the inevitability of kids getting hurt sometimes.
2. Mothers more frequently than fathers seem to side with their daughter's readiness to move into boy-girl relationships and all that goes with that: make-up, dates, style of dress, phone calls, and so on. Fathers frequently resist seeing their daughters move into dating young men.
3. Fathers and mothers often disagree on issues involving the family car.

4. Mothers usually have higher standards than fathers about neatness and cleanliness of the home.

The point is that mothers and fathers are different, and these differences, if each parent is to be real and honest, will inevitably emerge in conflicts between parents and their children. By airing honest differences between mothers and fathers in conflict-resolution—allowing their human-ness to show and be seen by their kids—parents discover that they receive from them a new kind of respect and affection. In this respect, kids are no different from adults—they, too, grow to love those who are human and they learn to distrust those who are not. They want their parents to be real, not playing a role of "parents," always voicing agreement with each other whether the agreement is real or not.

One Parent Using Method III, The Other Not

We are often asked in P.E.T. whether it is possible for one parent to resolve conflicts by the no-lose Method III approach while the other does not. The question comes up in our classes because not all participants enroll with their spouses even though we strongly urge that both parents enroll.

In some cases where only one parent is committed to change to the no-lose method, perhaps a mother, she simply starts resolving all her conflicts with the kids by using the no-lose method and permits the father to continue using Method I in his conflicts. This may not cause too many problems, except that the children, fully aware of the difference, often complain to the father that they no longer like his approach and wish he would solve problems the way their mother does. Some fathers respond to these complaints by enrolling in a subsequent P.E.T. class. Typical of such fathers is the one who showed up at the first session of a

P.E.T. class and admitted:

> "I'm here tonight in self-defense, I guess, because I began to see what good results my wife was getting with her new methods. Her relationship with the kids has improved and mine has not. They talk to her but they won't talk to me."

Another father, at the first session of the class in which he enrolled after his wife had been in a previous class, made this comment:

> "I want to tell you women who are taking this course without your husbands what you might expect from him. As you start using the new methods of listening and confronting and problem-solving with the children, he is going to feel hurt, left out. He will feel his role as a father is being taken away from him. You will be getting results, but he can't. I lashed out at my wife and said, 'What do you expect of me—I'm not taking the damn course.' Do you understand why I say now that I can't afford not to take the course?"

Some fathers who do not learn the new skills and remain content with their Method I approach are often given a bad time by their wives. One wife told us that she began to build up resentments and ended up being quite hostile toward her husband because she could not stand watching him resolve conflicts with power. "I see now just how much harm to the children Method I produces, and I just cannot sit by and watch him hurt the kids this way," she told the class. Another said, "I can see he is ruining his relationship with the kids and that makes me feel disappointed and sad. They need their relationship with him, but it is going down the drain rapidly."

Some mothers enlist the help of class members in P.E.T. to generate the courage to confront their husbands openly and honestly. I recall one attractive young mother who in class was helped to see how much she herself actually feared her husband and therefore had avoided confronting him with her feelings about using Method I. Somehow, by discussing this in P.E.T., she gained enough courage to go home and tell him the feelings she had identified in class:

> "I love my kids too much to stand by and see them hurt by you. I know what I have learned in P.E.T. is better for the kids and I want you to learn these methods, too. I've always been afraid of you and I can see you're doing the same to the kids."

The effects of her confrontation astonished this mother. For the first time in their relationship, he heard her out. He told her he hadn't realized how much he had dominated both her and the children, and subsequently agreed to enroll in the next P.E.T. class in their community.

It does not always work out as favorably as in this family, when one parent continues to use Method I. I am certain that in some families this problem never does get resolved. While we seldom hear about it, it is likely that some husbands and wives never do come together in their methods of resolving conflicts, or in some cases a parent who has been trained in P.E.T. methods may even return to her old ways under pressure of a spouse who refuses to give up using power to resolve conflicts.

"CAN WE USE ALL THREE METHODS?"

We occasionally encounter a parent who accepts the validity and believes in the effectiveness of the no-lose approach, yet is not willing to give up the' two win-lose approaches.

"Won't a good parent use a judicious mixture of all three methods, depending on the nature of the problem?" asked a father in one of my classes.

While understandable in view of some parents' fear of giving up all of their power over their children, this point of view is not tenable. As it is not possible "to be a little bit pregnant," it is not possible to be a little bit democratic in parent-child conflicts. In the first place, most parents who want to use a combination of all three methods really mean that they want to reserve the right to use Method I for the truly critical conflicts. Translated into simple language their attitude is: "On matters that are not too important to the children I will let them have a voice in the decision, but I will reserve the right to decide my way on issues that are very critical."

Our experience seeing parents try this mixed approach is that it simply does not work. Children, once given a taste of how good it feels to resolve conflicts without losing, resent it when the parent reverts back to Method I. Or they may lose all interest in entering into Method III on *unimportant problems* because they feel so resentful of losing on *the more important problems*.

A further outcome of the "judicious mixture" approach is that kids acquire a distrust of their parent when Method III is tried, because they have learned that when the chips are down and the parent has strong feelings on a problem, he will end up winning anyway. So, why should they enter into problem-solving? Anytime it gets to be a real conflict, they know Dad is going to use his power to win anyway.

Some parents muddle through by occasionally using Method I for problems where the kids do not have strong feelings—the less critical problems—but Method III should *always* be used when a conflict is critical, involving strong feelings and convictions on the part of the kids. Perhaps it is a principle in all human relationships that *when one doesn't care much about the outcome of a conflict, one may be willing to give in to another's power; but when one has a real stake in the outcome one wants to make sure to have a voice in the decision-making.*

DOES THE NO-LOSE METHOD
EVER FAIL TO WORK?

The answer to this question is, "of course." In our classes we have encountered some parents who for various reasons cannot put Method III to work effectively. While we have not made a systematic study of this group, their participation in class often reveals why they are unsuccessful.

Some are too frightened to give up their power; the idea of using Method III threatens their long-standing values and beliefs about the necessity of authority and power in bringing up children. Often these parents have a very distorted perception of the nature of man. To them, human beings cannot be trusted and they are sure that removing authority will only result in their children becoming savage, selfish monsters. Most of these parents never even try to use Method III.

Some of the unsuccessful parents have reported that their children simply refused to enter into no-lose problem-solving. Usually these have been older teen-agers who already have written off their parents or who are so bitter and angry at their parents that Method III appears to them to give far more to their parents than they deserve. I have seen some of these youngsters in private therapy, and I must admit that I have frequently felt that the best thing for them would be to find the courage to break away from their parents, leave home, and search for new relationships that might be more satisfying. One perceptive boy, a high-school senior, came to the conclusion on his own that his mother would never change. Having become very familiar with what is taught in

P.E.T. by virtue of his reading his parent's class notebook, this bright teen-ager shared with me these feelings:

"My mother is never going to change. She never uses the methods you teach in P.E.T. I guess I'll just have to stop hoping that she will change. It's a pity, but she is beyond help. Now, I have to find a way of earning my own living, so that I can leave home."

It is apparent to all of us in the P.E.T. program that an eight-week course does not change all parents—particularly those who have practiced their ineffective methods for fifteen or more years. For some of these parents, the program fails to produce a turn-around. This is why we feel so strongly about parents learning this new philosophy of child-rearing when their children are young. As in all human relationships, some parent-child relationships can become so fractured and deteriorated that they may be beyond repair.

14

How to Avoid Being Fired As a Parent

More and more often, children fire their parents. As they move into adolescence kids dismiss their mothers and fathers, write them off, sever their relationship with them. It is happening today in thousands of families, irrespective of social and economic class. By the droves, youngsters are leaving their parents, physically or psychologically, to find more satisfing relationships elsewhere, usually with groups of their peers.

Why is this happening? I am convinced by my experience in working with thousands of parents in P.E.T. that these kids have been driven out of their families by the behavior of their parents—a certain specific kind of behavior. Parents get fired by their kids when they hassle and harangue them to change cherished beliefs and values. Adolescents dismiss their parents when they feel they are being denied their basic civil rights.

Parents lose their opportunity to have a constructive influence on their children by too desperately and too persistently trying to influence them where kids are the most eager to determine their own beliefs and their own destiny. Here, as in our classes, I will examine this critical problem and offer specific methods for avoiding being fired as parents over these issues.

While the no-lose method can be dramatically effective when parents acquire the skills to put it to work, there are certain inevitable conflicts that parents *should not expect to be resolved,* even with skillful use of this method, because they are often not amenable to Method III problem-solving. And if parents try to involve their youngsters in conflict-resolution for these problems, they will more than likely fail. Getting parents to understand and accept this is a difficult task in P.E.T., because it requires giving up some age-old ideas and beliefs about the role of the parent in our society.

When family conflicts occur over issues involving cherished values, beliefs, and personal tastes, parents may have to handle these differently, because frequently kids are not willing to put these issues on the bargaining table or enter into problem-solving. This does *not* mean parents need to give up trying to influence their children by teaching them values. But to be effective, they will have to use a different approach.

A QUESTION OF VALUES

Conflicts inevitably arise between a parent and child over behaviors that are intricately related to a child's beliefs, values, style, preferences, philosophy of life. Take long hair as an initial example. For most boys today long hair has important symbolic meaning. It is not necessary for a parent to understand all components of the symbolic meaning of long hair; it *is* essential to recognize how important it is for a son to wear his hair long. *He values long hair.* It means something very important to him. He *prefers* long hair—in a sense, he *needs* to wear his hair long; he doesn't just want to.

Attempts by parents to frustrate this need, or strong efforts to take away from him what has strong value for him, will almost inevitably be met with tenacious resistance. Long hair is an expression of the youngster doing *his own thing, living his own life, acting out his own values and beliefs.*

Try to influence your son to cut his long hair and he will most likely tell you:

> "It's my hair."
> "I like it this way."
> "Get off my back."
> "I have a right to wear *my* hair the way *I* want it."
> "It's not affecting you in any way."
> "I don't tell you how to wear your hair, so don't tell me how to wear mine."

These messages, properly decoded, communicate to the parent "I feel I have a right to my value as long as I cannot see how it affects you in any tangible or concrete way." Assuming it were my own son, I would have to say he is right. How long he wears his hair in no conceivable way tangibly or concretely interferes with my meeting my own needs: it won't get me fired, it won't reduce my income, it won't stop me from having friends or making new ones, it won't make me a worse golfer, it won't prevent me from writing this book or practicing my profession, and it certainly will not prevent me from wearing *my* hair short. It won't even cost me money (in fact, it will cost me less money if I have been paying for his haircuts).

Yet, many behaviors, such as the way a boy wears his hair, are taken over by most parents and made into problems they feel they *"own."* Here is how it worked out for one parent who came to a P.E.T. class.

PARENT: I simply cannot stand your hair being so long. You look terrible. Why don't you get it cut?

SON: I like it this way.

PARENT: You can't be serious. You look like a hippie.

SON: So what?

PARENT: We've got to resolve this conflict someway. I can't accept your hair this way. What can we do?

SON: It's my hair and I'll wear it the way I want.

PARENT: Why don't you cut it a little bit, anyway?

SON: I don't tell you how to wear your hair, do I?

PARENT: No. But then I don't look like a slob.

SON: Come on now, I don't look like a slob. My friends like it—particularly the girls.

PARENT: I don't care, it disgusts me.

SON: Well, don't look at me then.

Obviously, the boy is not willing to enter into conflict-resolution about his hair because, as he puts it, "It's my hair." The final outcome, if the parent persists in pursuing the hair problem, is that the boy will withdraw—he will turn his parent off, walk away, get out of the house, or go to his room.

Parents nevertheless move in persistently to modify such behavior and this intervention almost invariably causes fights, resistance, and resentment from the children, and usually a serious deterioration of the parent-child relationship.

When children strongly resist attempts to modify behavior that they feel won't interfere with the parents' needs, their behavior is no different from that of adults. No adult wants to modify his behavior when his is convinced that it is not hurting someone else. Adults as well as children will fight vigorously to maintain their freedom when they feel someone is pushing them to change behavior that is not interfering with the other person.

This is one of the most serious mistakes parents make and one of the most frequent reasons for their ineffectiveness. If parents would limit their attempts to modify behavior to what interferes with the parents' needs, there would be far less rebellion, fewer conflicts, and fewer parent-child relationships that go sour. Most parents unwisely criticize, cajole, and harass their children to modify behaviors that have no tangible or concrete effect on the parent. In defense, children fight back, resist, rebel, or break away.

Not infrequently, kids react by overdoing the very things their parents are pressuring them not to do, as so often happens in the case of long hair. Other children, out of fear of parental authority, may give in to their parent's pressures but harbor deep resentment or hatred toward the parent for making them change.

Much of the rebellion of today's adolescents—their protests, their sit-ins, their fights against "the Establishment" —can be attributed to parents and other adults who put pressures on them to modify behavior that the kids feel is their own business.

Children do not rebel against *adults*—they rebel against adults' *attempts to take away their freedom.* They rebel against efforts to change them or mold them in the adults' image, against adults' harassment, against adults' forcing them to act according to what the adults think is right or wrong.

Tragically, when parents use their influence to try to modify behavior that does *not* interfere with the parents' own lives, they lose their influence to modify behavior that *does* interfere. My experience with children of all ages is that they are usually quite willing to modify their behavior when it is clear to them that *what they are doing does in fact interfere with someone else's meeting his needs.* When parents limit their attempts to modify children's behavior to what tangibly and concretely affects them, they generally find children quite open to change, willing to respect the needs of their parents, and agreeable to "problem-solve."

Styles of dress—like long hair—have tremendous symbolic value for kids. In my day it was faded yellow corduroy pants and dirty (always *very* dirty) saddle shoes. I remember it was a ritual for me, on buying new saddle shoes, to rub them with dirt before I would even consider wearing them. Today it's dirty jeans, ponchos, beads, open-toed sandals, Ben Franklin glasses, mini-skirts, no bras, and so on.

How I fought for my right to wear those corduroys and saddle shoes! I needed those symbols very much. Most importantly, my parents could not make a logical case that my wearing them tangibly and concretely affected them.

There are times when a child will understand and accept the fact that his way of dressing will have a tangible and concrete effect on his parents. An example is that of Jane and the plaid "raincoat problem," which I have cited repeatedly. In this situation it was clear to Jane that if she walked the several blocks to the bus without suitable protection from the rain, her clothes would then require dry cleaning or she might get a cold that would require her parents to buy medicine or spend time nursing her at home.

A second example of a problem amenable to no-lose problem-solving was the conflict over my daughter's wish to go to Newport Beach unchaperoned over the Easter weekend. In this case it was clear to her that we might lose sleep worrying or that we might be called out in the middle of the night if she happened to be in a group of kids that got hauled into Juvenile Court.

Even conflict over a son's long hair in rare instances might be amenable to problem-solving, as in one family I know. The father was a school principal. He felt that his job might be jeopardized in this conservative community, if people took his son's long hair as evidence that the father was too liberal for the job. In this family the son accepted this as a tangible and concrete effect of his long hair on his father's life. He agreed to trim his hair considerably shorter out of a genuine concern for his father's needs.

This might not have been the outcome in another family in

the same circumstances. The point is, *the child must accept the logic that his behavior is having a tangible and concrete effect on the parent.* Only then will he be willing to enter into no-lose problem-solving. The lesson for parents is that they had better be able to make a good case for some particular behavior having a tangible or concrete effect on their lives, or the child may not be willing to negotiate.

Here are other behaviors that some parents told us were not accepted as negotiable because their kids could not be convinced that their behavior would affect their parents in any tangible or concrete way:

> Teen-age daughter liking mini-skirts.
>
> Teen-age son wearing faded jeans and beat-up sneakers.
>
> Adolescent who preferred a group of friends his parents did not like.
>
> A child who dawdled when he did homework.
>
> Child wanting to quit college and become a pop musician.
>
> Teen-age girl who dressed hippie fashion.
>
> Four-year-old who still carried around his blanket.
>
> Daughter who wanted to get her ears pierced.
>
> Daughter who liked heavy eye shadow.
>
> Child who got in trouble with teachers by his clowning in class.
>
> Youngster who refused to go to church.

Method III is obviously not a method for molding children to suit parents. If parents try to use the method for this purpose, it is a sure bet that the children will see through it and resist. Parents then run the risk of killing any chance to use it on problems that do affect them—such as the children not doing chores, making excessive noise, destroying property, driving Dad's car too fast, leaving their clothes around the house, not wiping their dirty feet before coming into the house, monopolizing the TV set, not cleaning up the kitchen after making snacks, not putting Dad's tools back in the tool box, trampling through the flower garden, and countless other behaviors.

A QUESTION OF CIVIL RIGHTS

Parent-child battles over hair and other behaviors that kids feel do not tangibly or concretely affect their parents involve a question of *youth's civil rights*. They feel they have *a right* to wear their hair their own way, choose their own friends, wear their own kind of clothes, and so on. And youth today, as in other times, will defend this right tenaciously.

Youths, like adults or groups or nations, will fight to preserve their own rights. They will resist with all the resources they can muster any attempt to take away their freedom or their autonomy. These are important things to them, not to be negotiated or compromised or problem-solved away.

Why don't parents see this? Why don't parents understand that their sons and daughters are human beings and that *it is human nature to fight for freedom* whenever it is threatened by another? Why do parents fail to understand that we are dealing with something very basic and fundamental here—man's need to preserve his freedom? Why don't parents comprehend that civil rights must begin at home?

One reason why parents seldom think of their children as having civil rights is the widespread attitude that parents "own" their children. Holding this attitude, parents justify their efforts to mold their children, shape them, indoctrinate them, modify them, control them, brainwash them. Granting children civil rights or certain inalienable freedoms presupposes viewing children as separate human beings or independent persons, having *a life of their own*. Not many parents see their children this way when they first enter P.E.T. They have difficulty accepting our principle of allowing the child freedom to become what he wants to become, provided his behavior does not tangibly and concretely interfere with the parent becoming what he wants to become.

"CAN'T I TEACH MY VALUES?"

This is one of the most frequently asked questions in P.E.T., for most parents have a strong need to transmit their most cherished values to their offspring. Our answer is: "Of course—not only *can* you teach your values but inevitably you *will*." Parents cannot help but teach kids their values, simply because children are bound to learn their parents' values by observing what their mothers and fathers do, and hearing what they say.

The Parent as a Model

Parents, like many other adults with whom children will come into contact as they grow up, will be *models* for them. Parents are continuously modeling for their offspring—demonstrating by their actions, even louder than by their words, what they value or believe.

Parents *can* teach their values by actually living them. If they want their children to value honesty, parents must daily demonstrate their own honesty. If they want their children to value generosity, they must behave generously. If they want their children to adopt "Christian" values, they must behave like Christians themselves. This is the best way, perhaps the *only* way, for parents to "teach" children their values.

"Do as I say, not as I do" is not an effective approach in teaching kids their parents' values. "Do as I *do*", however, may have a high probability of modifying or influencing a child.

Parents who want children to be honest, will defeat their purposes if, when receiving an unwanted invitation over the phone, they lie in front of the children: "Oh, we'd love to come but we're expecting out-of-town guests." Or if Dad mentions at the dinner table how clever he was in padding his deductible expenses on his income-tax return. Or if Mother cautions her teen-age daughter, "Now let's not say anything to Dad about how much I paid for the new lamp." Or if both parents do not tell their kids the whole truth about life, about sex, about religion.

Parents who want children to value nonviolence in human relations, will seem like hypocrites when they use physical punishment to "discipline." I recall a poignant cartoon depicting a father paddling his son over his knee, shouting, "I hope this teaches you not to go around hitting your baby brother!"

Parents teach children values by *living their own lives accordingly*, not by *pressuring kids to live by certain rules*. I firmly believe that one of the principal reasons why adolescents today are protestingly rejecting many of the values of adult society is that they have detected how adults in so many ways, fail to practice what they preach. To their dismay, kids discover that their high-school textbooks do not tell the whole truth about our government and its history or that their teachers lie by omission of some of the facts of life. They cannot help feeling angry at adults who preach certain principles of sexual morality when they have been exposed on TV to movies and serials portraying adult sexual behavior that is inconsistent with the morality they espouse for their children.

Yes, parents can teach their values, if they live them. But how many parents do? Teach your values, yes you may, but by example, not by verbal persuasion or by parental authority. Teach whatever you have valued for *yourself,* but by being a model who practices his values.

What troubles parents is that their offspring *might not buy their values.* This is true—they may not. They may not like some values of the parents, or they may correctly see that some values held by parents produce results that kids don't like (as in the case of some of today's youth who reject patriotism because they see it as a value that produces behavior that often leads to war).

When they fear that youth might not buy their values, parents always fall back on the rationalization that they are justified in using their power to impose their values on their children. "They are too young to judge for themselves" is the most frequently expressed justification for imposing values on children.

Is it even *possible* to impose values on another healthy person by power and authority? I think not. More likely, the result is that those whose minds one wishes to influence will resist even more strongly such domination, often defending their beliefs and values all the more tenaciously. Power and authority may control the *actions* of others; they seldom control their *thoughts, ideas, beliefs.*

The Parent as a Consultant

In addition to influencing children's values by modeling, parents can use one other approach to teach what they feel is "right or wrong." They may *share with their offspring* their ideas, their knowledge and their experience, much as a consultant does when his services are requested by a client. There is a catch here. The successful consultant *shares* rather than preaches, *offers* rather than imposes, *suggests* rather than demands. Even more critical, the successful consultant shares, offers, and suggests usually no more than *once.* The effective consultant offers his clients the benefit of his knowledge and experience, yes, but does not hassle them week after week, does not shame them if they don't buy his ideas, does not keep pushing his point of view when he detects resistance on the part of his client. The successful consultant offers his ideas, then *leaves responsibility with his client for buying or rejecting them.* If a consultant behaved as most parents do, his client would inform him that his services were no longer desired.

Today's youth are discharging their parents—informing them that their services are no longer desired—because few parents are effective consultants to their kids. They lecture, cajole, threaten, warn, persuade, implore, preach, moralize, and shame their kids, all in an effort to force them to do what they feel is right. Parents go back to their kids day after day after day with their instructional or moralizing messages. They do not allow the child the responsibility for buying or rejecting, but assume responsibility themselves for the learning of their children. As consultants, most parents' attitude is that *their clients must buy;* if the clients don't, they feel they have failed.

Parents are guilty of the "hard sell." No wonder that in most families kids are desperately saying to their parents, "Get off my back," "Stop hassling me," "I know what you think, you don't need to keep telling me every day," "Stop lecturing me," "Too much." "Goodbye."

The lesson for parents is that they *can* be helpful consultants to their children—they can share their ideas, experience, wisdom—if they remember to act like an *effective* consultant so they do not get fired by the clients whom they wish to help.

If you believe you have some useful knowledge about the effects of cigarettes on the health of humans, tell your kids about it. If you feel religion has been an important influence in your life, tell your kids about it sometime. If you run across a good article about the effects of drugs on young people's lives, hand the magazine to your kids or read it out loud to the family. If you have data about the value of going to college, share it with the kids. If you learned in your youth how to make homework less irksome, offer your method to your kids. If you think you are an expert on the problem of premarital sex, report your findings to your kids at an appropriate time.

One further suggestion is based on my own experience as a consultant, when I learned that my *most valuable* tool in working with my clients was active listening. As I offered new ideas, my clients almost always reacted initially with resistance and defensiveness, in part because my ideas usually ran contrary to their own beliefs or habit patterns. When I could listen actively to these feelings, they generally disappeared and the new ideas were eventually adopted. Parents who want to teach kids their beliefs and values must be alert to resistance to their teaching, sensitive to objections to their ideas. When you hear resistance, don't forget active listening. It will come in handy when you are being a consultant to your kids.

So to parents in P.E.T. and parents reading this book, we say, "Sure, you can try to teach kids your values, but stop selling so hard!" State them clearly, but stop hammering! Share them generously, but no preaching. Offer them confidently, but don't impose them. Then retire gracefully and allow your "clients" to decide whether they will buy or reject your ideas. And don't forget to use active listening! If you do these things, your children might ask for your services again. They might put you on a retainer, convinced that you can be a helpful consultant for them. They just might not want to fire you.

"To Accept What I Cannot Change"

Readers may remember somebody's prayer that has been quoted often. I think it goes like this:

> Lord, grant me the courage to change what I can change;
>
> The serenity to accept what I cannot change;
>
> And the wisdom to know the difference.

"The serenity to accept what I cannot change" is relevant to what I have just been dealing with. For there are many behaviors of children that parents simply may not be able to change. The only alternative is to accept this fact.

Many parents strongly resist our idea of being just consultants to their children. They say:

> "But I have a responsibility to see to it that my child does not smoke cigarettes.
>
> "I must use my authority to prevent my daughter having premarital intercourse."
>
> "I'm not willing to act only as a consultant on smoking pot. I must do more to prevent my kids from this temptation."
>
> "I will not be satisfied letting my child not do his homework every night."

It is understandable that many parents feel so strongly about certain behaviors that they do not want to give up trying to influence their children, but a more objective view usually convinces them that they have no other feasible alternative except to give up—to accept what they cannot change.

Take cigarette smoking as an example. Assume that the parents have given their teen-ager all the facts (their own bad experience with the habit, the U.S. Public Health Report, magazine articles). Now, suppose the youngster still chooses to smoke. What can the parents do? If they try prohibiting him from smoking in the house, he will undoubtedly smoke when he is away from the house (and possibly smoke at home, too, when the parents are not there). Obviously they cannot accompany the child whenever he leaves the house, nor stay at home whenever he is at home. Even if they catch him smoking, what can they possibly do? If they ground him, he will simply wait until the grounding period is over and start smoking again. Theoretically, they might try threatening expulsion from the family, but few parents are willing to try such an extreme measure, realizing that they could end up having to follow through on their threat. So, in fact, parents have no feasible alternative than to accept their inability to make their teen-ager stop smoking. One parent stated her dilemma accurately when she said, "The only way I could stop my daughter from smoking would be to chain her to the bed post."

Homework, a problem that brings conflict in many families, is another example. What can parents do if the child won't do his homework? If they make him go to his room he will probably play his radio or "mess around" doing anything but homework. The point is, you just cannot make someone study or learn. "You can lead a horse to water but you can't make him drink" applies equally to making a child do his homework.

Well, what about premarital sex? The same principle applies here. It is impossible for parents to supervise their adolescent daughter all the time. A father in one of my P.E.T. classes admitted, "I might as well stop trying to prevent my daughter from premarital sex experience, because I sure can't 'ride shot gun' in the backseat of the car everytime she has a date."

Other behaviors can be added to our list of things that parents may have no power to change. Heavy make-up, drinking, getting into trouble at school, associating with certain kids, having dates with members of another race or religion, smoking grass, and so on. All a parent can do is to try to influence by being a model, being an effective consultant, and developing a "therapeutic" relationship with the kids. After that, what else? As I see it, a parent can only accept the fact that he ultimately has no power to prevent such behaviors, if the child is bent on doing them.

Maybe this is one of the prices for being a parent. You can *do* your best, then *hope* for the best, but in the long run you run the risk that your best efforts might not be good enough. Ultimately you, too, may then ask, "Lord, grant me . . . the serenity to accept what I cannot change."

THE DIVIDED-SHEET METHOD
FOR STARTING NO-LOSE PROBLEM-SOLVING

In families where parents have been using Method I or have been hassling and nagging their kids a lot about behavior that does not tangibly and concretely affect them, it is often difficult to start no-lose problem-solving because the relationships with the kids have deteriorated so much. The kids are already angry at their parents, they feel very defensive about any kind of intervention by the parents, and they are suspicious of any new attempt to modify their behavior. Then, when the parents approach them and suggest a session to try to resolve their conflicts, the kids either refuse to get involved or go into the session determined to scuttle the parents' newest effort to rob them of their freedom.

In P.E.T. we designed a surprisingly simple method for overcoming the resistance and distrust that kids bring to a problem-solving session. All parents need is a pen and a sheet of paper divided into two columns by a line drawn down the middle. The parents can start the session by saying something like:

> "We want to try a new way of resolving the con-
> flicts we have between us. In the past we have often

won and you lost, or you won and we lost. Now we would like to try to find solutions to our conflicts that would be acceptable to all of us—so no one loses. The rule in this new approach is that whatever we decide must be acceptable to everyone, and we will keep looking for solutions until we find one that we will all buy and be willing to carry it out.

"I've brought a sheet of paper divided down the middle. We'll list our problems and conflicts on this sheet as they are brought up by any of us. In the left column I'll write those conflicts we've had about behavior of you kids that really does not tangibly or concretely affect us, even though it might have bothered us. One I can think of immediately is your homework. In the right column I'll write down those conflicts we've had about behavior of you kids that really does affect us, things you do that interfere directly with our lives. An example would be your not carrying out the trash.

"When we've completed our list, then we'll promise not to hassle or nag you about any of the problems in the left column. We'll simply throw those problems away—no more bugging you. Take the homework, for example. We agree never to mention it—it will be up to you when you do it, or whether you do it. You are capable of taking care of this yourself.

"But all the problems in the right column will have to be worked out some way so that we come up with a solution for each that is acceptable to all of us—no one loses. Any questions about how we're going to operate here? [After answering questions] Okay, let's start listing the problems—anyone can bring up a problem. Then we'll take each one that's

brought up and decide whether it goes in the right
column or the left."

When families use this method, kids are so amazed and
delighted to have all the problems in the left column thrown
out the window, they then approach those in the right
column much more willing to negotiate, much more motivated to offer solutions, and to agree on one that would meet
the parents' needs as well as their own.

Following is the sheet of problems one family came up
with. In this family, as in most, there were far more problems
in the left column than in the right.

Problems Agreed to be Child's Responsibility (No mutual problem-solving)	Problems That Must Be Problem-Solved
1. His school work—how much he studies, when he studies, whether he studies. 2. How he wears his hair. 3. When he goes to sleep. 4. What he eats. 5. What clothes he wears to school. 6. His choice of his own friends. 7. How often he takes a bath. 8. How he decorates his room. 9. Where he goes when he goes out. 10. How he spends his allowance.	1. How much he contributes to the work required around the house. 2. The problem of allowance and what parents buy and child buys. 3. The problem of parents not being told when child will or will not be home for dinner. 4. The problem of the use of the family car. 5. The problem of the child not cleaning up his mess in the family room.

15

How Parents Can Prevent Conflicts by Modifying Themselves

The last concept that we offer parents is that they can prevent many conflicts between parent and child by changing some of their own attitudes. This idea is presented last because it can be somewhat threatening to parents to be told that sometimes *they* might be the ones who should change, rather than their children. It is far easier for most parents to accept new methods to change their *children* and new methods for modifying the *environment* than to accept the idea of making changes within *themselves*.

Parenthood in our society is considered more a way to influence the growth and development of children than the growth and development of parents. Too often parenthood means "raising" kids; they are the ones to adjust to parents. There are problem *kids*, but not problem *parents*. Supposedly there aren't even problem parent-child relationships.

Yet every parent knows that in his relationships with a spouse, a friend, a relative, a boss or a subordinate there are times when *he* must change in order to prevent serious conflicts or maintain the health of the relationship. Everyone has had the experience of changing his own attitude about someone else's behavior—becoming more accepting of another person's ways by changing his own attitude about the other's behavior. You may have been very upset over a friend's habitual tendency to be late for appointments. Over the years you begin to accept it, maybe chuckle about it, and kid your friend about it. Now you no longer get upset over it; you accept it as one of your friend's characteristics. His *behavior* has not changed. *Your attitude* about his behavior has. *You* have adjusted. *You* have changed.

Parents, too, can change attitudes about the behavior of children.

Peggy's mother became more accepting of her daughter's need to wear her skirts short when she thought back on the period in her own life when she slavishly followed the style of above-the-knee skirts and rolled stockings to the dismay of her own mother.

Jimmy's father became more accepting of his three-year-old son's hyperactivity after he heard in a discussion group with other parents that this kind of behavior was very typical of boys at that age.

A parent would be wise to realize, then, that he can reduce the number of behaviors he finds unacceptable by modifying himself so he becomes more accepting of the behavior of his child or children in general.

This is not as difficult as it may seem. Many parents become far more accepting of children's behavior after their first child, and often even more accepting after their second or third. Parents also can become more accepting of children after reading a book about kids or after hearing a lecture on parent education or after an experience as a youth leader. Direct exposure to children, or even learning about children from the experience of others, can markedly alter a parent's attitude. There are still more significant ways for parents to change so they become more accepting of children.

CAN YOU BECOME MORE ACCEPTING
OF YOURSELF?

Studies show that a direct relationship exists between how accepting people are of others and how accepting they are of themselves. A person who accepts himself as a person is likely to feel a lot of acceptance for others. People who cannot tolerate a lot of things about themselves usually find it difficult to tolerate a lot in others.

A parent needs to ask himself a penetrating question: "How much do I like who I am?"

If the honest answer indicates a lack of acceptance of himself as a person, that parent needs to re-examine his own life to find ways to become more fulfilled from his own achievements. Persons with high self-acceptance and self-regard are generally productive achievers who are using their own talents, who are actualizing their own potential, who accomplish things, who are doers.

Parents who satisfy their own needs through independent productive effort not only accept themselves but also *needn't seek gratification of their needs from the way their children behave.* They don't need their children to turn out in a particular way. People with high self-esteem, resting on a firm foundation of their own independent achievement, are more accepting of their children and the way they behave.

On the other hand, if a parent has few or no sources of satisfaction and self-esteem from his own life and must depend heavily on getting satisfaction from the way others evaluate his children, he is likely to be unaccepting of his children—especially those behaviors that he fears may make him look like a bad parent.

Relying upon this "indirect self-acceptance," such a parent will *need to have his children behave in certain specified ways.* And he is more likely to be unaccepting of them and upset with them when they deviate from his blueprint.

Producing "good children"—high achievers in school, socially successful, competent in athletics, and so on—has become a status symbol for many parents. They "need" to be proud of their children; they need their children to behave in a way that will make them look like good parents to others. In a sense, many parents are *using* their children to bring them a feeling of self-worth and self-esteem. If a parent has no other source of self-worth and self-esteem, which is unhappily true of many mothers in America (and some fathers, too) whose lives are limited to raising "good" children, the stage is set for a dependency on children that makes the parent over-anxious and severely needful that the children behave in particular ways.

WHOSE CHILDREN ARE THEY?

Many parents justify strong attempts to mold their children into a preconceived pattern by saying, "After all, they are *my* children, aren't they?" or "Don't parents have the right to influence *their own* children in whatever way they think best?"

A parent who feels possessive of a child, and therefore feels a right to mold the child in a certain way, will be much more inclined to feel unaccepting of the child's behavior when that behavior deviates from the prescribed mold. A parent who sees a child as someone quite separate and even quite different—not at all "owned" by the parent—is bound to feel accepting toward more of the child's behavior because there is no mold, no preconceived pattern for the child. Such a parent can more readily accept the uniqueness of a child, is more capable of permitting the child to become what he is genetically capable of becoming.

An accepting parent is willing to let a child develop his own "program" for life; a less accepting parent feels a need to program the child's life for him.

Many parents see their children as "extensions of themselves." This often causes a parent to try very hard to influence a child to be what the parent defines as a good child or to become what the parent regretfully failed to become himself. Humanistic psychologists these days talk a lot about "separateness." Evidence is accumulating that in healthy human relationships each person can permit the other to be "separate" from him. The more this attitude of separateness exists, the less the need to change the other, to be intolerant of his uniqueness and unaccepting of differences in his behavior.

In my clinical work with disturbed families and with P.E.T. classes, it frequently is necessary to remind parents: "You have created a life, now let the child have it. Let him decide what he wants to do with the life you gave him." Gibran has phrased this principle beautifully in *The Prophet:*

"Your children are not your children.

They are the sons and daughters of Life's longing for itself.

They come through you but not from you,

And though they are with you, yet they belong not to you.

You may give them your love but not your thoughts,

For they have their own thoughts . . .

You may strive to be like them, but seek not to make them like you.

For life goes not backward nor tarries with yesterday."

Parents *can* modify themselves, and reduce the number of behaviors that are unacceptable to them, by coming to see that their children are not *their* children, not extensions of themselves, but separate, unique. A child has the right to become what he is capable of becoming, no matter how different from the parent or the parent's blueprint for the child. This is his *inalienable* right.

DO YOU REALLY LIKE CHILDREN—OR JUST A CERTAIN TYPE OF CHILD?

I have known parents who profess a liking for children, but who by their behavior clearly demonstrate that they like only certain kinds of children. Fathers who value athletes often tragically reject a son whose interests and talents are nonathletic. Mothers who value physical beauty can reject a daughter who does not fit the cultural stereotype of female beauty. Parents whose lives have been enriched by music often show a nonmusical child how deeply disappointed in him they are. Parents who value academic and scholastic competence can cause irreparable emotional damage in a child who does not have this special type of intelligence.

Fewer behaviors will be unacceptable to parents if they realize that there is an infinite variety of children brought into this world and an infinite variety of ways in life for them to go. The beauty in nature, and the miracle of life, is this vast variety in the living forms.

I often tell parents, "Don't want your child to become something in particular; just want him to become." With such an attitude parents will inevitably find themselves feeling more and more accepting of each child and experiencing joy and excitement watching each become.

ARE YOUR VALUES AND BELIEFS THE ONLY TRUE ONES?

While parents are obviously older and more experienced than their children, it is frequently less obvious that their particular experience or knowledge has given them exclusive access to the truth or provided them with sufficient wisdom to judge always what is right and wrong. "Experience is a good teacher," but it does not always teach what is right;

knowledge is better than ignorance, but a knowledgeable person is not always wise.

It has impressed me to see how many parents in deep trouble in their relationships with their children are persons with very strong and very rigid concepts of what is right and wrong. It follows that *the more certain parents are that their own values and beliefs are right, the more they tend to impose them on their children* (and usually on others, too). It also follows that such parents are apt to be unaccepting of behaviors that appear to deviate from their own values and beliefs.

Parents whose system of values and beliefs is more flexible, more permeable, more amenable to change, less black-or-white, are inclined to be far more accepting of behavior that would appear to deviate from their values and beliefs. Again, it is my observation that such parents are far less likely to impose blueprints or try to mold their children into preconceived patterns. These are the parents who find it easier to accept their son's wearing long hair or beads, even though they may not value these for themselves; who find it easier to accept short skirts, changing patterns of sexual behavior, different styles of clothing, anti-Establishment protests, rebellion against school authority, antiwar demonstrations, or social mixing with children of a different race or cultural heritage. These are the parents who somehow seem to accept that change is inevitable, "that life goes not backward nor tarries with yesterday," that the beliefs and values of one generation are not necessarily those of the next, that our society does need improvements, that some things should be vigorously protested, and that irrational and repressive authority often deserves to be strongly resisted. Parents with such attitudes find much more of the behavior of youth understandable, justified, and genuinely acceptable.

IS YOUR PRIMARY RELATIONSHIP WITH
YOUR SPOUSE?

Many American parents look to their *children* for their
primary relationship, rather than to their *spouse*. Mothers,
particularly, rely heavily on their children to give them
satisfactions and pleasures that more appropriately should
come from the marriage relationship. Frequently this leads to
"putting the children first," "sacrificing for the children," or
counting heavily on the children "turning out well," because
of the parents' heavy investment in the parent-child
relationship. Their children's behavior means *far too much* to
these parents. How the kids behave is too crucial. These parents feel that children must be constantly watched, directed,
guided, monitored, judged, evaluated. It is very difficult for
such parents to allow their children to make mistakes or
stumble in their lives. They feel their children must be
protected against failure experiences, shielded against all
possible danger.

Effective parents are able to have a more casual
relationship with their children. Their marriage relationship
is primary. Their children have a significant place in their
lives, but it is almost a secondary place—if not secondary, at
least no more important than the place of the spouse. Such
parents seem to allow their children much more freedom and
independence. These parents enjoy being with their children
but only for limited times; they also like to spend time alone
with their marriage partner. Their investment is not solely in
their children; it is also in their marriage. How their children
behave or how much they achieve, therefore, is not so critical
to them. They are more apt to feel that the children have their
own lives to live and should be given more freedom to shape
themselves. Such parents seem to correct their children less
frequently and monitor their activities less intensely. They
can be there when the children need them, but they do not

feel strong needs to intervene or push into the lives of the children without being asked. They generally do not neglect their children. They certainly are concerned about them but not anxious. They are interested, but not smothering. "Children are children" is their attitude, so they can be more accepting of what they are—children. Effective parents more often feel amused at their children's immaturity or their foibles, rather than devastated.

The parents in this latter group obviously are inclined to be much more accepting—fewer behaviors will upset them. They will have less need to control, limit, direct, restrict, admonish, preach. They can allow their children more freedom—more separateness. Parents in the first group are inclined to be less accepting. They *need* to control, limit, direct, restrict, and so on. Because their relationship with the children is the primary one, these parents have strong needs to monitor their behavior and program their lives.

I have come to see more clearly why parents who have an unsatisfactory relationship with their spouse find it so difficult to be accepting of their children: They are too needful of their children bringing them the joys and satisfactions that are missing in the marital relationship.

CAN PARENTS CHANGE THEIR ATTITUDES?

Can this book—or an eight-week P.E.T. course bring about a change in such parental attitudes? Can parents learn to become more accepting of their children? Six years ago I would have been skeptical. Like most practitioners in the helping professions, I had certain biases carried over from my formal training. Most of us were taught that people don't change much unless they go through intensive psychotherapy under the guidance of a professional therapist, usually lasting from six months to a year or even longer.

In recent years, however, there has been a radical shift in

the thinking of professional "change agents." Most of us have watched people make significant changes in attitudes and behaviors as a result of having an experience in "growth groups"—sensitivity training, basic encounter groups, week-end marathon groups, human-potential training groups, leaderless encounter groups, couples' groups, live-in family workshops, Synanon groups, sensory-awareness workshops, and so on. Most professionals now accept the idea that people can change significantly when they get the opportunity to have a group experience and can talk openly and honestly with each other, share feelings and discuss problems in an atmosphere where they feel empathically understood and warmly accepted.

P.E.T. apparently is one such experience. Parents share their feelings and problems with each other in an informal classroom. They sit in a circle; anyone can talk whenever he wants; they are encouraged to talk about their feelings about their children; they learn that most parents have the same problems as they; the instructor listens and demonstrates understanding with his active listening; their ideas or their arguments are not judged and evaluated; they are not put down by the instructor; and they become aware via experience that people really care about them.

In P.E.T. there are no examinations or grades. Attendance is voluntary. The new concepts and new methods are offered but not imposed. Parents are made to feel free to express disagreement, to talk openly about any resistance to the new ideas and methods. Parents are given opportunity to practice the new methods in the safe atmosphere of the classroom before they are encouraged to try them out at home, and their initial clumsiness in using the new methods is accepted and understood by the group.

Almost all the parents who enroll in P.E.T. realize, and often openly admit in class, that their present attitudes and methods as parents leave much to be desired. Many know they already have been ineffective with one or more of their children; others are scared about what their present methods might ultimately do to the children; all are acutely aware of how many kids are getting into trouble and how many parent-child relationships deteriorate when the children move into adolescence.

Consequently, most parents in P.E.T. have a readiness and willingness to change—to learn new, more effective methods, to avoid mistakes of other parents (or their own), and to discover any technique that might make their job easier. We have yet to meet a parent who does not want to do a better job of raising his children.

With all these things going for us in P.E.T., it is not surprising that the training experience brings about significant changes in parents' attitudes and behavior. Here is a small sample of statements taken from letters or from the evaluation forms that parents fill out anonymously at the end of the course:

> "We only wish we had been able to take this course years ago before our kids were teen-agers."
>
> "We now treat our kids with the same kind of respect we show our friends."
>
> "I feel fortunate to have been one of the parents who have taken the course. More than that, I feel my outlook toward the whole human race has broadened, and I have become much more accepting of others as they are, not as I used to see them."
>
> "I have always liked children, but now I am learning to respect them as well. P.E.T. is not just a class in child-rearing. To me, it seems a way of life."
>
> "It made me realize how much I had underestimated my children and weakened them through

> my overprotectiveness and overconscientiousness.
> I had been a member of a really fine child study
> group, but it had only reinforced my guilt feelings
> and kept me trying to be a "perfect Mommy."
>
> "I was so skeptical and had such little faith in my
> children I can hardly believe it. When I found out
> that they coped with their feelings and problems
> much better than I ever had, I felt the weight of the
> world had been lifted from my shoulders. I started
> living for myself. I went back to school, and I was a
> much happier, self-fulfilled person, therefore, a
> better parent."

Not all parents within the eight-week time period are able
to make the changes in attitudes required to become more
accepting of their children. Some come to realize that their
marriage is not mutually fulfilling, so that one or both cannot
be effective with the children. Either they seldom find the
time and energy because so much of it goes into their own
marital conflicts, or they find that they cannot be accepting of
their children because they are not feeling accepting of
themselves as husband and wife.

Other parents find it difficult to throw off the oppressive
value system, acquired from their own parents and now
causing them to be excessively judgmental and unaccepting
of their children. Still others have trouble modifying their
attitude of "owning" their children or their deep commitment
to a goal of making their children fit a preconceived mold:
this attitude is found mostly in parents who have been
strongly influenced by the dogmas of a few religious sects
that teach parents to have a moral obligation to make
converts out of their children, even though it may mean using
the power and authority of the parent or using methods of
influence not too dissimilar from brainwashing and thought
control.

For some parents whose own basic attitudes they find hard to modify, the P.E.T. experience, for whatever reason, opens the door to seek other kinds of help—group therapy, marital counseling, family therapy, or even individual therapy. Quite a few of these parents have said that before P.E.T. they never would have consulted a psychologist or psychiatrist for help. Apparently, P.E.T. creates greater self-awareness and the motivation and desire for people to change, even when P.E.T. itself may not be enough to bring about significant change.

After the P.E.T. course some parents ask to continue meeting with a smaller group of mothers and fathers so they may be helped to work through the attitudes and problems that prevent them from effectively employing the new methods they have learned. In these "advanced groups" parents deal mainly with their marriage relationship, their relationship with their own parents, or basic attitudes about themselves as persons. Only after their experience in these deeper therapeutic groups do these parents acquire the insight and bring about the changes in attitudes that then permit them to use P.E.T. methods effectively. So for some parents P.E.T. may not in itself produce enough change in attitudes, but it does start a process of change or encourages them to start down the road to greater effectiveness as a person and parent.

Obviously, reading this book cannot be the same as taking an eight-week course with a group of other parents, under the guidance and coaching of a trained instructor. Nevertheless, I feel that most parents will be able to obtain a sound understanding of this new philosophy of raising children by reading and conscientiously studying this book. Many parents will be able to acquire from this book a reasonable level of competence in the specific skills required to put the philosophy to work at home. These skills can be practiced by the reader frequently and long after they have finished reading the book—not only in your relationship with your children but also in your relationship with your spouse, your business associates, your parents, your friends.

Our experiences tell us that becoming more effective in raising responsible children will take work—diligent work—whether the exposure comes from the P.E.T. program or reading this book, or both. But after all, what job doesn't take work?

16

The Other Parents of Your Children

Throughout their lives your children will be exposed to the influence of other adults to whom you delegate certain parental responsibilities. Since those people carry out parental functions with your children, they, too, will have a strong influence on your youngsters' growth and development. I refer, of course, to grandparents, relatives, and babysitters; teachers, principals, and counselors; coaches, camp directors, and recreational leaders; YMCA and YWCA program directors, Boy Scout and Girl Scout troop leaders, Camp Fire Girls leaders, Sunday School teachers, and Little League managers; and parole and probation officers.

When you turn your children over to such surrogate parents, what assurance do you have about their effectiveness? Will these adults create relationships with your sons and daughters that will be "therapeutic" and constructive or "nontherapeutic" and destructive? How effective will they be as helping agents for your youngsters? Can you turn your children over to these youth workers and trust that they will not be damaged?

These are important questions because your childrens'

lives will be strongly influenced by all adults with whom they develop relationships.

Many of these parent surrogates enroll in our P.E.T. classes. We have also worked with such people in our other specially designed training programs: Teacher Effectiveness Training, Counselor Effectiveness Training, and Leader Effectiveness Training. We have learned that most of these professional people are remarkably similar to parents in their attitudes toward kids and in their methods of dealing with them. They, too, usually fail to listen to children; they, too, talk to children in ways that put them down and damage their self-esteem; they, too, rely heavily on authority and power to manipulate and control children's behavior; they, too, are locked into the two win-lose methods of conflict-resolution; they, too, hassle and harangue and preach and shame children in attempts to shape their values and beliefs and mold them into their own image.

Naturally, there are exceptions, just as there are exceptions among parents. But, by and large, the adults who touch the lives of your children lack the basic attitudes and skills to be effective helping agents. Like parents, they have not been adequately trained to be effective "therapeutic agents" in an interpersonal relationship with a child or adolescent. And so, unhappily, they can do damage to your children.

I will use school teachers and school administrators as examples, but this does not imply that they are the most ineffective or most needful of training. But because they spend so much time with your children, they have the greatest potential for influencing them, for good or bad. Drawing on our experience of working in many school districts, it is clear to me that schools, with very few exceptions, are basically authoritarian institutions that modeled their organizational structure and leadership philosophy after military organizations.

Rules and regulations for student conduct are almost

invariably determined unilaterally by adults at the top of the hierarchy, without participation of youngsters who are expected to obey them. Infractions of these rules bring punishments—in some cases, believe it or not, physical punishment. Even classroom teachers are not given a voice in establishing rules of conduct that they are expected to enforce. Yet, these teachers are usually judged more on how effectively they maintain order in the classroom than on how effective they are in encouraging learning.

Schools also impose on children a curriculum that most kids consider dull and not at all relevant to what is going on in their lives. Then, recognizing that such a curriculum is not likely to motivate students by virtue of interest and relevance, the schools almost universally employ a system of rewards and punishments—the ubiquitous grades—that almost insures that a certain rather large percentage of children will be labeled "below average."

In the classroom, children are frequently scolded and put down by their teachers. They are rewarded for their ability to recite back what they have been told to read, and often chastised for dissent or disagreement. Almost universally, at least in the upper elementary-school grades and in junior and senior high school, teachers are quite ineffective in getting their classes to participate in meaningful group discussions because many teachers habitually respond to students' contributions with the "twelve roadblocks." So open and honest communication from the students is discouraged by all but a few teachers.

When children "act up" in class, as they naturally will in such a "nontherapeutic" and uninteresting climate, the conflicts are usually handled by Method I, in some cases by Method II. Kids are often ordered to go see the principal or the counselor, who are supposed to try to resolve these teacher-student conflicts—*although one member of the conflict is not present*—namely, the teacher. So, usually, the prin-

cipal or counselor *assumes* the child is at fault and forthwith
either punishes or lectures him, or extracts a promise to
"cease and desist."

In most schools, students are blatantly denied civil
rights—the right of free speech, the right to wear their hair as
they prefer, the right to wear the clothes they like, the right
to dissent. Schools also deny children the right to refuse to
testify against themselves, and if kids get into trouble,
administrators seldom follow the customary procedures of
"due process of law" guaranteed to citizens by the judicial
system.

Is this a distorted picture of our schools? I think not. Many
other observers of the school system are seeing the same deficiencies.* Furthermore, one need only ask youngsters how
they feel about schools and school teachers. Most kids say
they hate school and that their teachers treat them
disrespectfully and unfairly. Most kids come to experience
school as a place where they *must* go; they experience
learning as something that is seldom pleasant or fun; they
experience studying as tedious work; and they see their
teachers as unfriendly policemen.

When children are assigned to adults whose treatment of
them produces such negative reactions, parents cannot be
expected to shoulder all the blame for the way their kids turn
out. Parents can be blamed, yes, but other adults must share
the blame.

What can parents do? Can they exert constructive
influence on the other parents of their children? Can they
have a voice in deciding how their children are talked to and
treated by other adults? I believe they can, and they must.
But they must become much less passive and submissive than
they have been in the past.

First, they must alert themselves to detect in all the

* See references in the *Supplementary Reading List* to books by Glasser, Holt,
Neill, Rogers.

institutions that serve youth any evidence that their children are controlled and suppressed by adults arbitrarily exercising power and authority. They must stand up and fight against those who advocate "being tough with kids," who sanction the use of power in dealing with kids under the banner of "law and order," who justify authoritarian methods on the grounds that one cannot trust children to be responsible or self-disciplined.

Parents must get off the bench and go to bat to protect their childrens' civil rights whenever they are threatened by adults who feel that kids do not deserve such rights.

Parents can also advocate and support programs that offer innovative ideas and methods for bringing about reform in the schools—such as those that provide curriculum change, eliminate the grading system, introduce new instructional methodologies, give students more freedom to learn on their own and at their own pace, offer individualized instruction, give kids a chance to participate with adults in the schools' governing process, or train teachers to be more humanistic and therapeutic in relating to kids.

Such programs are already available in communities that want to improve their schools. Many more are in the planning stage. Parents need not be afraid of such new educational programs, but rather should welcome them, encourage administrators to try them out and test their effects.

The program with which I am most familiar is our own, consisting of three courses: Teacher, Counselor, and Administrator Effectiveness Training. In the last two years this program has been introduced in more than fifty schools, chiefly in California. The results we have seen so far have been encouraging.

In one junior high school in Cupertino, California, our program was responsible for the Principal involving both teachers and students in a project to rewrite all the student-conduct regulations. This participative adult-student problem-solving group discarded their old thick rule book and substituted two simple rules: no one has the right to interfere with another's learning, and no one has the right physically to harm another! The Principal reported this effect:

> "The reduced use of power and authority over the entire student body resulted in a more self-directed student population with pupils assuming more responsibility for their own behavior as well as the behavior of others."

In another school, in Palo Alto, California, by using our Method III conflict-resolution procedure in a classroom that had all but disintegrated because of lack of discipline, a teacher reduced the number of "unacceptable and disruptive acts" from thirty per class hour to an average of 4.5 per class hour. A follow-up questionnaire revealed that 76 per cent of the students felt that the class had accomplished more work since the problem-solving sessions and ninety-five per cent felt the classroom atmosphere was either "improved" or "greatly improved."

The principal of Apollo High School in Simi Valley wrote about the effects of Teacher Effectiveness Training on him and on his school:

1. Discipline problems have decreased at least fifty percent. I find it to be a satisfactory and effective method of handling behavior problems without suspending students. I learned that suspension only eliminates the problem for three or four days; and it does nothing to counteract the causes of the behavior. The skills I learned in the P.E.T. class facilitate problem-solving within the student; between the staff and administration, and between teachers and students.

2. We have instituted school meetings wherein we feel we prevent conflicts before they arise. We use Dr. Gordon's problem-solving method, and have been successful in preventing conflicts from becoming behavioral problems.
3. My relationships with students have improved immensely, by allowing students to have the responsibility for their actions and behavior and to have the privilege of dealing with their own problems.

The Principal of an elementary school in La Mesa wrote this evaluation of the Effectiveness Training program:

As an elementary-school principal working with a large number of staff members trained in the Teacher Effectiveness Training program (sixteen out of twenty-three) I have observed behavioral changes in both students and faculty directly attributable to this program:

1. Teachers feel confident in their own abilities to handle difficult behavior problems.
2. The emotional climate of classrooms is far more relaxed, far healthier.
3. Children are involved in establishing the rules under which their school experiences are structured. Therefore, they have a personal commitment to these rules.
4. Children are learning how to solve social problems without using force or manipulation.
5. Far fewer "discipline cases" are referred to me.
6. Teacher behavior is far more appropriate, i.e., student counseling is done now when the student has a problem, not when the teacher has a problem.

7. Teachers are far more effective in solving their own problems without resorting to use of force with children.
8. Teacher ability to conduct meaningful parent-teacher conferences has increased.

Significant changes *can* be produced in schools by giving administrators and teachers training in the same skills that we have been teaching parents in P.E.T. But we have learned that schools are not open to change in those communities where most of the parents are committed to maintaining the status quo, are frightened of change, or are steeped in the tradition of authoritarian tratment of youth.

My hope is that more parents can be influenced to start listening to their kids when they complain about the treatment they receive from many teachers, coaches, Sunday School teachers, and youth leaders. They can begin to trust the validity of their youngsters' feelings when they say they hate school or resent the way they are treated by adults. Parents can find out what is wrong with these institutions by listening to the kids and not always defending the institutions.

Only by aroused parents will these institutions be influenced to become more democratic, more humanistic, and more therapeutic. What is needed more than anything I know, is nothing less than an entirely new philosophy for dealing with children and youth, a new Bill of Rights for youth. No longer can society treat children as children were treated two thousand years ago, any more than it can sanction the way minority groups have been treated in the past.

I offer one such philosophy of adult-child relationships, in the form of a credo, upon which our P.E.T. programs have been built. Written several years ago in an attempt to put the P.E.T. philosophy into a succinct and easily understood statement, it is handed to the enrollees in our courses, and offered here as a challenge to all adults:

A CREDO FOR MY RELATIONSHIPS WITH YOUTH

You and I are in a relationship that I value and want to keep. Yet each of us is a separate person with his own unique needs and the right to try to meet those needs. I will try to be genuinely accepting of your behavior when you are trying to meet your needs or when you are having problems meeting your needs.

When you share your problems, I will try to listen acceptingly and understandingly in a way that will facilitate your finding your own solutions rather than depending upon mine. When you have a problem because my behavior is interfering with your meeting your needs, I encourage you to tell me openly and honestly how you are feeling. At those times, I will listen and then try to modify my behavior, if I can.

However, when your behavior interferes with my meeting my own needs, thus causing me to feel unaccepting of you, I will share my problem with you and tell you as openly and honestly as I can exactly how I am feeling, trusting that you respect my needs enough to listen and then try to modify your behavior.

At those times when either of us cannot modify his behavior to meet the needs of the other and find that we have a conflict-of-needs in our relationship, let us commit ourselves to resolve each such conflict without ever resorting to the use of either my power or yours to win at the expense of the other losing. I respect your needs, but I also must respect my own. Consequently, let us strive always to search for solutions to our inevitable conflicts that will be acceptable to both of us. In this way, your needs will be met, but so will mine—no one will lose, both will win.

As a result, you can continue to develop as a person through meeting your needs, but so can I. Our relationship thus can always be a healthy one because it will be mutually satisfying. Each of us can become what he is capable of being, and we can continue to relate to each other with feelings of mutual respect and love, in friendship and in peace.

While I have no doubt that this credo, if adopted and practiced by adults in institutions serving youth, would in time bring about constructive reforms, I also realize that such reform may be a long time in coming. After all, today's adults are yesterday's children and are themselves the products of ineffective parenthood.

We need a *new* generation of parents who will accept the challenge of learning the skills for raising responsible children in the home. For this is where it all must start. And it can start there today, this minute—in your home.

Appendix

1. LISTENING FOR FEELINGS *(An Exercise)*

DIRECTIONS: *Children communicate to parents much more than words or ideas. Behind the words often lie feelings. Following are some typical "messages" children send. Read each separately, trying to listen carefully for feelings. Then in the right-hand column, write the feeling or feelings you heard. Discard the "content" and write in only the feeling —usually one or several words. Some of the statements may contain several different feelings—write in all the main feelings you hear, numbering each different feeling. When you have fnished, compare your list with those in the Key, scoring each item according to the scoring directions.*

Child Says	Child is Feeling
EXAMPLE: I don't know what is wrong. I can't figure it out. Maybe I should just quit trying.	(a) Stumped. (b) Discouraged. (c) Tempted to give up.
1. Oh boy, only ten more days until school's out.	
2. Look, Daddy, I made an airplane with my new tools!	
3. Will you hold my hand when we go into the nursery school?	
4. Gee, I'm not having any fun. I can't think of anything to do.	
5. I'll never be good like Jim. I practice and practice and he's still better than me.	
6. My new teacher gives us too much homework. I can never get it all done. What'll I do?	
7. All the other kids went to the beach. I don't have anyone to play with.	
8. Jim's parents let him ride his bike to school, but I'm a better rider than Jim.	

9. I shouldn't have been so mean to little Jimmy. I guess I was bad.

10. I want to wear my hair long—it's my hair, isn't it?

11. Do you think I'm doing this report right? Will it be good enough?

12. Why did the old bag make me stay after school, anyway? I wasn't the only one who was talking. I'd like to punch her in the nose.

13. I can do it myself. You don't need to help me. I'm old enough to do it myself.

14. Arithmetic is too hard. I'm too dumb to understand it.

15. Go away; leave me alone. I don't want to talk to you or anybody else. You don't care what happens to me anyway.

16. For awhile I was doing good, but now I'm worse than before. I try hard, but it doesn't seem to help. What's the use?

17. I would sure like to go, but I just can't call her up. What if she would laugh at me for asking her?

18. I never want to play with Pam anymore. She's a dope and a creep.

19. I'm sure glad that I happened to be born the baby of you and Daddy rather than some other parents.

20. I think I know what to do, but maybe it's not right. I always seem to do the wrong thing. What do you think I should do, Dad, work or go to college?

NOW, USE THE SCORING KEY ON THE NEXT PAGE AND SCORE YOUR RESPONSES:

1. Score each item just to the left of the numbered items.
2. Total all of your item scores and write in the total score on the Scoring Key page.

SCORING KEY:

Listening for Feelings

DIRECTIONS:

Give yourself a 4 on those items where you feel your choices closely match those on the Scoring Key.

Score yourself a 2 on items where your choices only partially match or where you missed a particular feeling.

Give yourself a 0 if you missed altogether.

1. (a) Glad.
   (b) Relieved.
2. (a) Proud.
   (b) Pleased.
3. (a) Afraid, fearful.
4. (a) Bored.
   (b) Stumped.
5. (a) Feels inadequate.
   (b) Discouraged.
6. (a) Feels job is too hard.
   (b) Feels defeated.
7. (a) Left behind.
   (b) Lonely.
8. (a) Feels parents are being unfair.
   (b) Feels competent.
9. (a) Feels guilty.
   (b) Regrets his action.
10. (a) Resents interference of parents.

11. (a) Feels some doubt.
    (b) Not sure.
12. (a) Angry, hateful.
    (b) Feels it was unfair.
13. (a) Feels competent.
    (b) Doesn't want help.
14. (a) Frustrated.
    (b) Feels inadequate.
15. (a) Feels hurt.
    (b) Feels angry.
    (c) Feels unloved.
16. (a) Discouraged.
    (b) Wanting to give up.
17. (a) Wants to go.
    (b) Afraid.
18. (a) Angry.
19. (a) Grateful, glad.
    (b) Appreciates parents.
20. (a) Uncertain, unsure.

YOUR TOTAL SCORE_____

HOW YOU RATE IN RECOGNIZING FEELINGS:

61–80	Superior recognition of feelings.
41–60	Above average recognition of feelings.
21–40	Below average recognition of feelings.
0–20	Poor recognition of feelings.

2. RECOGNIZING INEFFECTIVE MESSAGES
(An Exercise)

DIRECTIONS: *Read each situation and the message sent by the parent. In the column,* FAULTY SENDING BECAUSE, *write in the reason why the parent's message was not effective sending, using the following list of "sending errors."*

Undershooting.	Sending solutions, orders.
Blaming, judging.	Venting secondary feelings.
Indirect message, sarcasm.	Name-calling.
	Hit and run.

Situation and Message	Faulty Sending Because:
EXAMPLE: Ten-year-old left open Scout knife on floor of baby's room. "That was so stupid. The baby could have cut herself."	Blaming, judging.
1. Kids fighting about which TV program to watch. "Stop that fighting and turn the TV off this minute."	
2. Daughter arrives home at 1:30 A.M. after agreeing to be in by midnight. Parent has been quite worried that something might have happened to her. Parent is relieved when she finally arrives. "Well, you cannot be trusted, I see. I'm so angry at you. You are to be grounded for a month."	
3. Twelve-year-old left gate to pool open, endangering two-year-old. "What did you want to do, drown your baby brother? I'm furious with you!"	
4. Teacher sent note home stating that eleven-year-old was doing too much loud and "filthy" talking in class. "Come in here and explain why you want to embarrass your parents with your dirty mouth."	

5. Mother is angry and very frustrated because child is dawdling and making her late for an appointment. "Mother would like for you to be more considerate of her."

_____

6. Mother comes in house and finds living room all messed up after she had asked kids to keep it clean for company. "I hope you both had a lot of fun this afternoon at my expense."

_____

7. Father is repulsed by the sight and odor of daughter's dirty feet. "Don't you ever wash your feet like other human beings? Get up there in that shower."

_____

8. Child is disturbing you because he is getting attention of your guests by turning somersaults. Mother says, "You little show-off."

_____

9. Mother angry at child because dishes were not put away after washing. As child is running off to schoolbus, Mother shouts: "I am very upset with you this morning, do you know that?"

Compare your answers with these:
1. Sending solution.
2. Blaming, judging.
   Venting secondary feeling.
   Sending solution.
3. Blaming, judging.
   Venting secondary feeling.
4. Blaming, judging.

5. Blaming, judging.
   Undershooting.
6. Indirect message.
7. Indirect message.
   Sending solution.
   Blaming, judging.
8. Name-calling.
9. Hit and run.

(For further instructions please see following page.)

WRITE DOWN CONGRUENT "I-MESSAGES" FOR EACH OF THE ABOVE SITUATIONS, AVOIDING ALL OF THE "SENDING ERRORS."

1.

2.

3.

4.

5.

6.

7.

8.

9.

3. SENDING "I MESSAGES" (*An Exercise*)

DIRECTIONS: *Read each situation, examine the "you message" in the second column, then write in an "I message" in the third column. When you have finished, compare your "I messages" with those in the Key on page 315.*

Situation	"You Message"	"I Message"
1. Father wants to read paper. Child keeps climbing on lap. Father irritated.	"You shouldn't ever interrupt someone when he is reading."	
2. Mother using vacuum cleaner. Child keeps pulling plug out of socket. Mother is in a hurry.	"You're being naughty."	
3. Child comes to table with very dirty hands and face.	"You're not being a responsible big boy. That's what a little baby might do."	
4. Child keeps postponing going to bed. Mother and Dad want to talk about a private problem of concern to them. Child keeps hanging around, preventing them from talking.	"You know it's past your bedtime. You're just trying to annoy us. You need your sleep."	

(Exercise continues on following page.)

5.	Child keeps pleading to be taken to a movie, but he has not cleaned up his room for several days, a job he agreed to do.	"You don't deserve going to a movie when you have been so inconsiderate and selfish."
6.	Child has been sulking and acting sad all day. Mother doesn't know reason.	"Come on now. Stop this sulking. Either brighten up or you'll have to go outside and sulk. You're taking something too seriously."
7.	Child is playing phonograph so loud it is interfering with conversation of parents in next room.	"Can't you be more considerate of others? Why do you play that so loud?"
8.	Child promised to iron napkins to be used for dinner party. During day she dawdled; now it's one hour before guests arrive and she hasn't started the job.	"You have dawdled all day and fallen down on your job. How can you be so thoughtless and irresponsible?"
9.	Child forgot to show up at agreed upon time she was to be home so Mother could take her to buy shoes. Mother is in a hurry.	"You should be ashamed. After all, I agreed to take you and then you are careless about the time."

KEY

1. "I can't read the paper and play too. I really feel irritated when I can't have a little while alone to relax and read the paper."
2. "I'm in a big rush and it really makes me angry to be slowed down by replacing the plug. I don't feel like playing when I have work to get done."
3. "I can't enjoy my dinner when I see all that dirt. It makes me feel kind of sick and lose my appetite."
4. "Mother and I have something very important to discuss. We can't talk about it when you're here and we don't like waiting around for you to finally go to bed."
5. "I don't feel very much like doing something for you when you don't stick to your agreement about your room. I feel like I'm being taken advantage of."
6. "I'm sorry to see you be so unhappy but I don't know how to help because I don't know why you're feeling so blue."
7. "I feel kind of cheated. I want to spend some time with your father and the noise is driving us mad."
8. "I really feel let down. I've worked all day to get ready for our party and now I still have to worry about the napkins."
9. "I don't like it when I carefully plan my day so we can shop for your new shoes and then you don't even show up."

4. USE OF PARENTAL AUTHORITY *(An Exercise)*

DIRECTION: *Below is a list of typical things parents do in their relationship with their children. By being objective and honest with yourself on this exercise, you will learn about one important aspect of your role as a parent—how you use your parental authority.*

You are to read each statement and then indicate on the Answer Sheet whether it is likely or unlikely for you as a parent to do what is stated (either exactly what is stated or something similar).

If you do not yet have children, or if the item applies to a child older or younger or of a sex other than your own, simply predict how you would behave. Circle only one of the alternatives. Only if you do not understand an item or feel very uncertain, should you circle the "?."

    U.   Unlikely for you to do this or something similar.

    L.   Likely for you to do this or something similar.

    ?.   Uncertain or do not understand.

So that you understand the terms used in this exercise, read the following definitions:

"Punish."	Cause some kind of unpleasantness for the child through denying him something he wants or inflicting physical or psychological hurt.
"Reprimand."	Strongly worded criticism, "scolding," or "bawling out," dressing down, negative evaluation.
"Threaten."	Warn the child of possible punishment.
"Reward."	Cause some kind of pleasantness for the child through giving him something he wants.
"Praise."	Evaluate the child positively or favorably; say something good about him.

EXAMPLE: Require your ten-year-old child to ask permission to speak when he is in a gathering of adults.   U   L   ?

             By circling the *U,* you would indicate you are unlikely to require this.

INDICATE YOUR ANSWERS ON THE *ANSWER SHEET*

1. Physically remove your child from the piano when he refuses to stop banging on it after you have told him it is becoming unbearable to you.

2. Praise your child for being consistently prompt in coming home to dinner.

3. Scold your six-year-old child if he demonstrates objectionable table manners in front of guests.

4. Praise your adolescent boy when you see him reading the right kind of literature.

5. Punish your child when he uses an objectionable swear word.

6. Give a reward when your child has indicated on a chart that he did not miss a single time for brushing his teeth.

7. Make your child apologize to another child he has treated very discourteously.

8. Praise your child when she remembers to wait at school for you to pick her up in the car.

9. Make your child eat almost everything on his plate before being allowed to leave.

10. Make it a requirement that your daughter take a bath each day and give her a reward for not missing a single day for a month.

11. Punish or deny your child something when you catch him telling a lie.

12. Offer your adolescent boy some kind of reward or grant him a privilege if he will change his long-hair style to a crew-cut.

13. Punish or reprimand your child for stealing money out of your purse.

14. Promise your daughter something she wants if she will refrain from using too much make-up.

15. Insist that your child perform when he is asked to do so for relatives or guests.

16. Promise your child something you know he wants if he practices his piano lessons a certain amount of time each day.

17. Make your two-year-old remain on the toilet until he has performed his "duty," when you know he has to go.

18. Set up a system whereby your child can earn some kind of rewards if he regularly does his chores around home.

19. Punish or threaten to punish your child if he eats between meals after you have told him not to.

20. Promise some kind of reward to encourage your boy always to come home on time after dates.

21. Punish or scold your child for not cleaning up his room after making a mess of it during play.

22. Set up some system of rewards as an incentive for your daughter to limit the length of her phone calls.

23. Scold your child for carelessly breaking or ruining one of his expensive toys.

24. Promise some kind of reward for your thirteen-year-old girl if she refrains from smoking.

25. Punish or scold your child for "sassing" you or saying something disrespectful.

26. Promise your child some kind of reward if she will stick to her study schedule in order to improve her grades.

27. Make your child stop bringing his toys into the living room when it gets too cluttered.

28. Tell your daughter you are proud of her or pleased with her choice when you strongly approve of the boy she is dating.

29. Make your child clean up his own mess when he carelessly spills food on the rug.

30. Tell your child she is a good girl or reward her when she remains still while you are combing her hair.

31. Punish your child for continuing to play in his room after you thought he had gone to sleep at his bedtime.

32. Set up system of rewards for your child if he habitually washes his hands before coming to the table.

33. Make your child stop or punish him when you catch him fingering his genitals.

34. Set up some kind of system of giving your child rewards for promptness in getting ready for school.

35. Punish or reprimand your children for fighting loudly with each other over a toy.

36. Praise or reward your child for not crying when he doesn't get his way or has his feelings hurt.

37. Threaten to punish or reprimand your child for telling you he won't go on an errand after you have asked him several times.

38. Tell your daughter that you will buy her something she has been wanting if she keeps her dress clean until you go out to dinner a couple of hours from now.

39. Punish or reprimand your child when you see him pulling up the skirt of the girl next door and embarrassing her.

40. Offer to give your child some kind of monetary reward for every course in which he pulls his grade up on his next report card.

ANSWER SHEET:
Use of Parental Authority

1.	U	L	?	21.	U	L	?
2.	U	L	?	22.	U	L	?
3.	U	L	?	23.	U	L	?
4.	U	L	?	24.	U	L	?
5.	U	L	?	25.	U	L	?
6.	U	L	?	26.	U	L	?
7.	U	L	?	27.	U	L	?
8.	U	L	?	28.	U	L	?
9.	U	L	?	29.	U	L	?
10.	U	L	?	30.	U	L	?
11.	U	L	?	31.	U	L	?
12.	U	L	?	32.	U	L	?
13.	U	L	?	33.	U	L	?
14.	U	L	?	34.	U	L	?
15.	U	L	?	35.	U	L	?
16.	U	L	?	36.	U	L	?
17.	U	L	?	37.	U	L	?
18.	U	L	?	38.	U	L	?
19.	U	L	?	39.	U	L	?
20.	U	L	?	40.	U	L	?

(Directions for scoring appear on following page.)

DIRECTIONS FOR SCORING:

1. First, count all of the *L*'s circled after the *ODD* numbers (1, 3, 5, 7, etc.).
2. Second, count all of the *L*'s circled after the *EVEN* numbers (2, 4, 6, 8, etc.).
3. Place these two figures in the table below and write in the sum of all *L*'s.

Number

Odd L's		This number indicates the degree to which you use *punishment* or threaten to use punishment to control your child or to enforce your solutions to problems.
Even L's		This number indicates the degree to which you use *rewards* or *incentives* to control your child or enforce your solutions to problems.
Total L's		This number indicates the degree to which you use both sources of your *parental* power to control your child.

Use of Punishment		*Use of Reward*		*Use of Both Kinds of Power*	
Score	Rating	Score	Rating	Score	Rating
0–5	Very little.	0–5	Very little.	0–10	Anti-authoritarian.
6–10	Occasionally.	6–10	Occasionally.	11–20	Moderately authoritarian.
11–15	Often.	11–15	Often.	21–30	Considerably authoritarian.
16–20	Very often.	16–20	Very often.	31–40	Very authoritarian.

5. A CATALOG OF EFFECTS OF THE TYPICAL WAYS PARENTS RESPOND TO CHILDREN

ORDERING, DIRECTING, COMMANDING

These messages tell a child that his feelings or needs are not important; he must comply with what his parent feels or needs. ("I don't care what you want to do; come into the house this minute.")

They communicate unacceptance of the child as he is at the moment. ("Stop fidgeting around.")

They produce fear of the parent's power. The child hears a threat of getting hurt by someone bigger and stronger than he. ("Go to your room—and if you don't, I'll see to it that you get there.")

They may make the child feel resentful or angry, frequently causing him to express hostile feelings, throw a tantrum, fight back, resist, test the parent's will.

They can communicate to the child that the parent does not trust the child's own judgment or competence. ("Don't touch that dish." "Stay away from your baby brother.")

WARNING, ADMONISHING, THREATENING

These messages can make a child feel fearful and submissive. ("If you do that, you'll be sorry.")

They can evoke resentment and hostility in the same way that ordering, directing, and commanding do. ("If you don't get to bed right away, you're going to get paddled.")

They can communicate that the parent has no respect for the child's needs or wishes. ("If you don't stop playing that drum, I'm going to get cross.")

Children sometimes respond to warnings or threats by saying, "I don't care what happens, I still feel this way."

These messages also invite the child to test the firmness of the parent's threat. Children sometimes are tempted to do something that they have been warned against, just to see for themselves if the consequences promised by the parent actually happen.

EXHORTING, MORALIZING, PREACHING

Such messages bring to bear on the child the power of external authority, duty or obligation. Children may respond to such "shoulds," "oughts," and "musts" by resisting and defending their posture even more strongly.

They may make a child feel the parent does not trust his judgment—that he had better accept what "others" deem is right. ("You ought to do the right thing.")

They may cause feelings of guilt in a child—that he is "bad." ("You shouldn't think that way.")

They may make a child feel the parent does not trust his lidity of others' blueprints or values. ("You should always respect your teachers.")

ADVISING, GIVING SUGGESTIONS OR SOLUTIONS

Such messages are often felt by the child as evidence that the parent does not have confidence in the child's judgment or ability to find his own solution.

They may influence a child to become dependent on the parent and to stop thinking for himself. ("What should I do, Daddy?")

Sometimes children strongly resent parents' ideas or advice. ("Let me figure this out myself." "I don't want to be told what to do.")

Advice sometimes communicates your attitudes of superiority to the child. ("Your mother and I know what's best.") Children can also acquire a feeling of inferiority. ("Why didn't I think of that?" "You always know better what to do.")

Advice can make a child feel his parent has not understood

him at all. ("You wouldn't suggest that if you really knew how I felt.")

Advice sometimes results in the child devoting all his time reacting to the parents' ideas to the exclusion of developing his own ideas.

LECTURING, GIVING LOGICAL ARGUMENTS

The act of trying to teach another often makes the "student" feel you are making him look inferior, subordinate, inadequate. ("You always think you know everything.")

Logic and facts often make a child defensive and resentful. ("You think I don't know that?")

Children, like adults, seldom like to be shown they are wrong. Consequently, they defend their position to the bitter end. ("You're wrong, I'm right." "You can't convince me.")

Children generally hate parental lectures. ("They go on and on and I have to just sit there and listen.")

Children often resort to desperate methods of discounting parental facts. ("Well, you are just too old to know what's going on." "Your ideas are outmoded and old-fashioned." "You're a square.")

Often children already know very well the facts parents insist on teaching them, and resent the implication that they are uninformed. ("I know all of that—you don't need to tell me.")

Sometimes children choose to ignore facts. ("I don't care." "So what." "It won't happen to me.")

JUDGING, CRITICIZING, DISAGREEING, BLAMING

These messages, probably more than any of the others, make children feel inadequate, inferior, stupid, unworthy, bad. A child's self-concept gets shaped by parental judgment and evaluation. As the parent judges the child, so will the child judge himself. ("I heard so often that I was bad, I began to feel I must be bad.")

Negative criticism evokes counter-criticism. ("I've seen you do the same thing." "You're not so hot yourself.")

Evaluation strongly influences children to keep their feelings to themselves or to hide things from their parents. ("If I told them I'd just be criticized.")

Children, like adults, hate to be judged negatively. They respond with defensiveness, simply to protect their own self-image. Often they become angry and feel hatred toward the evaluating parent, even if the judgment is correct.

Frequent evaluation and criticism make some children feel that they are no good and that the parents do not love them.

PRAISING, AGREEING

Contrary to the common belief that praise is always bene-ficial to children, it often has very negative effects. A positive evaluation that does not fit the child's self-image may evoke hostility: "I am *not* pretty, I'm ugly." "I hate my hair." "I did *not* play well, I was lousy."

Children infer that if a parent judges positively, they can also judge negatively some other time. Also, the absence of praise in a family where praise is used frequently can be interpreted by the child as criticism. ("You didn't say anything nice about my hair so you must not like it.")

Praise is often felt by the child as manipulative—a subtle way of influencing the child to do what the parent wants. ("You're just saying that so I'll study harder.")

Children sometimes infer that their parents don't understand them when they praise. ("You wouldn't say that if you knew how I really felt about myself.")

Children are often embarrassed and uncomfortable when praise is given, especially in front of their friends. ("Oh, Daddy, that's not true!")

Children who are praised a lot may grow to depend on it and even demand it. ("You didn't say anything about my cleaning up my room." "How do I look, Mother?" "Wasn't I a good little boy?" "Isn't that a good drawing?")

NAME-CALLING, RIDICULING, SHAMING

Such messages can have a devastating effect on the self-image of a child. They can make a child feel unworthy, bad, unloved.

The most frequent response of children to such messages is to give one back to the parent. ("And you're a big nag." "Look who's calling me lazy.")

When a child gets such a message from a parent who is trying to influence him, he is much less likely to change by looking at himself realistically. Instead, he can zero in on the parent's unfair message and excuse himself. ("I do *not* look cheap with my eye shadow. That's ridiculous and unfair.")

INTERPRETING, ANALYZING, DIAGNOSING

Such messages communicate to the child that the parent has him "figured out," knows what his motives are or why he is behaving the way he is. Such parental psychoanalyzing can be threatening and frustrating to the child.

If the parent's analysis or interpretation happens to be accurate, the child may feel embarrassed at being so exposed. ("You are not having dates because you are too shy." "You are doing that just to get attention.")

When the parent's analysis or interpretation is wrong, as it more often is, the child will become angry at being accused unjustly. ("I am not jealous—that's ridiculous.")

Children often pick up an attitude of superiority on the part of the parent. ("You think you know so much.") Parents who frequently analyze their children communicate to them that the parents feel superior, wiser, cleverer.

The "I know why" and "I can see through you" messages frequently cut off further communication from the child at the

moment, and teach the child to refrain from sharing problems
with his parents.

REASSURING, SYMPATHIZING, CONSOLING, SUPPORTING

Such messages are not as helpful as most parents believe.
To reassure a child when he is feeling disturbed about some-
thing may simply convince him that you don't understand him.
("You couldn't say that if you knew how scared I am.")

Parents reassure and console because they are not comfortable with their child feeling hurt, upset, discouraged, and
the like. Such messages tell a child that you want him to stop
feeling the way he does. ("Don't feel bad, things will turn
out all right.")

Children can see through parents' reassurances as attempts
to change them and often distrust the parent. ("You're just
saying that to make me feel better.")

Discounting or sympathizing often stops further communication because the child senses you want him to stop feeling
the way he does.

PROBING, QUESTIONING, INTERROGATING

To ask questions may convey to children your lack of trust,
your suspicion or doubt. ("Did you wash your hands like I
told you?")

Children also see through some questions as attempts "to get
them out on a limb," only to have it sawed off by the parent.
("How long did you study? Only an hour. Well, you *deserve*
a C on that exam.")

Children often feel threatened by questions, especially
when they don't understand why the parent is questioning
them. Note how often children say, "Why are you asking
that?" or "What are you driving at?"

If you question a child who is sharing a problem with you,
he may suspect that you are gathering data to solve his problem for him, rather than let him find his own solution. ("When

did you start feeling this way? Does it have anything to do with school? How is school?") Children frequently do not want their parents to come up with answers to their problems: "If I tell my parents, they will only tell me what I should do."

When you ask questions of someone who is sharing a problem with you, each question limits the person's freedom to talk about whatever he wants to—in a sense each question dictates his next message. If you ask, "When did you notice this feeling?" you are telling the person to talk *only* about the onset of the feeling and nothing else. This is why being cross-examined as by a lawyer is so terribly uncomfortable—you feel you must tell your story exactly as demanded by his questions. So interrogating is not at all a good method of facilitating another's communication; rather, it can severely limit his freedom.

WITHDRAWING, DISTRACTING, HUMORING, DIVERTING

Such messages can communicate to the child that you are not interested in him, don't respect his feelings, or are downright rejecting him.

Children are generally quite serious and intent when they need to talk about something. When you respond with kidding, you can make them feel hurt and rejected.

Putting children off or diverting their feelings may for the moment appear successful, but a person's feelings do not always go away. They often crop up later. Problems put off are seldom problems solved.

Children, like adults, want to be heard and understood respectfully. If their parents brush them aside, they soon learn to take their important feelings and problems elsewhere.

6. SUGGESTED READING FOR PARENTS

Axline, Virginia M. *Dibs: In Search of Self.* New York; Ballatine Books, 1969.

A moving story of a child's growth and change in the process of therapy with the author, who is one of the pioneers in client-centered play therapy. Demonstrates active listening and the power of the language of acceptance.

Axline, Virginia M. *Play Therapy.* Boston: Houghton Mifflin, 1947.

The first book describing the application of the client-centered approach to therapy with children. Demonstrates use of active listening. Deals with concept of limits. Presents a variety of case material and recorded interviews. Techniques described may be applied by parents in the home.

Baruch, Dorothy W. *New Ways in Discipline.* New York: McGraw-Hill, 1949.

One of the most widely read books for parents. Written in simple style. Illustrates use of active listening. Deals with problems of reward and punishment. Shows how parents can apply methods of play therapy at home.

Bettelheim, Bruno. *The Children of the Dream.* New York: Macmillan Co., 1969.

A penetrating study of children and child-rearing in the kibbutz of Israel. Draws lessons for the American parent and presents implications for our methods of child-rearing and education, particularly in the slums. Will help parents enlarge their conceptions about how our society might bring up its children more effectively.

Bronfenbrenner, Urie. *Two Worlds of Childhood: U.S. and U.S.S.R.* New York: Russell Sage Foundation, 1970.

A scholarly report of a comparative study of child-rearing practices in America and in the Soviet Union. Shows how American parents have driven their children to be brought up by their peers and TV. Shows parents how they fail to provide freedom to children and how, in contrast to Soviet parents, we are neglecting training of children to be cooperative, altruistic, and self-disciplined.

Button, Alan DeWitt. *The Authentic Child.* New York: Random House, 1969.

A penetrating analysis of the characteristics of the child who becomes authentic from his relationship with authentic parents. Stresses the importance of parents' acceptance, honesty, and willingness to be human. Will help parents see beauty in their children and experience joy in a mutual, nonpower relationship. Rejects pat solutions in parent education in favor of developing spontaneously open relationships with children.

Donovan, Frank R. *Wild Kids.* Harrisburg, Pennsylvania: Stackpole Books, 1967.

An eye-opener for people who are unaccepting of today's children and their behavior. Shows how kids have been rebelling against authority throughout history. Shows how children have been exploited and dominated in all generations by adults.

Dreikurs, Rudolph. *Children: The Challenge.* Des Moines, Iowa: Meredith Press (Duell, Sloan and Pearce), 1964.

A widely read book for parents that presents an approach to child-rearing rooted in Adlerian theory. Dreikurs' approach has some distinct similarities to the P.E.T. philosophy, but also some differences, particularly in the area of discipline and conflicts. Parents will find this book helpful in understanding their children better, even though certain recommended techniques will be seen as inconsistent with the P.E.T. approach.

Ginott, Haim G. *Between Parent and Child.* New York: Macmillan Co. 1965.

Best-selling, easy-to-read book that shows parents the difference between destructive and constructive (therapeutic) conversation with children. While rich in brief examples, the book does not present longer cases showing how active listening can be used in counseling children. Unlike the P.E.T. philosophy, Ginott's approach to discipline sanctions parents' setting limits and rules. This book is full of helpful ideas for dealing with specific problems—jealousy, getting up and getting dressed, bedtime, TV, sex, etc. For some of these problems, the author quite strongly advocates a "correct" solution.

Ginott, Haim G. *Between Parent and Teenager.* New York: Macmillan Co., 1969.

Focuses primarily on how parents can use the language of acceptance to respond to teen-agers' messages. Shows destructive effects of criticism, insults, praise, and lecturing. Offers parents advice on handling problems of dating, dress, sex, drinking, drugs. Author is often strong on how parents "should" act. Presents a philosophy of discipline different from the P.E.T. approach. Rich in cases, but offers no theory to cement together all of his examples.

Glasser, William. *Schools Without Failure.* New York: Harper and Row, 1969.

A highly critical appraisal of American schools, showing how teachers, grading, and imposed curricula contribute to children's failure. Introduces classroom methods for giving children more freedom to talk and think. Deals with the problem of how to achieve discipline without punishment.

Gordon, Thomas. *Group-Centered Leadership.* Boston: Houghton Mifflin, 1955.

One of the first attempts to apply the client-centered philosophy to the field of leadership, supervision, and administration. Shows the origins of Dr. Gordon's group-centered problem-solving approach. Useful for parents wanting to learn group leadership skills for family conferences. Will be most helpful to parents who occupy leadership roles outside the home and want to apply group-centered principles to release the creative potential of their groups.

Holt, John. *How Children Fail.* New York: Dell Publishing Co., 1964.

A teacher provides a penetrating analysis of what teachers and classes do to children to make them fail—even children who get good grades. Shows effects of evaluation. Shows how schools make children bored, afraid, and confused. Parents, as well as teachers, will find this book fascinating.

Holt, John. *The Underachieving School*. New York: Pitman Publishing Corp., 1969.

A critical examination of the deficiencies of American schools. Holds that teachers should be more effective as helping agents, that evaluation and authoritarian control seriously interfere with the child's learning. An important book—one that will help parents acquire new insights about how children should be treated and educated.

Hymes, James L. *The Child Under Six*. Englewood Cliffs, New Jersey: Prentice-Hall, 1963.

Will help parents acquire more understanding of young children and how they develop. Little attention given to the parent-child relationship and the communications process between them. Weak on discipline and how to deal with conflicts.

Jourard, Sidney M. *The Transparent Self*. New York: D. Van Nostrand, 1964.

Offers the hypothesis that man can be healthier, more fully functioning, and more helpful to others if he gains courage to be his real self with others. Concealing feelings and thoughts prevents intimate relationships and brings on emotional sickness

Katz, Robert L. *Empathy*. New York: The Free Press of Glencoe, Macmillan Co., 1963.

The most scholarly and complete treatment of empathy in human relationships—what it is and what it can do to help another person grow. Useful for parents who want a deeper understanding of this essential attitude and skill of the helping agent.

Missildine, W. Hugh. *Your Inner Child of the Past*. New York: Simon and Schuster, 1963.

Helpful for parents who want to understand themselves better, in terms of what influence their parents had on *their* personalities. Will help parents to reach a deeper understanding of the complexities of parent-child relationships and how much parents can influence their children.

Neill, A. S. *Summerhill.* New York: Hart Publishing Co., 1960.

Report of a pioneering school in England in which an attempt has been made to incorporate in an education institution the principles of democracy and the elements of a therapeutic community.

Neill, A. S. *Freedom—Not License.* New York: Hart Publishing Co., 1966.

Neill takes the philosophy underlying his Summerhill School and applies it more specifically to the adult-child relationship, pointing out the difference between freedom and excessive permissiveness. Will provide parents with more understanding of the power of trusting children. Reinforces some of the P.E.T. concepts.

Putney, Shell, and Putney, Gail. *The Adjusted American.* New York: Harper, 1964.

One of the best books for understanding self and others. Clearly written, insightful and penetrating. Shows parents how they contribute to child's maladjustive behavior. Will help parents understand their relationship with their own parents. Strongly recommended.

Rogers, Carl R. *Client-Centered Therapy.* Boston: Houghton Mifflin, 1951.

The basic text on the theory and practice of client-centered psychotherapy, from which the ideas of acceptance and active listening were derived. Excellent for parents who want a deeper understanding of what it takes to be a helping agent for others. This book contains the origins of much of Dr. Gordon's philosophy and basic attitudes about persons.

Rogers, Carl R. *On Becoming a Person.* Boston: Houghton Mifflin, 1963.

A collection of Rogers' papers, covering his thinking about therapy, education, the self, the healthy individual, and the helping relationship. Useful to parents wanting to understand the broader implications of client-centered therapy and to capture the essence of Rogers as a person.

Rogers, Carl R. *Freedom to Learn.* Columbus, Ohio: Charles E. Merrill, 1969.

Presents the application of client-centered theory and Rogers' philosophy to schools and to classroom teaching. Demonstrates how teachers can create a classroom climate of freedom and help students become fully functioning and self-directing.

Spock, Benjamin. *The Common Sense Book of Baby and Child Care.* New York: Duell, Sloan and Pearce, 1957.

The revised version of Spock's classic and world-famous book for parents. Gives practical and easy-to-understand suggestions for hundreds of problems. Excellent for helping parents deal with problems of feeding, daily care, illness, sex, sleeping, play. One of the best sources for understanding what children are like. The focus, however, is not on the parent-child relationship, nor will parents learn how to communicate with children or resolve conflicts. Spock presents a very ambiguous and incomplete point of view about discipline.

How to Find Out About P.E.T. Classes in Your Area

As this book went to press, Parent Effectiveness Training courses were being offered by qualified instructors in most states, with plans for continuing expansion throughout the remainder of the United States and in foreign countries.

Readers who wish to inquire about the availability of classes in any community or region are invited to write to:

P.E.T. INFORMATION
Effectiveness Training Associates
110 South Euclid Avenue
Pasadena, California 91101

Acknowledgments

I wish to acknowledge the following for their continuous support of the Parent Effectiveness Training program, for their confidence in me, and for what they have generously given to foster the growth of P.E.T.

The Los Angeles Altrusa Foundation

Mr. and Mrs. Howard Preston

Mr. and Mrs. John Lovelace

Mr. and Mrs. Robert Schrimmer

Mr. Gordon Gumpertz

Mr. Frederick Llewllyn

Mr. Ralph Carson

The California P.E.T. Instructors

T.G.

Index